D1711045

"*Bite-Sized Parenting* has the answer to all of the 'is this normal?' questions you have during the first year, without making parents feel stressed that they're doing things wrong. It is the perfect handbook for new parents to navigate the first year with trustworthy and relatable advice!"
— Kacie Barnes, MCN, RDN, founder of Mama Knows Nutrition

"Sharon Mazel's *Bite-Sized Parenting* is a must-have for every expectant parent! Her easy-to-understand graphics are full of evidence-based information that will put every new parent's mind to ease. *Bite-Sized Parenting* is the only book you will need to feel confident and thrive throughout your baby's first year of life!"
— Liesel Teen, BSN, RN, founder of Mommy Labor Nurse

"*Bite-Sized Parenting: Your Baby's First Year* by Sharon Mazel is a must-have resource for new parents. This comprehensive book covers all aspects of baby development including sleep, feeding, gross motor, fine motor, communication, and cognitive development. Using clear explanations and visuals, this book is organized by age, making it easy to find information specific to your child's stage. Whether you are a first-time parent or an experienced one, *Bite-Sized Parenting* is sure to provide valuable insights and practical tips to care for your baby until their first birthday."
— Dr. Allison Mell, PT, pediatric physical therapist, founder of Tots on Target

BITE-SIZED PARENTING

Your Baby's 1st Year

The Essential Guide to What Matters Most, from Sleeping + Feeding to Development + Play

SHARON MAZEL
Illustrations by Kara Western

BenBella Books, Inc.
Dallas, TX

Bite-Sized Parenting: Your Baby's First Year copyright © 2023 by Sharon Mazel

BenBella

BenBella Books, Inc.
10440 N. Central Expressway
Suite 800
Dallas, TX 75231
benbellabooks.com
Send feedback to feedback@benbellabooks.com

BenBella is a federally registered trademark.

Printed in China
10 9 8 7 6 5 4 3 2 1

Library of Congress Control Number: 2022046869
ISBN 9781637742655 (trade paperback)
ISBN 9781637742662 (electronic)

Illustrations by Kara Western
Editing by Leah Wilson
Copyediting by Leah Baxter
Proofreading by Jenny Bridges and Karen Wise
Indexing by WordCo.
Text design and composition by Kit Sweeney
Cover design by Sarah Avinger

To Gaby and Kenny
for being great parenting role models

To Daniella, Arianne, Kira, and Sophia
for giving me the greatest job in the world

To Zara
for letting me practice all over again

And to Jay, my everything
There's no one I'd rather be with on
this journey of life than you

CONTENTS

MONTH TWELVE 287

INTRODUCTION

Welcome to one of the most exciting—and perhaps also one of the most daunting—chapters in your life: parenthood.

If there's one truth about being a parent, it's that it's overwhelming. The responsibility of caring for a tiny and seemingly helpless infant is monumental, yet soon after birth you're set free without much guidance to go home and "parent." Determined to be the best possible mom or dad you can be, you start down the rabbit hole of oversized parenting books, online blogs, social media posts, Dr. Google, and more . . . where instead of getting the reassurance you need and the simple answers you seek, you're bombarded with conflicting, confusing, sometimes inaccurate, and oftentimes scary parenting advice. The result: You end up even more overwhelmed, more unsure, and more stressed.

What I've learned in my more than twenty-five years as a parenting expert, author, and mom of four is that when there's too much information, there is, in effect, no information at all. And that's not helpful to parents. *Bite-Sized Parenting: Your Baby's First Year* sets out to change that dynamic by cutting through the cacophony of conflicting parenting advice, reducing information overload, and empowering instead of frightening. This book offers simplified, practical, evidence-based answers to the most important parenting questions, separating facts and science from opinions and preferences, in a digestible month-by-month format that is actionable and easy to understand, with exactly the information you need to make the best parenting choices for you and your baby.

I know what keeps moms and dads up at night (besides, of course, a crying baby)—and it's these big topics that figure prominently in *Bite-Sized Parenting*. I like to categorize them into what I call the big three, the secondary two, and the relegated one.

The "big three" are sleeping, pooping, and eating, and most of your days in your baby's first year will be consumed with these parenting concerns. *Is my baby eating enough? Why isn't my baby napping? I can't believe how much my baby is pooping/spitting up/burping! How do I start solids? When will my baby sleep through the night?* The bulk of the topics in this book tackle these types of pressing questions.

The "secondary two" are milestones and play/learning, topics that tend to come up whenever you're not mired in the big three. Whether it's wondering when your baby will roll over, sit, crawl, pull up, walk, smile, say words, wave, clap, or point; deliberating on how to handle behavior issues from crying and fussiness to separation anxiety and biting; or wondering about ways to stimulate your baby's growing mind, this book's got you covered.

Finally, no less important but often not touched upon in parenting guides is the "relegated one": you and your life as a parent. The information in these pages will help you feel more confident as a mom or dad, deal with everyone's unsolicited advice (believe me, you'll get plenty!), avoid comparisons, make time for adult relationships, ask for help, deal with the mental load of parenting, and more.

In *Bite-Sized Parenting,* you won't have to read endless paragraphs to get to the bottom line (because, let's face it, what new parent has time for that anyway?). You'll get the snapshot of each topic in a beautifully illustrated infographic—a visual learning aid that makes it easy to remember what you need to know. And if that's all you want or have time for, that's great. But when you're ready or interested to learn more, you'll be able to turn to each topic's "A Closer Look" section for a deeper dive into the content, with additional nuance, information, and guidance.

Because the book is organized month-by-month, you can read each chapter as your baby grows, giving you the freedom to enjoy every precious moment of your little one's first year as it comes instead of stressing about topics that aren't applicable yet. Or you can choose to read ahead and get an early start on what to know for the months to come.

In short, you get to choose how to consume the material in these pages—and what to do with that information after you've acquired it. Which is exactly what you'll be doing as a parent—making choices for you and your family based on what works for you and on your instincts (they're remarkably strong, even in newbie parents!).

There's a lot to learn in parenting your new baby, but the good news is, aside from abiding by safety recommendations (such as those about medical care or the safest sleep position), whatever and however you choose to parent, you aren't going to get it wrong. Parenting isn't black and white, and most of the choices you'll be making in your baby's first year won't have one "perfect" answer. There is no one parenting path that every parent must travel, no singular answer to any parenting challenge, and no specific approach that will feel right to every mom or dad. Which means that however you choose to soothe your crying baby, whether you decide to sleep train or not, which method you opt to start solids with, or which toys you break out to entertain your little one, you and your baby will not only survive, but—with the confidence that comes with a little expert guidance—thrive.

Feeling good about the parenting choices you make will turn you into the exact parent your baby needs—and that means you'll be able to enjoy your little one's first twelve months with less stress and with more confidence. You've got this!

MONTH ONE

It's the first month with your new baby and the beginning of an amazing twelve months ahead.

What was once an abstract idea, a bunch of kicking limbs from within, and a smushed face on a 3D image, is now a reality, ready to grow and develop into an individual with a unique personality and temperament that'll undoubtedly keep you on your toes.

The first month with your newborn will be filled with sleepless nights, endlessly busy days, lots of worry (on your part), and lots of poop (on your baby's part). The next twelve months will challenge you in ways you never expected (and maybe in some ways you did) and bring you to heights of joy you never thought possible. Give yourself the time and space to learn what it means to be a parent, to learn about your baby, and to figure out who he or she is. Little by little you'll gain the confidence to parent in the way that feels right for you—because, after all, that is the best way to parent. Let the adventure begin!

MONTH ONE OVERVIEW

BIRTH TO ONE MONTH OLD

SLEEPING

14-18 HOURS
Total time your baby may sleep in a 24-hour day

4-5
Number of naps your baby may take each day

30-60 MINUTES
Time your baby may be awake between naps

EATING

8-12
Number of liquid meals your baby may have each day

16-32 OUNCES
Total amount of breast milk or formula your baby may drink each day

2-4 HOURS
Time between feedings

GROWING

1-1½ INCHES
Length your baby may grow this month

1-2 POUNDS
Weight your baby may gain this month

A CLOSER LOOK

Your baby is a unique individual, on his or her own developmental timeline, growing at his or her own pace, with his or her own distinctive temperament, personality, desires, and needs. That means that how much (or how often) he sleeps, how many feedings she has, how tall he is, or how much she weighs will be unique to your little one.

This overview (and the monthly overviews to come) represents what a baby *might* be doing, sleeping, or gaining this month. But because every child is different, your baby won't necessarily fit perfectly into these averages. That's okay. Use these overviews as rough guides to help you gauge what might be happening with your baby each month, recognizing that the range of normal is wide. And then enjoy your baby wherever he or she happens to land.

As with the growth and sleep estimates, the feeding amounts in these monthly overviews are also only approximations, since all babies have different feeding needs. If you're feeding formula, expect your baby, on average, to drink around 2.5 ounces of formula a day for every pound of body weight. It's easy to measure formula or breast milk amounts that are given in a bottle, but if you're nursing, you'll have to trust that your baby is getting the right amount of breast milk based on clues like weight gain and diaper output (see page 13 for more). Still, in these early months, feeding on demand and listening to your baby's hunger and satiety cues (see page 37) will be the name of the game, whether you're nursing or bottle feeding. Never push your baby to finish a bottle to match the numbers in these overviews—listen to your baby instead.

WHAT YOU'LL NOTICE
ABOUT YOUR NEWBORN

YOUR BABY'S BODY

A pointy head   A pushed-in nose   Swollen or puffy eyes that look crossed   Swollen breasts or genitals

Soft downy hair on the body and head   Peeling skin   Skin covered in vernix   Fast-growing nails

YOUR BABY'S QUIRKS

No tears when crying   Hiccups often   Sneezes in the light/sun   Funny reflexes

Spits up a lot   Red face when pooping   Has explosive poops   A frog position during sleep

YOUR BABY'S BEHAVIORS

Cries a lot   Sleeps a lot   Not on a schedule   Wants to be held all the time

A CLOSER LOOK

Your new baby is of course adorable, but she may have arrived with a few surprising physical features, quirks, and behaviors. Here are some things you may notice about your newborn in the first few weeks after birth.

Your baby's body. Sorry to burst your bubble, but the baby you bring home may not look like the perfectly proportioned newborn of your dreams. Instead, your newborn may have a pointy head and a squished nose (thanks to the journey through the birth canal), swollen eyes that look crossed (don't worry, they'll coordinate soon), and swollen genitals and breasts (due to leftover hormones from mom). You may notice soft downy hair on her shoulders, back, forehead, and cheeks, which may remain for the first few months; peeling or wrinkled skin (especially prominent if your baby was overdue); and a white, creamy, almost waxy coating called vernix that protected your baby in utero (more evident if your baby was born before term). Some newborns sport birthmarks of varying colors, sizes, and locations. These newborn features are temporary. By the time your baby is a few weeks old, most of them will be gone, though some birthmarks may take a few months to fade, and others don't ever disappear.

One feature that will remain for a number of months is the soft spot, or fontanel, on the top of your baby's head (there's also another, less noticeable one, toward the back of the head). This opening in the skull helped your baby pass through the birth canal, and it's not unusual to notice it throbbing or see it bulge slightly when your baby cries.

Another thing you'll notice is your baby's umbilical stump, which should fall off within the first two weeks or so. No need for any special care—just keep the stump dry and avoid tub baths until the stump falls off (see page 44 for more on bathing your baby).

What will need attending to, however, are your little one's nails. They'll grow fast and furious right from the start, so be sure to have safe baby nail scissors, an electric or manual baby file, or clippers on hand. Expect your baby's nails to be soft at first, but they'll begin to harden after the first few weeks.

Your baby's quirks. You'll notice plenty of newborn quirks in the early weeks:

- Your baby will cry a lot, but you probably won't see tears yet. That's because your baby's tear ducts won't be fully up and running until sometime between one and three months old.

- Those hiccups that were a common occurrence in utero will also happen regularly these days. The good news is that they aren't bothersome for your baby.

- Your baby will likely sneeze often to rid her tiny nasal passages of common irritants like dust, mucus, and even breast milk. She may also sneeze in the sunlight, likely a result of her brain still trying to work out which nerves stimulate which reaction. And you'll notice several newborn reflexes—involuntary muscle movements or reactions that protect babies outside the womb. Some of the key newborn reflexes include the startle reflex, the rooting reflex (see page 38), and the sucking reflex.

- Grab some burp cloths and bibs . . . your little baby may be doing a lot of spitting up, especially as she starts to take in larger quantities of breast milk or formula. Read all about spitting up on page 84.

- Your baby's face may turn red when she poops. Don't worry . . . that's normal and doesn't mean she's constipated. Straining, grunting, fussing, and crying to poop or pass gas is normal, too, and will go away eventually. See page 39 to learn more about your baby's poop.

- Those poops will be explosive and loud. Your baby's digestive system is still immature, and it hasn't quite figured out how to move gas and stool quietly through the gastrointestinal tract. Give it one or two months . . . things will eventually get quieter.

- Your baby will sleep with her legs in a froggy position, though she'll start to straighten in a few weeks.

Catch these cute baby quirks before it's too late—they'll disappear over the coming months!

Your baby's behaviors. Your baby will spend a lot of her early days crying. Though it may be hard to handle, remind yourself that it's your baby's only way of communicating. Try to reframe how you think about crying and focus on the different sounds, tones, pitches, and cadences of those cries so you can learn to discern what your baby needs (see page 16 for more on what to do when your baby cries).

When your baby isn't crying, she'll be sleeping a lot, though not for long stretches of time. That's a good thing, since your newborn will need to eat every 2 to 4 hours, but it also means you won't be getting much sleep this month. Your baby will begin to consolidate sleep patterns when she's closer to four or five months old, and you'll start to see your baby settling into more of a routine around then, too. But until then, be prepared for your baby's sleep to adhere to little to no schedule at all.

Your newborn's favorite spot will undoubtedly be in your arms, skin-to-skin on your chest, or in a baby carrier. Feeling the closeness and the movement that comes along with being held will be comforting for your newborn, so hold your baby when you can. Don't worry—you can't spoil a newborn, even if you end up holding her all day.

SAFE SLEEP FOR YOUR BABY'S FIRST YEAR

Always put your baby on his back for sleep

Use a firm mattress in a safe crib or bassinet with a tight-fitting sheet

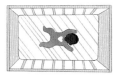

Keep the crib or bassinet bare, free of soft bedding and toys

Keep sleeping surfaces flat—if your baby falls asleep in an inclined seat, move him to a flat surface as soon as possible

Room share

Offer a pacifier

Stop swaddling as soon as your baby starts to roll over

A CLOSER LOOK

Perhaps you're stressing about just the right amount of white noise for your baby's room . . . or which swaddle is the most comfortable for your precious bundle . . . or how to get your baby to sleep when not in your arms. Those are definitely top concerns in the first few months, but don't let those worries distract you from the most important thing to think about when it comes to sleep: safety.

The reason safe sleep is such an important topic is because tragically, according to the Centers for Disease Control and Prevention (CDC), more than 3,400 babies in the US alone die annually during sleep from SIDS (sudden infant death syndrome), or what experts now prefer to call unexplained sudden death in infancy. Fortunately, since the early 1990s, the rate of these tragic deaths has declined dramatically. This positive trend can be attributed to the following safe sleep recommendations from the American Academy of Pediatrics (AAP).

Always place your baby on his back for sleep. Back sleeping is the safest way to sleep, period. Though it's true that some babies sleep better on their tummies or sides, study after study has shown that young babies are safest when sleeping on their backs. Be sure to put your baby to sleep on his back both at night and for naps throughout the entire first year.

Once your baby can roll over on his own, sometime after month three or four, you don't have to worry if he ends up sleeping on his tummy. While you should always place your baby in the crib on his back, there's no need to flip him over if he rolls onto his tummy on his own (see the box on page 94 for more).

Use a firm mattress in a safe crib or bassinet with a tight-fitting sheet. The safest sleep location for your baby is in a crib or bassinet that meets current safety standards. You can certainly opt to use a crib from day one, but some newborns feel cozier in a smaller space, and many parents prefer the portability of a bassinet for the first three or so months. The choice is yours.

Whether you start with a crib or bassinet, use a firm mattress that sits snugly inside, with a sheet that fits tightly. Cushioned sleepers, in-bed sleepers, or sleepers with thick padding around the sides are not recommended because your baby's face can get pushed against the padding and his breathing can become obstructed.

Keep the crib or bassinet bare, free of toys and soft bedding. Pining after a decked-out nursery like the ones you've seen on social media or in magazine spreads? Save yourself the money because your baby doesn't need fancy bumpers or blankets to get a good night's sleep. In fact, bumpers are dangerous and have been banned for sale in the US and other countries because of suffocation and entrapment risks. Your baby's sleeping environment will be much safer without bumpers and without pillows, blankets, comforters, stuffed animals, positioners, and inserts, which pose similar risks. Even mesh liners are not recommended because they still present a chance of entrapment. What's left in the crib? Nothing—other than your baby.

Afraid that your baby will injure himself without bumpers? Don't worry—your little one won't be able to bang his head hard enough to get hurt. And if your baby does get his arm or leg stuck in the crib slats, you'll be able to help free it, and your baby won't be any worse for the wear.

Keep sleeping surfaces flat. You've already learned that back sleeping is the safest way for your baby to sleep. But there's more to that bedtime story. Your baby should also always sleep on a flat surface. With little to no neck strength, young babies are prone to slumping their heads to the side or forward when sleeping in an inclined position (even on an incline as small as 10 degrees). When this happens, there's a chance their airways may become obstructed. So don't use inclined sleepers, swings, car seats, or baby seats as sleep surfaces for your baby. If your baby falls asleep in an inclined seat, transfer him to the crib or bassinet as soon as you can. No need to panic if your baby falls asleep in the car seat during a drive, but transfer him to a flat sleeping surface when you arrive at your destination.

Room share. Get ready for a new roommate! The AAP recommends that your baby share your room for the first six months or longer to help decrease the risk of SIDS. That means your baby's crib or bassinet is in your room, within arm's reach.

Wondering about bed sharing? For safety reasons, the AAP strongly advises against having your baby sleep in your bed with you. If you do choose to bed share, make sure you do it safely: Keep pillows and blankets away from your sleeping baby, and make sure there's no opportunity for him to get trapped between the headboard and mattress.

Offer a pacifier. Pacifiers during sleep may help to reduce the risk of SIDS, since sucking on a pacifier opens the airways. Don't force your baby to take a pacifier if he doesn't want one. Some babies love the pacifier because it's soothing; other babies never take to the pacifier, and that's fine, too. If your little one uses a pacifier, there's no need to shove the paci back in his mouth if it falls out during sleep . . . and definitely don't attach the pacifier to your sleeping baby's clothes, neck, or hands. If your little one is a binky lover, rest assured that using a pacifier often is fine in the newborn stage, and it won't result in your baby preferring the artificial nipple over mama's (a worry that some parents have). However, once your baby is a little older, say five to six months old, it's best to limit the pacifier just to sleep times.

Stop swaddling as soon as your baby starts to roll over.
Considering a swaddle for your baby? That's great—you can read more about swaddling in the box on page 12. If you do end up swaddling your little one, you'll need to stop swaddling as soon as your baby shows signs of starting to roll over, something that can happen as early as two months old. A swaddled, confined baby who rolls over to his tummy is at a higher risk of SIDS in that tummy-down position for two reasons. First, the swaddle (and a baby's inability to move when he's wrapped up) may make it difficult for him to reposition himself if he's not getting enough oxygen. Second, the tightness of a swaddle makes it harder for a baby to wake up if he's having trouble breathing. This second reason is actually why some parents like to swaddle their babies—the decreased arousal mechanism helps babies sleep longer and wake less easily. That's okay on the back, but not on the tummy. Though it may be tempting to keep your baby in a swaddle longer, especially if it helps him sleep better, it's not safe past the first few months. Once your baby starts showing signs of rolling over, use a sleep sack or footed sleeper that allows for freedom of movement instead. And avoid weighted sleep sacks when you make the transition—the AAP considers them unsafe.

It's important to note that the risk of SIDS is highest in the first six months, but you should continue to practice these safe sleep recommendations until your baby is twelve months old. After your baby's first birthday, you can add a blanket to the crib if you'd like, but there's no need to add a pillow. You can introduce a pillow when your baby makes the switch to a bed, which usually happens after age two and a half.

SWADDLING YOUR BABY

There are many good reasons to swaddle your baby, but swaddling is not a must do. In fact, plenty of babies hate being swaddled and sleep just as well without being tightly blanketed like a burrito.

First the pros: Swaddling can make your baby feel safe and secure and can be helpful if your baby has difficulty calming down. Swaddling may help your baby sleep better and more soundly—both because your baby can feel comfier in a swaddle when on his back, and because he's less likely to startle awake when tightly cocooned.

But there are also some downsides to swaddling. Swaddling limits your baby's freedom of movement, an important component of motor and cognitive development (though you can prevent this downside by swaddling only at night or by keeping your baby's legs or arms out of the swaddle). Swaddling can lead to overheating when babies are too bundled up—and overheating can lead to SIDS. And there's also a risk of hip problems if your baby spends a significant part of the day and night tightly wrapped in a swaddle—though making sure your baby's legs are bent up and out while in the swaddle or using a sleep sack that allows the legs freedom of movement can help reduce this risk.

Remember, if you decide to swaddle your baby, it's important that you stop swaddling as soon as he starts working on rolling over. In some babies, that's as early as eight weeks old.

SIGNS YOUR BABY IS GETTING ENOUGH TO EAT

Your baby is gaining weight at a steady rate

Your baby seems content after feedings

You hear your baby gulping and swallowing during feedings

Your baby has at least 3 to 4 large poops per day

Your baby has at least 6 to 8 wet diapers per day

Your baby's pee is colorless or pale yellow

A CLOSER LOOK

It's a common new mom and dad question: *Is my baby getting enough to eat?* If you're bottle feeding, you won't have much trouble getting your answer, since you'll see the precise amount of fluid going in. If you're nursing, it'll be harder to know for sure how much milk your baby is drinking. Luckily, babies are really good at listening to their appetites and regulating their intake. The vast majority of babies will eat when they're hungry and stop eating when they're full (a good reason not to push your baby to eat more than she wants)—which means that it's likely your little one is getting enough to eat, especially if you see the following reassuring signs.

Your baby is gaining weight at a steady rate. The most reliable sign that your baby is getting enough to eat is weight gain. If your baby is putting on ounces at a steady rate—an ounce a day in the first month on average—you can rest assured that your baby is getting the right amount of food. (It doesn't matter which percentile your little one falls into on the growth chart, just that she's following her own curve; see page 32.) Weigh-ins at the doctor's office during well-baby visits will help you track her weight gain.

Your baby seems content after feedings. A well-fed baby will be a happy baby, at least most of the time, and certainly after feedings. Obviously, your baby will cry—all babies do—but if your baby seems content after most meals, it's a good sign she's getting enough to eat. If your baby seems to be in pain after a meal, or struggling during or after a feeding, speak to your pediatrician.

You hear your baby gulping and swallowing during feedings. If you're bottle feeding, you'll see how much swallowing your baby is doing. But with nursing, it's harder to gauge whether your baby is extracting milk, let alone the amount your baby is taking in. So, you'll want to listen for gulping and swallowing. Once letdown happens (that's the feeling of fullness or the tingling sensation you may experience when your milk releases from your milk ducts), your baby will start suckling and swallowing, and you'll hear a rhythmic grunt with each suck-swallow-breath. Check for motion in your baby's ear and cheek—that'll also let you know she's swallowing.

If you're nursing and your baby doesn't seem to be getting a good latch, is unable to suck and swallow well, or seems to have difficulty at the breast, a discussion with a lactation consultant may help get things back on track. If you suspect the cause of your baby's breastfeeding difficulties is a tongue-tie (when the band of tissue that connects the underside of the tongue to the floor of the mouth is too short), check with your pediatrician to see if any intervention is needed. Most of the time, clipping a tongue-tie is not considered necessary.

Your baby has at least three to four large poops per day.
What goes in must come out, usually in the form of poop, so you'll
be paying close attention to your baby's diaper contents for the first
month or so. Though the frequency of bowel movements varies
widely from one baby to another, you'll be looking for at least three
to four large poops each day in the newborn period starting on day
five. (Before day five, your baby might only have one or two poopy
diapers.) After six weeks old, your baby may go a few days without
pooping, something that's perfectly normal and nothing to worry
about, but for now keep an eye on those poops.

Early bowel movements, usually during the first 24 hours
of life, will be blackish green in color, with a consistency that's
very sticky, like tar. This is meconium, which filled your baby's
intestines in the uterus. Once your baby starts to eat, you'll
notice transitional stool—darkish green-yellow in color, loose,
sometimes seedy, and mucousy. After three to four days of that,
the appearance of your baby's poops will depend on what she's
eating (see page 40 for more).

Your baby has at least six to eight wet diapers per day.
When looking at your baby's diaper contents for reassurance she's
getting enough to eat, don't stop at poop. After the first week,
your baby should have at least six to eight wet diapers per 24-
hour day. If you're using cloth diapers, you'll have no problems
feeling wetness or noticing that the diaper feels stiffer after your
baby has peed. But if you're using disposable diapers, unless the
diapers you're using have a wetness indicator line, you won't
always be able to tell that the diaper is wet, especially if there's
also poop in there. But because newborns don't yet have the
sphincter control to hold in urine during a bowel movement,
you can safely assume that your little one has peed when she's
pooped. You can also squish the diaper around a little. If it feels
crunchy when you squeeze, it's dry. If it feels jelly-like, it's wet.

Your baby's pee is colorless or pale yellow. Your baby's pee
should appear light yellow or have no color at all. Anything dark
yellow or brown warrants a call to the pediatrician, since it could
mean your baby is not getting enough to eat.

SOOTHING STRATEGIES WHEN YOUR BABY IS CRYING

Rock your baby

Offer a pacifier

Get some fresh air

Feed your baby

Massage your baby

Swaddle your baby

Sing to your baby or play soft music

Bathe your baby

Hold your baby in different positions and go skin-to-skin

Play white noise or whisper "shhh"

Bring your baby into a dark room

Burp your baby

A CLOSER LOOK

Your baby will be doing a lot of crying. And let's be real . . . it's going to be hard on you. But crying is a good thing, since it lets your baby communicate his needs to you. So, embrace the crying as best as you can, even when things get rough. Remind yourself that crying does not mean you're not a good mom or dad, or that your baby is angry at you, or that you're doing something wrong. Your baby is telling you that he's hungry or tired, that something is bothering him, that he needs to suck for comfort, or that he needs some cuddles, rocking, jiggling, or just a change of scenery. And the more you get used to your baby's different cries, the better you'll be able to respond.

Respond with comfort. Sometimes a fussy baby just needs a little soothing, so rock your baby, put him in a sling or carrier to create comforting closeness, try kangaroo care (skin-to-skin contact), or offer a pacifier. You can also try a warm bath (see page 44), some white noise, a massage (see page 87), a swaddle, or a trip in the stroller outdoors for a change of scenery and fresh air. Playing soft music or singing a lullaby can also soothe a fussy baby.

Respond by feeding. If your baby is hungry, offer the breast or bottle. This is called feeding on demand, and especially in the early months, you'll want to respond to a hunger cry (or better yet, hunger cues; see page 37) with a feeding, which will happen every 2 to 3 hours if you're breastfeeding and every 3 to 4 hours if you're formula feeding. But remember, a crying baby doesn't always indicate a hungry baby, and responding to every cry with a feeding could lead to your baby being overfed and uncomfortably full, which in turn can lead to more crying.

Offer relief from pain. If your baby seems out of sorts, try repositioning your baby, burping him (see page 42), or bicycling his legs to relieve gas. If your baby seems to be in a lot of pain, call your pediatrician for advice.

Put your baby to sleep. If your baby is tired, lay him down to sleep or rock him to sleep in your arms or in a carrier.

The most important takeaway: Always respond to your baby's cries. You can't spoil your newborn by holding him too much or by responding to his needs every time—even if you're not 100 percent sure what those needs are. By responding to his cries, you're sending a message to your baby that you love him, you're here for him, and you can be relied on. And that's what a newborn needs most.

COLIC AND UNEXPLAINED CRYING

Did you know that the typical newborn cries for about 2 hours a day (if you add it all up)? But what if your baby seems to be crying more than expected?

Beginning at two to five weeks old, if your baby cries for more than 3 hours per day, for more than 3 days each week, continuing for at least 3 weeks, it could be colic. Babies who have colic sometimes pull up their knees or arch their backs during crying spells, which often sound urgent or painful.

Or perhaps it's PURPLE crying. PURPLE doesn't refer to the color your baby might turn when crying, but rather is an acronym. P stands for *Peak of crying* and refers to the crying bouts themselves, which increase each week and peak in the second month; U stands for *Unexpected*, meaning crying can come and go without a clear reason; R stands for *Resists soothing*, meaning your baby is impossible to calm; P stands for *Pain-like face*, meaning your baby may look like he's in pain, but isn't; L stands for *Long-lasting*, meaning that the crying can last for hours; and E stands for *Evening*, since that's when the crying is more likely to occur.

Or maybe it's just the "witching hour(s)"—the period in the late afternoon, evening, and early night hours when your usually happy-go-lucky baby turns into a fussy, inconsolable demon who won't stop crying.

Experts aren't really sure why some babies cry more than others, but some suggest excessive crying in an otherwise healthy baby is a normal developmental phase. Others think that it could be the result of a slight decrease in a nursing mom's milk supply in the afternoon and evening hours, too much stimulation in your busy house late in the afternoon, or overfeeding and the discomfort that a baby feels when he's too full.

Ultimately it doesn't really matter what the crying is officially called. Whether you call it colic, purple crying, or the witching hour, it's draining, exhausting, and feels like it will never end. But it will pass eventually. These crying bouts, which often peak around week six, usually come to an end around the three-month mark.

If your baby's crying is incessant, however, don't keep quiet about it. Describe the crying to your pediatrician, because there will be babies for whom this type of crying signals something else going on, and it's important to have a medical professional guiding you through this trying time.

GETTING STARTED WITH TUMMY TIME

Start as early as the first week of life

Wait 10 to 20 minutes after a feeding

Aim for short bursts of time

Always supervise

Make it fun

Don't worry if your baby struggles at first

A CLOSER LOOK

You've heard that for safety's sake babies should sleep only on their backs (see page 9 for reasons why). Along with that safe sleep advice comes another important recommendation: Place your baby on her tummy during play time. Tummy time gives babies the chance to strengthen the upper body, arm, and back muscles that they're not working out if they're on their backs all the time. Babies who spend little time on their tummies while awake will be slower to reach certain milestones like rolling over and crawling than babies who get plenty of tummy time during play. Plus, tummy time helps prevent a baby's head from flattening or becoming misshapen from being in the same position all day and all night (see the box on page 23). Here are some tips to help get you and your baby started with tummy time.

Start as early as the first week of life. The sooner you get started, the sooner your baby will get used to being on her tummy—and you can start from day one. You don't even have to wait until the belly button stump falls off to start tummy time on the floor, but if you're worried about putting your baby on a hard surface, you can lay your baby tummy-down on your chest or stomach instead.

Wait 10 to 20 minutes after a feeding. Give your baby a little time to digest after a feeding before putting pressure on her tummy. But don't worry if she spits up during tummy time, even if it's been a while after the last feed. Some babies are prolific spitters, and it doesn't mean there's anything wrong. See page 84 for more on spitting up.

Aim for short bursts of time. Start off doing tummy time two to three times a day for a few minutes each time during the first month. Then slowly work your way up, adding to the time your baby spends on her tummy each session by a minute here and there. By the end of the newborn stage (eight weeks old) your baby should be on her tummy a cumulative 15 to 30 minutes per day. By four to five months old, aim for about 40 minutes to an hour a day cumulative in tummy time.

Remember, some tummy time is better than no tummy time, and even a minute or two here and there adds up, so keep trying.

Always supervise. When doing tummy time, be sure that both you and your baby are awake and alert and you're constantly supervising. This ensures your baby won't fall asleep on her tummy without you noticing, since that could be risky.

Make it fun. Here are some ideas to make tummy time more enjoyable and exciting for your little one:

- Put a rolled blanket or a pillow under your baby's chest to help her lift her head.

- Lay your baby tummy-down on your own tummy. Make funny faces or sing an engaging song.
- Lie stomach down on the floor, face to face with your baby.
- Position your baby perpendicularly across your lap, tummy-down.
- Position your baby tummy-down on an exercise ball (keeping a hand on her for support).
- Carry your baby tummy-down in a football hold.
- Place her on surfaces that offer different sensory sensations—a play mat or fluffy blanket one day, a crinkly surface the next . . .
- Rotate the toys that your baby has within her field of vision or reach.
- Put a mirror in front of your baby—she'll find her face fascinating!
- Massage your baby when she's on her tummy (see page 87 for more on baby massage).
- Change the location or room for tummy time every so often so that your baby has something new to look at.
- Let someone else lead the tummy time session instead of you. A new face might pique her interest.

Don't worry if your baby struggles at first. If your baby whimpers a little during tummy time, that's okay—most babies dislike it in the beginning. Of course it's hard for your baby to lift her heavy head and use muscles she hasn't strengthened yet. That's the whole point of tummy time—and there's nothing wrong with letting your baby experience a little bit of frustration (that's how learning and problem-solving happen). So, give her the opportunity to work at it. She'll rise to the challenge of lifting her head eventually, and with practice she'll fight tummy time less and less.

That said, if it feels especially challenging to keep your baby on her tummy, don't force it. If she's crying a lot or really struggling, take her out of tummy time and try again later (or even take a break from tummy time for a day or two).

As your baby grows, you'll want to give her plenty of time in different positions on the floor during play—on her back, on her tummy, on her sides, and eventually sitting, on hands and knees, and standing up. This will help her strengthen all the muscles needed to reach the vast array of first-year motor milestones. Outside of transport, limit time in containers (swings, strollers, bouncer seats, jumpers, stationary exercisers, etc.) to no more than 15 to 30 minutes at a time, twice a day, to allow your baby the freedom to move and explore her environment. These opportunities will promote both physical and cognitive development.

MINIMIZING YOUR BABY'S FLAT HEAD

Because your little baby will spend a lot of time sleeping, you may notice a flat spot developing on the back or side of her head. You can help minimize this flattening by alternating your baby's position in the crib—head facing one direction during sleep on the first day and then feet facing that direction on the second day—so your baby doesn't put pressure on only one side of the head. Babies like to look at windows or other landmarks in a room and will turn towards them when lying down, so swapping positions will encourage your baby to turn her head in the opposite direction. Your pediatrician will keep an eye on head shape, and, if your baby's head looks especially flattened, might prescribe treatment down the road.

By the way, a bald spot on the back of your baby's head is nothing to worry about. It's just because your baby spends a lot of time on her back in the early months. The hair will grow back eventually.

STIMULATING YOUR BABY IN THE FIRST MONTH

Place objects 8 to 12 inches away from your baby's face

Get in close (your baby loves faces)

Introduce toys with bold contrasting colors

Read books with black and white patterns

Play music or sing lullabies

Talk to your baby in a higher-pitched voice

A CLOSER LOOK

Your newborn may seem like a blob, but there's a lot going on in that cute little brain of his—which means you can start boosting brain development right from the start. Here's how you can stimulate your baby in the first month (if you can find the time between those endless feedings and naps!).

Place objects 8 to 12 inches away from your baby's face. Any farther than 12 inches away will be a blur to your newborn. Don't worry, though . . . your baby's range of vision will increase quickly over the next few months. In the meantime, it's pretty clever that newborns have the ability to see only around 8 to 12 inches away at first, since that's the perfect distance for a baby in your arms to be able to gaze into your face.

Get in close (your baby loves faces). Your face is one of the most exciting things for your newborn to look at! Plus, your face can teach your baby so much. Lean in close so he can make out the expression in your eyes and mouth, see what a smile looks like, and observe how your lips move when you talk.

Introduce toys and books with bold contrasting colors and black and white patterns. After human faces, newborns are most drawn to highly contrasting patterns and bright colors. Give your baby lots of colorful mobiles, toys, and books to gaze at. Black and white patterns will also capture your newborn's attention and will keep your baby's interest longer than objects with lots of similar soft colors, such as subtle shades of pastels.

Play music or sing soft lullabies. A baby's hearing is well developed at birth, which means your newborn will be able to respond to music very early on. But music is not just for enjoyment. Research shows that music enhances connectivity in brain circuitry, and that every time you sing to your baby or sway with him to the beat of a song, his brain pathways are strengthened. Moving together to music is also a great way to strengthen your relationship with your new baby, since it triggers the release of oxytocin (the feel-good bonding hormone) in you both.

Talk to your baby in a higher-pitched voice. Ever notice that you naturally raise the pitch of your voice when speaking to your baby (or any baby, for that matter)? That's because you innately know that babies respond better to high frequency sounds. But it's not just a higher pitch that stimulates your baby's ears. It's also the exaggerated way you speak when talking to your baby— widening your eyes, elongating your syllables, and making fuller movements with your mouth. You're nurturing your little one in exactly the way nature intended, so keep up the good work—it's precisely what your baby needs and responds to best!

NEW PARENT MYTHS

Myth: Bonding with your baby happens immediately

Myth: You'll enjoy every minute of being a parent

Myth: Breastfeeding comes naturally

Myth: You'll be able to manage it all on your own

Myth: It's bad to need a break from your baby

Myth: You're doing something wrong if your baby cries

A CLOSER LOOK

New moms and dads have lots of expectations of what being a parent will look and feel like. But often those expectations aren't met (maybe because they're not realistic), leaving them feeling bad, sad, or both. Here are some new parent myths to bust right now, so that you can lower the bar you—or your friends, or society—set for yourself and enjoy your newborn without the guilt, worry, or self-doubt.

Myth: Bonding with your baby happens immediately.
Though some parents fall in love with, and feel a deep
connection to, their baby the moment they set eyes on her, for
other new moms and dads, the puffy-faced, crying, squirmy baby
they meet doesn't engender much love or attachment at first. Not
only is that normal, it also doesn't make you a bad parent. The
love that you're hoping for will come with time and through every
interaction with your new baby.

Myth: You'll enjoy every minute of being a parent. Yes, you
will enjoy being a parent. Maybe you'll love it most of the time.
But there will be times (and for some new moms and dads, lots
of times) when you won't. It's hard to care for a squalling baby
who rarely sleeps, needs to be fed seemingly all the time, doesn't
smile or interact much, and needs round-the-clock attention.
And you may feel anxiety about doing everything "right" bubble
up and sap the joy out of parenting. What you're feeling is
extremely common. Appreciate that you're brand new at this, and
that not only are there bound to be fumbles, but also moments
of dissatisfaction and despair. And certainly don't feel guilty
or upset when it's hard to feel good about your new reality. If
you're feeling especially unhappy, however, be sure to seek help.
Postpartum depression is common but very treatable, so speak
up if you're suffering.

Myth: Breastfeeding comes naturally. It's recommended that
you put your baby on your breast right in the delivery room, as
soon after birth as possible. Amazingly, your baby's instinctual
ability to find the breast and suck is extremely strong after birth,
so it's really the perfect time for that first introduction to nursing.
But just because breasts are made for breastfeeding doesn't mean
that breastfeeding will be effortless at first. After all, you're both
learning what to do. So don't worry if it doesn't feel perfect on the
first day. Or on the third day. Or even in the second week. It can
take weeks (and perhaps some help from a lactation consultant) for
breastfeeding to become second nature. So, give it time and don't
give up (unless, of course, you're absolutely miserable—nursing
isn't for everyone, so do what feels best for you).

Myth: You'll be able to manage it all on your own. Every new
parent can use a helping hand (or two), and there's no shame in

needing and asking for help (see page 208). Trying to manage it all on your own is certainly doable for some new parents, but you're not going to get a medal or win a prize for handling it solo. Ask for help from your partner, your family, your friends, a neighbor, paid help if you can afford it, or anyone else willing to lend a hand.

Something else to keep in mind: Becoming a new parent can sometimes feel lonely. If your friends aren't in the baby business yet, you may feel disconnected from them. Your relationships with coworkers may change now that you have competing priorities. If family isn't close by (or if they're not helpful), you may feel isolated. Creating for yourself a new network of parents, whether it's at the neighborhood playground or on social media, can help make the first year a little less lonely. Talking about your emotions (with a friend, your partner, or a therapist) can help ease your struggle. Even taking a walk outdoors with your baby and making eye contact with strangers can make you feel less isolated than sitting alone at home.

Myth: It's bad to need a break from your baby. Something that may surprise you about becoming a new parent is how all-consuming it is. There's never a time when you don't have something to do or think about, and there's never enough time in the (exhausting) day to get things done. Truth is, while there's little natural opportunity for "me time," it's good practice to take a break from your baby when you can—and not feel guilty about it. Not only is there nothing bad about needing a respite from your baby, but a little time away can help you recharge so you feel ready to tackle another day. Even a few minutes in a different room can make a world of difference.

Myth: You're doing something wrong if your baby cries. All babies cry. Period. Full stop. It's the way they communicate their needs. You're not doing anything wrong if (when) your baby cries. In fact, you're likely doing everything right, because you're responding as best you can. Continue to remind yourself, even (or especially) when things get rough, that when your baby cries, you're learning about what she needs, likes, wants, and feels—and that's a good thing!

LEARN MORE

Here are some other topics in the chapters to come that may be relevant this month:

- Distinguishing night from day (page 34)
- Sleep cues (page 55)
- Establishing a bedtime routine (page 58)
- Dressing your baby for sleep (page 36)
- Hunger signs (page 37)
- Bottle or breast refusal (page 61)
- Your baby's poop: What's normal (page 39)
- Diaper rash (page 69)
- Pimples, cradle cap, and other common rashes (page 89)
- Gassiness (page 66)
- Burping your baby (page 42)
- Spitting up (page 84)
- Bathing your baby (page 44)
- Baby massage (page 87)

MONTH TWO

Welcome to month two! You're more than halfway through the newborn period now, and though you've undoubtedly seen some amazing changes in your adorable baby already, get ready for even more exciting developmental achievements to come.

This month will reward you with your baby's first social smile, first coos and gurgles of communication, and first attempts at hand-eye coordination during play. You might even be rewarded with more than an hour or two of sleep (or at least a few minutes to shower) as your baby begins to regulate his or her sleep-wake pattern into something slightly more predictable.

You're no longer a newbie parent, but it's still helpful to remind yourself that parenting has a learning curve. You won't become an expert overnight (especially when those overnights leave you sleep deprived), and you shouldn't assume you'll have it all figured out by now. Being a mom or dad is hard, so pat yourself on the back for accomplishing as much as you have already, and lower any expectations about where you "should be" by now.

You've got this!

MONTH TWO OVERVIEW

ONE TO TWO MONTHS OLD

SLEEPING

14–18 HOURS
Total time your baby may sleep in a 24-hour day

3–5
Number of naps your baby may take each day

45–60 MINUTES
Time your baby may be awake between naps

EATING

8–12
Number of liquid meals your baby may have each day

16–32 OUNCES
Total amount of breast milk or formula your baby may drink each day

2–4 HOURS
Time between feedings

GROWING

**7 LBS–11 LBS 15 OZ
19¾–22½ IN**
Average range of weight and height for a baby girl this age

**7 LBS 8 OZ–12 LBS 9 OZ
20–23 IN**
Average range of weight and height for a baby boy this age

A CLOSER LOOK

Your baby is a unique individual on his or her own developmental timeline, growing at his or her own pace, with his or her own distinctive temperament, personality, desires, and needs. That means that how much (or how often) he sleeps, how many feedings she has, how tall he is, or how much she weighs will be unique to your little one.

This overview (and the other monthly overviews in this book) represents what a baby *might* be doing, eating, or gaining this month. But because every child is different, your baby won't necessarily fit perfectly into these averages. That's okay. Use these overviews as rough guides to help you gauge what might be happening with your baby each month, recognizing that the range of normal is wide. And then enjoy your baby wherever he or she happens to land.

A note about the average ranges for height and weight listed in each month's overview: These numbers represent the third and ninety-seventh percentiles on the World Health Organization's (WHO) growth charts for babies, which both the AAP and CDC recommend doctors and parents use to measure a baby's growth. There's no need to concern yourself with which percentile your baby falls into. The most important factor to pay attention to is how your baby's growth is tracking along his or her own growth curve. It doesn't matter if he or she is in the tenth percentile, ninetieth percentile, or somewhere in between—all percentiles are healthy and normal. Remember, babies come in all shapes and sizes!

MILESTONES CHECK-IN

At each of your baby's regular checkups, your pediatrician will use milestone checklists to assess whether your little one is meeting the developmental expectations for his or her age. But remember, the range of normal is extremely wide. Some babies may be faster to reach some milestones and slower to reach others, and that's okay. That said, flagging developmental lags is important to identifying children who may benefit from additional evaluation and, if necessary, intervention. Early identification of a developmental or motor delay can lead to earlier intervention, which can make a big difference when it comes to your little one's learning and development.

The CDC and the AAP use checklists that highlight the milestone expectations for the seventy-fifth percentile—meaning 75 percent or more of children can be expected to reach those milestones by a given age. There's no reason to overthink these milestone checklists (remember, every baby is on his or her own timeline), but if your baby doesn't seem to be meeting any one of these milestones, mention it to your pediatrician.

Seventy-five percent of babies will be able to do at least the following by the end of the second month:

- Look at your face
- Watch you as you move
- Seem happy to see you
- Smile when you smile or talk to them
- Calm down when you pick them up or talk to them
- Make sounds other than crying
- React to loud sounds
- Look at a toy for longer than a few seconds
- Hold their head up during tummy time
- Open their hands briefly

Note: If your baby was born early, you'll use his or her adjusted (or "corrected") age when tracking milestones. You can calculate adjusted age by taking the number of weeks since your baby was born and subtracting the number of weeks your baby was preterm.

HELPING YOUR BABY DISTINGUISH BETWEEN NIGHT AND DAY

AT NIGHT

Establish a
bedtime routine

Keep the
room dark

Minimize interactions

DURING THE DAY

Make a big deal
of the morning

Keep your baby
active when awake

Keep the room
light during naps

A CLOSER LOOK

Your baby spent the nine months of your pregnancy in the dark, where there wasn't much difference between day and night. But now you'd like your little one's schedule to match the rest of your family's (and the world's). Here are some tips to help your newborn learn to distinguish between night and day.

Establish a bedtime routine. Even little babies benefit from a bedtime routine, and implementing one will help your baby learn about the transition from day to night. For now, the routine doesn't need to include much more than a bath, a lullaby, some rocking, and a feeding. You can add more steps to the bedtime routine as your baby gets older (see page 58).

Keep the room dark at night. When it's nighttime, keep your baby's room dark—even when it's time for a feed or diaper change (a very dim nightlight can help you find your way). Keeping the lights off will reinforce for your baby that when it's dark, it's nighttime—and time for sleep.

Minimize interactions during night feedings. Make nighttime downtime, even during those night feedings. Soft lullabies and soothing words are fine, but avoid excitement. If you're swaddling your newborn (no worries if you don't since it's not a must do; see the box on page 12), keep your baby swaddled for night feedings (but change his diaper first). You'll feed him unswaddled during the day.

Make a big deal of the morning. Create some excitement when your baby wakes up in the morning. Sing a good morning song, open the shades to let the morning sun in, and generally start the day with a bustle of activity. Since you'll be keeping night wake-ups low-key, your baby will begin to notice the difference.

Keep your baby active when awake. Though there won't be much time between naps in the early weeks (only around 30 to 60 minutes—you'll know your baby is ready for a nap again when you notice sleep cues; see page 55), try to keep your baby active between those daytime naps. Take your baby for a walk and talk to him. Bring him along on chores and narrate as you work. Play music and offer some toys to get your little one engaged (see pages 24 and 46 for some ideas). You can also keep daytime feeds stimulating—talk and sing to your baby while he's eating.

Keep the room light during naps. During daytime naps it's okay to keep the room light (no need to close the shades) and the house noisy—at least in the newborn stage (after the second month, your baby will sleep better in darkness). Another great way to help your baby's circadian rhythms adapt to a day versus night schedule is to expose him to sunlight every day (weather permitting). Getting fresh air will be great for you, too!

DRESSING YOUR BABY FOR SLEEP

Keeping your baby at a comfortable temperature can make for better and healthier sleep. Once your baby is past the first week or two of life, his ability to regulate his temperature is pretty sophisticated. That means you can dress your little one for sleep as you would yourself—for example, in a one-piece outfit or other warm pajamas plus a (non-weighted) sleep sack or swaddle layer (the equivalent of your blanket, since your baby can't use a blanket in the first year; see page 8 for more on safe sleep). Never put your baby to sleep with a hat on. In fact, your baby doesn't need a hat indoors at all after the first few hours of life. That could lead to overheating, which increases the risk of SIDS.

Check to make sure your baby is neither too cold nor too warm with a quick feel to the back of his neck or his chest. Don't use his fingers or the tip of his nose as a temperature gauge, since those body parts tend to be colder than the core body temperature.

SIGNS YOUR BABY IS HUNGRY

EARLY HUNGER CUES

Sucking sounds, sucking on the lips, or opening and closing the mouth

Sucking on hands or fingers

ACTIVE HUNGER CUES

Fidgeting, squirming, sniffing around your chest

Rooting reflex

LATE HUNGER CUES

Moving head frantically side to side

Crying

A CLOSER LOOK

In the first few months of your baby's life, you'll be feeding your little one every 2 to 4 hours. Even though you'll be following the clock somewhat to know when it's time for a feeding, you'll really be feeding on demand—in other words, feeding your baby whenever she wants to be fed. And that means you'll need to be on the lookout for hunger cues.

Early hunger cues. Early hunger cues might include lip licking, sucking, or smacking; her mouth opening and closing; or finger or hand sucking.

Active hunger cues. Active hunger cues can include fussing or squirming, fast breathing, and sniffing and turning toward your chest. This turning toward the side to try to find food is called the rooting reflex. This reflex, which can also be elicited by touching your baby's cheek (even when she isn't hungry), lasts until your baby is around four months old.

Late hunger cues. Late hunger cues include your baby moving her head frantically from side to side in search of a meal—and, of course, crying. Because it's much harder for a baby to latch on properly and suck effectively when she's crying hysterically, you'll ideally want to offer the breast or bottle before she reaches this late hunger cue.

If your baby is the type who tends to sleep through mealtime instead of showing these hunger cues, your pediatrician may have advised that you wake her regularly for feedings until she's around eight weeks old.

If your baby falls asleep during feedings before she's eaten her fill, you can wake her by burping her (see page 42 for burping tips), undressing her (newborns don't like to be cold), changing her diaper, switching feeding positions, moving her elbow and arm up and down (she'll look like a chicken, but it works!), or running a cool washcloth over her forehead or back.

YOUR BABY'S POOP: WHAT'S NORMAL

A breastfed baby's poop is usually mustard-colored, seedy, and loose

A formula-fed baby's poop is usually yellow or brown with a pasty peanut butter–like consistency

Constipation is when poop is small, round, and hard—not when a baby doesn't poop every day

After the first month or two, your baby may not poop every day

Your baby's poop will change when he starts solids

It's normal for a baby to grunt while pooping out even soft poop

A CLOSER LOOK

With all the diapers you've been changing, you would think you'd have a handle on their contents by now. But as with many things parenting, you may be in for surprises at each diaper change. Here's what normal (and what's not) when it comes to your baby's poop.

Color and consistency. Remember when you changed your baby's early newborn diapers? Those first few poops, called meconium, were blackish green in color, with a sticky and almost tar-like consistency. Transitional stool came next—darkish green-yellow in color, loose, sometimes seedy and mucousy. But now, the color and consistency of your baby's poop will depend on what your baby is eating.

If you're feeding your baby breast milk, his bowel movements will most often be a mustard-yellow color with a loose, seedy consistency. Those seeds, by the way, are undigested fat globules. But because there's a lot of variation across normal infant poop, the color can vary from brownish to yellow to green. Green, watery, frothy stool in a breastfed baby may mean your baby is getting more foremilk (the lower-fat milk that comes out first) than hindmilk (the more calorie-rich milk that's released in the second part of a breastfeeding session). If that's the case with your baby, be sure you aren't removing him from the breast too soon—keep him latched on until your breast is well drained before switching to the second side. If your baby is content and gaining weight, there's no reason to be concerned about green poop.

If you're feeding your baby formula, he will likely have soft, paste-like stool that's yellow to brown to brown-green in color.

Once your baby starts solids at six months old, your baby's poop will change again. Expect it to look brown or dark brown, though don't be surprised if it comes out blue from the blueberries he ate, orange from the carrots, red from the beets, green from the spinach, and so on. It will be firmer and thicker but still mushy, and occasionally appear to have chunks of undigested food in it (not to worry if that happens from time to time—your baby's chewing and digestion are still maturing). It'll also be smellier than when your baby was on a liquid-only diet.

By the way, if you ever notice blood in the stool, it could mean your baby is allergic or sensitive to something (most often dairy) in your diet or in the formula. Mention it to your pediatrician. Also mention to your doctor if your baby's poop is very watery, mucousy, and greener than usual *and* your baby is showing signs of fever or greater-than-usual irritability. That could signal diarrhea, and your baby will need an evaluation to make sure he's not sick or dehydrated. And if your baby's poop is black (after the first week of life), white, gray, or red, call your doctor to get your baby checked out.

Frequency. Expect at least three to four poops daily for some babies in the early months. Some might be very messy (cue the poop blowouts!), but these poops will let you know your baby is getting enough to eat (see page 15).

Once your baby is over six weeks old, you don't have to count dirty diapers anymore. In fact, it's totally normal for your baby not to poop daily, especially if your baby is breastfed. That's because his body becomes proficient at using up most of the nutrients and components of breast milk, leaving little left to poop out. Some breastfed babies may even go a few days to a week without pooping after the newborn stage.

Don't mistake frequency (or infrequency) of bowel movements for constipation in the first year. If your baby's stool is infrequent yet soft, even if it has some form to it, he's not constipated. Constipation is when poop is in small, hard, round balls that are difficult to pass. If you notice constipation in your baby, let your pediatrician know.

Sound effects. It's also not a sign of constipation if your baby seems to struggle while pooping. Straining is normal for little poopers because it's hard work to coordinate all the muscles needed to push out those bowel movements—even soft ones. In time, your baby will learn to poop without making such a scene. Until then, don't worry if he grunts, groans, and contorts his face. And be prepared for the poops themselves to be explosive and loud. Things will quiet down eventually.

BURPING YOUR BABY

BURPING POSITIONS

Place your baby
over your shoulder

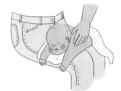

Lay your baby
across your lap

Support your
baby sitting up

BURPING TECHNIQUES

Pat or rub your
baby's back

Focus on the left side
of your baby's back

Use a burp cloth
to catch spit-up

A CLOSER LOOK

Burping your baby helps your little one bring up excess air swallowed during feeding and crying, easing discomfort. If you're nursing, burp your baby before you switch to the second breast. If you're bottle feeding, stop halfway through the bottle to burp your baby. End feedings with a final burp.

Burping positions. You can burp your baby over your shoulder, lying tummy-down on your lap, or sitting up on your lap with your baby leaning forward and her chest and chin supported by your arm and hand. Some days one position will work better than the other, so don't feel you have to stick with only one burping position. And here's a quick baby burping hack: If you're not getting a burp, it may help to lay your baby down for a minute or two and then pick her back up again. Often the change in position brings up a burp faster.

Burping techniques. You can either rub or pat your baby's back. When doing so, focus on your baby's left side, since that's the side where her tummy is located.

Parents are often surprised at how much force they sometimes need to use to get their baby to produce a burp. You don't want to punch your baby or hit her very hard, obviously, but don't tap too lightly, either. A firm tap is not going to hurt your baby.

Don't be upset if your baby doesn't burp every time. Try for a few minutes and then stop. There's no need to burp your baby for longer than 5 minutes if it's unproductive. In fact, in some babies, burping may not do any good—they either aren't burpers or the burping itself makes things more uncomfortable. If burping doesn't work for your baby, don't bother with it.

Spitting up. Grab a burp cloth to catch spit-up. Not all babies spit up during burps, but if yours does, you'll want to protect your clothing. Read more about gassy babies and spitting up on pages 66 and 84.

GIVING YOUR BABY A BATH

Until the umbilical cord stump falls off, give only sponge baths

Fill the bath with warm water no higher than your baby's chest

Gather what you need before putting your baby in the bath

Keep your eyes and hands on your baby at all times

Use a gentle soap or cleanser

Wash from cleanest to dirtiest areas (usually top to bottom)

A CLOSER LOOK

Bath time may become a cherished and relaxing part of your baby's day. Or maybe it won't. Some babies love a bath, while others loathe being lathered. Luckily, babies don't need daily baths—bathing your baby two or three times a week is just fine. There's also nothing wrong with giving him a daily bath if you want to and if your baby enjoys a good soak in the tub. Here's how.

Until the umbilical cord stump falls off, give only sponge baths. Before the umbilical cord stump falls off (usually within a week to ten days after birth), you'll be sponge bathing your baby by cleaning the diaper area, under the neck, in your baby's curled fists, and so on with a washcloth. When the stump falls off, you can start giving full baths in a baby bathtub.

Fill the bath with warm water no higher than your baby's chest. When you're giving a bath, make sure the room you're doing the bathing in is warm (around 75° to 80°F, if possible). After filling the baby bath, test the water's temperature with your elbow or the back of your hand to ensure it's comfortably warm before putting your baby in. The water level should reach no higher than your baby's chest.

Keep safety in mind. Gather everything you need for the bath before you place your baby in the tub—the towel, body wash, washcloth, shampoo—and have it all within arm's reach so you don't have to scramble mid-bath. Hold your baby securely in a semi-reclining position or use a bath with built-in supports. Even with those supports, however, it's always best to keep your hand on your small baby for safety's sake. Skip the bath seats, even once your baby can sit well, since most safety experts recommend against using them. Your undivided attention during bath time (which means no texting or talking on the phone) will help keep your baby safe.

Use a gentle soap or cleanser. Choose a gentle body wash or body wash/shampoo combo with baby-safe ingredients (look for ones that are tear-free).

Wash from the cleanest to dirtiest areas. Using your hands or a washcloth, wash your baby from the cleanest to dirtiest areas—usually from top to bottom. If you prefer to skip shampooing at some bathtimes, that's fine. Once or twice a week is probably enough when it comes to washing your baby's hair (that is, until your baby starts putting food in his hair instead of his mouth during feeding time).

One of the areas you don't have to clean is inside your baby's ears. You can clean the outer ears during bath time, but using a cotton swab or even your finger inside the ear canal can be dangerous. Wax will naturally make its way out of the ear, so don't pick out wax—even wax you can easily see.

STIMULATING YOUR BABY IN THE SECOND MONTH

Gently stretch your baby's hands up and say, "So big!"

Join your baby tummy-down on a mat

Shake a rattle or toy for your baby to follow with her eyes

Give your baby a massage

Put on music and slow dance with your baby

Clap your baby's hands together and sing *Patty-Cake* or other nursery rhymes

A CLOSER LOOK

Your baby, while still blob-like, is interacting more with you these days—especially with that emerging social smile. Here are some ways to play with your baby in the second month.

Gently stretch your baby's hands up and say, "So big!"

Finger- and hand-play games will be a big part of your repertoire when interacting with your baby during the first year. Start with this simple game: Lift your baby's arms up and say, "Soooo big!" In a few months' time, your baby will do her own heavy lifting, bringing up her arms whenever you ask, "How big is baby?"

Join your baby tummy-down on a mat. You already know why tummy time is so important for your little one. Make it fun by getting in the game yourself! And check out pages 21–22 for other ways to make tummy time more fun for your baby.

Shake a rattle or toy for your baby to follow with her eyes. It might seem like no biggie for a baby to track (or follow) an object, such as a rattle, with her eyes. But the truth is, the ability to synchronously move her eyes in the same direction is a big milestone for your baby to reach, and most babies only hit it sometime after month two. You can help encourage development of this visual milestone by holding a toy or rattle (which adds auditory interest, too) in front of your baby and slowly moving it from side to side. Watch how your baby follows it!

Give your baby a massage. Babies learn a lot through their sense of touch, which is well developed by birth. That's why massaging your infant is good for her emotional (and even physical) well-being. Massage can be a powerful form of communication between babies and their parents, making it a great bonding experience. It also increases your little one's serotonin levels, helping to relax and soothe her. Check out page 87 for baby massage tips.

Put on music and slow dance with your baby. Introduce your baby to the world of music by letting her listen to the stimulating sounds of your voice, musical toys, or your favorite playlist. Slow dancing will also delight your baby, and the movement will help her learn to hold her head steady and gain strength in her core. Be sure to keep volume levels low so you don't hurt those precious baby ears, and hold your baby's head securely to make sure it doesn't flop around.

Clap your baby's hands together and sing *Patty-Cake* or other nursery rhymes. Talking, singing, and playing with your baby helps stimulate crucial communication skills. Carrying on conversations with your baby (even though she doesn't understand a word of it) is one of the most important ways to stimulate your baby. Nursery rhymes, especially when repeated, help your baby learn about sounds, language, and emotions. Coupling them with finger movements also helps promote important small motor skills such as clapping, waving, and fine finger movements down the road.

THINGS THAT ARE OKAY WHEN YOU'RE A NEW PARENT

It's okay if you still don't feel an intense connection with your baby

It's okay if you still feel overwhelmed

It's okay if your baby still fusses all the time

It's okay if being a parent feels very hard

It's okay if you need medication and/or therapy to help with mental health

It's okay if you don't want to or can't breastfeed

A CLOSER LOOK

There is a lot of pressure placed on new parents—by themselves, by others, by family members. Being a new mom or dad is hard enough without that added burden, so give yourself a break. Know that it's okay if you feel overwhelmed, don't love being a parent, don't meet all the expectations you had for yourself, or don't fit into what society's idealized version of parenthood looks like. You're doing a great job no matter what your parenthood journey looks like!

It's okay if you still don't feel an intense connection with your baby. It's been nearly two months with your new roommate and you would think that by now you'd not only be used to having him around, but also that you'd be feeling that special parent–baby bond. But your baby is not interacting much yet, is sleeping most of the day, and is almost certainly keeping you up most of the night. Those are reasons enough to keep you from feeling super bonded to your mini-roomie. Don't worry. Not feeling an immediate connection to your baby in these early months is quite normal. In time, your newborn blob will become a little baby with a big personality and a bond will grow without you even realizing—a bond that comes from the experiences you share and the love and attention you shower on him every day.

It's okay if you still feel overwhelmed. Feeling like a hamster in a wheel? Going, going, going, but never getting anywhere? These first months with a new baby can be overwhelming. You're up all night nursing a cluster-feeding baby and spending all day changing diapers and messy outfits. Your nipples and washing machine never seem to catch a break, and neither do you. Becoming a new parent is challenging because everything is so new. Know that all new parents feel overwhelmed, if not every day then at least many of them. And that's okay. Things will get easier, and you will get through this, one day at a time!

It's okay if your baby still fusses all the time. All babies fuss. It's what babies do—their way of communicating with you. But some may fuss a lot more than others, and quite a few babies this age cry or fuss endlessly, often with no clear reason (see the box on page 18). Remind yourself again and again that you're not doing anything wrong, your baby is okay, and you both will survive this trying time. These days with a fussy baby may feel like they're lasting an eternity, but there are lots of smiles and giggles headed your way soon.

It's okay if being a parent feels very hard. As you finish changing your tenth poop blowout of the week, you may feel very done with this whole parenting thing. Truth is, parenting a newborn (and a baby, and a toddler, and a teenager) is hard. Endless baby care takes a toll on you, and it's okay to acknowledge how hard it is. After all, you can't leave the house anymore without worrying about when your baby needs to eat. You'd rather stay out until the wee hours of the night with friends than spend the wee hours of the night begging your baby to close his eyes. You'd prefer to have time for yourself instead of feeling like you barely have time to pee in peace. This is all normal, and you're not the only new parent feeling this way. Being a parent is the hardest job you'll ever have, so don't feel guilty if (when) you're ready to give up or feel crushed under the burden of it all. Hang in there. For every moment of difficulty, there's an equal moment of reward, and pretty soon those rewarding parts of parenting will outweigh the challenging ones.

It's okay if you need medication and/or therapy to help with mental health. Approximately 10 percent of new moms experience postpartum depression (PPD) or postpartum anxiety (PPA). New fathers aren't immune from mental health issues either. Around 5 percent of new dads also experience PPD or PPA. Both are highly treatable with therapy and/or medication. You don't have to suffer alone or in silence if you're feeling down or anxious and just can't seem to shake it. There's no shame in asking for help and treatment if you need it, and it can make a huge difference when it comes to feeling better and being the best parent you can be to your little one.

It's okay if you don't want to or can't breastfeed. There are plenty of good reasons to breastfeed your baby, and yes, breast milk is tailor-made for your growing little one. But it's certainly okay if you choose not to or can't breastfeed, whatever the reason. Ultimately, fed is best, and doing what feels right for you and your baby is the best way to parent. Breast or bottle, breast milk or formula, your little one will be just fine.

You know what else is also okay? If you're feeling great, loving every minute of new parenthood, and on cloud nine with your new baby. Every new mom or dad is different, and your experience will be uniquely yours. Embrace your new role as parent no matter what emotions come with it!

LEARN MORE

Here are some other topics in the chapters to come that may be relevant this month:

- Sleep cues (page 55)
- Establishing a bedtime routine (page 58)
- Bottle or breast refusal (page 61)
- Diaper rash (page 69)
- Pimples, cradle cap, and other common rashes (page 89)
- Gassiness (page 66)
- Spitting up (page 84)
- Baby massage (page 87)

MONTH THREE

Welcome to the third month! You've made it through the newborn stage, and your baby has morphed from a curled-up blob to an unfurled, more alert, awake, and engaged companion—one who has been growing by leaps and bounds and who has almost certainly outgrown those adorable newborn clothes.

Listen for your little one's gurgles and squeals, revel in those adorable smiles, and pay attention to your baby's cues so you'll know when he or she could use some stimulation (a book, a mirror, a toy), needs a nap, is ready for another feeding, or would rather just watch the world go by (such as during a walk outdoors).

The most exciting toy for your baby this month is you, and there's nothing more engaging to him or her than the sound of your voice. Talk, sing, and interact with your baby. You're setting the stage for amazing language and social–emotional growth to come.

MONTH THREE OVERVIEW

TWO TO THREE MONTHS OLD

SLEEPING

14–16 HOURS
Total time your baby may sleep in a 24-hour day

3–4
Number of naps your baby may take each day

60 MINUTES
Time your baby may be awake between naps

EATING

6–10
Number of liquid meals your baby may have each day

16–32 OUNCES
Total amount of breast milk or formula your baby may drink each day

3–4 HOURS
Time between feedings

GROWING

8 LBS 13 OZ–14 LBS 5 OZ
21–24 IN
Average range of weight and height for a baby girl this age

9 LBS 11 OZ–15 LBS 7 OZ
21½–24½ IN
Average range of weight and height for a baby boy this age

A CLOSER LOOK

Your baby is a unique individual, on his or her own developmental timeline, growing at his or her own pace, with his or her own distinctive temperament, personality, desires, and needs. That means that how much (or how often) he sleeps, how many feedings she has, how tall he is, or how much she weighs will be unique to your little one.

This overview (and the other monthly overviews in this book) represents what a baby *might* be doing, eating, or gaining this month. But because every child is different, your baby won't necessarily fit perfectly into these averages. That's okay. Use these overviews as rough guides to help you gauge what might be happening with your baby this month, recognizing that the range of normal is wide. And then enjoy your baby wherever he or she happens to land.

SIGNS YOUR BABY IS SLEEPY

Eyes that look
red, less focused,
or glazed over

Slower sucking
on the pacifier,
bottle, or breast

A decrease
in activity

Yawning

Thumb
sucking

Hair pulling, eye
rubbing, ear pulling

Fussiness,
clinginess

Crying

A CLOSER LOOK

One of the best things you can do for your baby is establish a
good foundation for healthy, quality sleep. Noticing your baby's
tiredness cues—and then responding by putting your baby down
to sleep—is one important step. Not all babies exhibit the same
sleepy signs, but the more attuned you are to your little one, the
more likely you'll recognize her signs of tiredness. Here are some
examples of sleep cues.

Eyes that look red, less focused, or glazed over. As your baby
becomes drowsy, her eyes will appear unfocused and glassy.
Redness around the eyes or even around the eyebrows can also
be a clue.

Slower sucking and/or a general decrease in activity. If your baby is sucking on the breast, her bottle, or a pacifier, you might notice a slowdown in sucking. If your baby is batting at a toy bar, you might observe a decrease in playful motions. Another tired cue could be if your baby has shifted from social butterfly to apathetic (though it could simply indicate your baby is overstimulated and needs a break).

Yawning. Unsurprisingly, yawning is a tired cue. Listen, too, for deep sighs—they're another a sign of drowsiness.

Thumb sucking. Your baby's thumb or fingers may find their way to her mouth—a comfort habit that could be a sign of tiredness. (Of course, finger sucking can also mean your baby is seeking comfort for another reason or because she's hungry; see page 37. You'll learn how your little one uses thumb/finger sucking the more you get to know your baby.)

Hair pulling, eye rubbing, ear pulling. Your baby's later sleepy cues might include pulling her hair (if your baby's got some), rubbing her eyes, or pulling on an ear.

Fussiness or clinginess. As your baby gets more and more tired, you'll see more and more fussiness and perhaps clinginess. Older babies may seem harder to please or become easily irritated. If you haven't gotten your baby down to sleep yet, now is the time!

Crying. If your baby is very grouchy or crying, you're at a late-stage sleep cue. Waiting any longer to put her to sleep will result in an overtired baby.

It's more difficult for an overtired baby to fall asleep, stay asleep, and sleep well. So, pay attention to your baby, watch for those sleepiness cues, and put her to sleep before she reaches the point of overtiredness.

Keep in mind that, as your baby gets older, sleep cues shouldn't be the only way you determine sleep times. Yes, watching and responding to your baby will still be important to know when it's time for a nap. But it'll be equally important to set up a nap schedule to ensure your baby is getting enough sleep. This may mean putting your baby down for naps at her usual time, even if she's not showing any overt sleepy signs. Each month's overview (see page 53 for this month's) will give you average wake windows (the amount of time your baby stays awake between naps) to help you set up a flexible and workable daily schedule.

ESTABLISHING A BEDTIME ROUTINE

A warm bath	A massage	PJs	Final feeding (bottle or breast)

A book	A lullaby	Some cuddles and/or rocking	Good night

A CLOSER LOOK

Healthy sleep habits start with a consistent bedtime routine—and you can implement one even when your baby is only a few months old. A bedtime routine helps soothe your baby, marking the transition from activity to calm and letting your baby know that it's time for sleep. A bedtime routine will also be key when you're helping your baby learn to sleep through the night (see page 103). Here are some steps you can incorporate into your baby's bedtime routine.

A warm bath. While a baby doesn't *need* to be bathed every night, especially if he hasn't gotten dirty during the day, a rubdown in the tub can become a favorite part of the before-sleep routine. Many parents find incorporating a bath into the bedtime routine helps calm their babies after an action-packed day. See page 44 for bath time tips.

A massage. Some babies love being massaged; others, not so much. If yours does, this calming practice can be incorporated into your bedtime routine. Even if you don't make it a formal massage, merely rubbing lotion into your baby's damp skin can be a soothing part of the pre-bed ritual. Read more about baby massage on page 87.

PJs. Since a bedtime routine is all about marking the difference between daytime and nighttime, changing into pajamas can help your baby get the message that playtime is over and it's time for a (hopefully) restful night. What those PJs consist of will depend on room temperature and your baby's age. The box on page 36 will help you decide how to dress your baby for sleep. The box on page 12 will answer your questions about swaddling.

Final feeding. Now's a good time in the bedtime routine for that final bottle or nursing. If you find your baby is falling asleep during this feeding, you can move it earlier in the routine, since it's best to let your baby fall asleep on his own in the crib. There's certainly nothing wrong with your baby falling asleep while nursing or drinking from a bottle (especially at this young age), and if it works for you, go for it. But know that it may make those nighttime wake-ups harder down the road, since your baby will become acclimated to only falling asleep while feeding. See page 105 for more on sleep associations. By the way, never give your baby a bottle in the crib. It could lead to choking and tooth decay, plus can result in your baby associating food with being in the crib.

A book. Don't let your baby's young age stop you from reading to him. An early introduction to books will help foster a love of reading and boost your baby's language development, and any book with a soothing cadence can be the perfect coda to your bedtime routine. For a baby this young, a short book with high-contrast patterns and few words will suffice, and as he grows, you can increase the complexity. Read more about reading to your baby on page 153.

A lullaby, some cuddles, and/or some rocking. The final part of the bedtime routine can be a soft lullaby, some gentle rocking, some kisses and hugs, and a brief goodnight. Avoid rocking your baby completely to sleep if possible, placing him down in the crib just before he's been lulled into dreamland so that he gets used to falling asleep on his own instead of in motion in your arms.

Repeating this process nightly will help your baby know what to expect, and the routine will become an anticipated element of his (and your) evening.

IF YOUR BABY REFUSES THE BREAST OR BOTTLE

IF YOUR BABY REFUSES THE BREAST

Relax so the milk flows

Pump first if the issue is slow letdown

Offer expressed breast milk in a bottle

Treat thrush

IF YOUR BABY REFUSES THE BOTTLE

Try different types and styles of bottles and nipples

Warm the bottle nipple

Have someone besides mom offer the bottle

Offer the bottle when your baby is sleepy

FOR BOTH BREAST AND BOTTLE REFUSAL

Don't wait too long to feed a hungry baby

Be sure your baby is actually hungry

Clear your baby's nose

Try again . . . and again . . . and again

A CLOSER LOOK

You thought you had the baby feeding process in the bag, but suddenly (and seemingly out of the blue) your little one is refusing the breast or bottle. Here's how to tackle both nursing and bottle strikes.

Nursing strikes—when your baby refuses to suckle from the breast—are happily short-lived, usually lasting only a day or two. What brings on a nursing strike? Maybe you've changed your deodorant or you're using a new moisturizer, and your scent is unfamiliar to your baby. Or perhaps your baby is starting to teethe and her gums are sore, making it hard to suckle on your breasts. Or maybe you're ovulating (something that would be less likely but not impossible if you're exclusively breastfeeding), have your period, or are newly pregnant, and your breast milk tastes different due to a hormonal shift. Here are some strategies to try if you're dealing with a nursing strike.

Relax so the milk flows. Babies are pretty attuned to their moms' stress levels, and if you feel anxious, your baby might also feel unsettled and refuse the breast. Take a deep breath, meditate, listen to some soothing music . . . whatever it takes to relax before you bring your baby to the breast. Nursing in a quiet, dimly lit room that's free of distractions can also help relax both you and your little one.

Pump first if the issue is slow letdown. Does it take a while for your milk to start flowing? Slow letdown can sometimes be the reason behind a nursing strike. Your hungry baby becomes impatient and frustrated, then unlatches in despair. You can work around this issue by pumping just enough milk right before a feeding to jumpstart letdown and get the milk flowing.

Offer expressed breast milk in a bottle. Try offering breast milk in a bottle instead of from your breasts for a few feeds. Your baby may be more amenable to a meal that way. And since you'll be pumping, your milk supply won't suffer.

Treat thrush. Thrush, an oral yeast infection, can make nursing painful for babies. You'll know your little one has thrush if you see white, cottage cheese–like spots inside your baby's mouth, on her tongue, and/or at the corners of her mouth. These spots won't wipe off easily, unlike milk residue, which will appear as a white tongue or white spots in your baby's mouth, so don't confuse the two. There's no need to discontinue nursing, but because thrush can be easily transmitted between you and your baby, your doctor will likely treat both of you. You'll use an antifungal cream on your nipples, which may appear pink, shiny, and crusty, and your baby will be treated with a topical oral antifungal medication. The infection should clear up after about a week, hopefully ending the nursing strike as well.

Whatever is causing the nursing strike, remind yourself that it's only temporary and not an indication that your baby wants to wean.

Bottle refusals are also often only temporary. They are more likely to happen in a baby who's going back and forth between the breast and bottle, who's only recently been introduced to the bottle, or who's with an unfamiliar caregiver or in a new environment (such as day care). Here are some strategies to try if you're dealing with bottle refusal.

Try different types of bottles and nipples. There are many bottle and nipple shapes and sizes on the market, so try a few options to determine which style your baby likes best. Perhaps it's one that mimics a breast or that has a more orthodontic shape. Or maybe your baby prefers a nipple made from a different material (silicone, for instance, versus latex). Make sure, too, that you're using the correct nipple size for your baby's age. A nipple that's too big or too small, or has a flow that's too fast or slow, may make sucking challenging for your baby, resulting in a refusal to feed.

Warm the bottle nipple. Maybe your baby is protesting a cold nipple, especially if she's used to mom's warm one. A quick nip dip in warm water may make the bottle more palatable to your baby. Experiment with the temperature of the milk, too. Some babies prefer warmed milk, but most babies are fine with room temperature or even cold milk. As a general rule, you do not have to warm formula or breast milk. Your baby can drink both straight from the refrigerator or at room temperature.

Have someone besides mom offer the bottle. Nursing babies are used to the warmth of their moms' bodies, their smell, touch, and everything else that comes along as a bonus during nursing sessions. Babies sometimes refuse a bottle from mom, or when mom is nearby, because they know those familiar breasts are teasingly close. If possible, having someone other than the nursing parent offer the bottle may help curb the refusal, as may having mom stay out of the room so your baby doesn't get distracted by her presence and the promise of what's under her shirt.

Offer the bottle when your baby is sleepy. A stubborn baby may be less determined to reject the bottle if she's sleepy and too tired to put up a fight. Don't turn this into a habit (see page 105 for reasons why), but it's a good tactic to try in the short term to deal with bottle refusal.

For both a nursing strike and bottle rejection, you can try the following.

Don't wait too long to feed a hungry baby. A baby who's frantic for a meal may be so out of sorts that she unwittingly refuses a feeding no matter what source it comes from, rejecting the bottle or even the breast out of frustration without realizing the consequences (continued hunger). Watch your baby for early hunger signs (see page 37) so you can offer her a meal before she gets hangry.

Be sure your baby is actually hungry. Unsurprisingly, a baby may reject the bottle or breast because she's not hungry. Remember, crying doesn't always indicate hunger, and responding to every wail with a feeding instead of seeing if there's another reason for the fussiness could be the reason your baby is not interested in eating. See page 16 for soothing strategies to try when your baby is crying for reasons other than hunger.

Clear your baby's nose. Colds and even dry indoor air can cause nasal congestion in babies, making it more difficult for them to eat. You can help clear your baby's nose by using saline drops and a nasal aspirator to suction out the mucus. Don't go overboard with the nasal aspirator, however. Using it more than two to three times a day can irritate your baby's tender nasal lining and make her even more congested. Save the aspirator for when the congestion is interfering with your baby's ability to eat or breathe. Running a humidifier in your baby's room to keep the air moist can also help clear nasal passages.

Try again. Just because your baby rejects the breast or bottle once (or five times) doesn't mean she will also refuse it the next time, so try again and again. Feeding strikes are temporary, and often over as quickly as they began. If none of these tips work, try others: Vary the feeding position, nurse or bottle feed when in motion, and/or give your baby extra attention and skin-to-skin contact when not feeding. It may take some time to figure out the cause of the feeding refusal, but once you do, you'll hopefully be able to bring it to an end.

PREVENTING AND TREATING GASSINESS

Feed your baby before crying starts

Keep your baby's head higher than his tummy during feedings

Don't let air get into bottle nipples

Burp your baby during feedings

Bounce your baby on your lap

Bicycle your baby's legs

Gently massage your baby's tummy

Offer probiotics

A CLOSER LOOK

Most babies are gassy babies. Little ones tend to gulp in a lot of air during feeding and while crying. Add to that an immature digestive system that's still working out the kinks, and it's a recipe for gassiness. Signs of gas include arching the back, pulling the legs up to the stomach, and general squirminess. Luckily, there are strategies you can use to try to prevent excess gassiness and bring some relief when gassiness occurs.

Feed your baby before crying starts. You've already learned that crying is a late hunger cue (see page 37). Ideally, you'll want to get your baby on the breast or bottle before frantic crying begins, not only because it's easier to feed a calm baby, but also because your baby will gulp in less air, resulting in less gassiness.

Keep your baby's head higher than his tummy during feedings. Another way to prevent excess air from troubling your baby's tummy is to keep him more upright during feedings. It's easy to do if you're bottle feeding, and it's possible even if you're nursing: Position your baby in your arms so his head is higher than his tummy.

Don't let air get into bottle nipples. Tilting your baby's bottle so that the milk fills the entire nipple will help reduce the amount of air your little one swallows. Choosing bottles that promise to reduce air intake might also help.

Burp your baby during feedings. Burping your baby during and after feedings will help bring up excess air, making your baby feel more comfortable. Read all about burping your baby on page 42.

Bounce your baby on your lap. When your baby's got gas, try bouncing it out. Hold your baby securely on your lap and slowly bounce him up and down—you can do this in a chair or on an exercise ball. Don't overdo it, and try not to bounce too closely to the end of a feed, since doing so may elicit lots of spit-up. But gentle bouncing may help move air bubbles through the upper digestive tract, expelling trapped gas.

Bicycle your baby's legs. Burping and bouncing help with air in the upper digestive tract, but gas can also form in the intestines. If your baby seems uncomfortable, try bicycling your cutie's legs. The leg movement can help air pockets in the lower digestive tract move down and out (cue the farts!).

Gently massage your baby's tummy. A tummy massage can also help get trapped air moving through the body, and it's most effective when your baby is calm. It's best not to use massage as a gas-relieving technique too soon after feedings, though, as that can be uncomfortable for your baby and even cause vomiting. When rubbing your baby's tummy to move gas along, do so in a clockwise direction, which follows the path of the intestinal tract.

Offer probiotics. Ask your pediatrician if probiotic drops might be a good idea for your baby. There's research suggesting these good bacteria can help reduce gastric inflammation and ease gas discomfort.

What about gripe water? Before you turn to this popular remedy, know that there's no scientific evidence showing that gripe water relieves gas discomfort. Baby gas medication drops also probably don't help, but gas drops are likely a safer option than gripe water, which sometimes has questionable ingredients.

BREASTFEEDING AND GAS

If you're breastfeeding, you may think that you need to watch what you eat to ensure your baby doesn't become gassy. The good news is that most breastfed babies are not sensitive to what their moms eat. Yes, you may hear friends swear that what they eat impacts their babies' tummies and causes gas and discomfort, but the actual scientific data doesn't back this up. Many babies have tummy discomfort whether they're breastfed or formula fed. It's just the way babies' tummies are. In other words, you don't have to avoid broccoli or chocolate when you're breastfeeding.

That said, there are always exceptions to the rule, and if you suspect that your baby has a sensitivity to something you've eaten (maybe caffeine or cabbage), you can eliminate that food from your diet for at least two to three weeks before reintroducing it. Once you reintroduce the food, watch your baby closely to see if there's an increase in tummy trouble, which could mean your baby is sensitive to it.

Additionally, a small fraction of babies are sensitive (or even allergic) to the cow's milk proteins that get into a mom's milk from the dairy she consumes (often blood in a baby's stool, rather than gas, is a clue). If you suspect that's the case with your little one, discuss with your pediatrician whether you should eliminate dairy from your diet.

PREVENTING AND TREATING DIAPER RASH

Change dirty diapers promptly

Use gentle, unscented wipes on your baby's bottom

After wiping, dry your baby's bottom completely

Use a thick layer of diaper cream or ointment

Give your baby some diaper-free time

For a tougher case, a prescription cream may be necessary

A CLOSER LOOK

You probably never realized just how many diapers you'd be changing in the early months (by now you're a pro!). Something else you may not have expected is diaper rash, which is very common on baby bottoms. Luckily there are strategies you can use to prevent (and cure) diaper rash.

Change dirty diapers promptly. Prolonged exposure to pee and poop can irritate skin, so change those diapers when they get dirty.

Use gentle, unscented wipes. Water-based wipes or the unscented, gentle varieties are kinder to your baby's bottom than those with irritating ingredients, reducing the chance of diaper rash. Not a fan of wipes? No problem. Water and a little gentle soap on a washcloth can work just as well.

After wiping, dry your baby's bottom completely. Once you've cleaned your baby's bum, expose it to the air. A smart parenting hack is to fan your baby's bottom with a clean diaper until it's dry to the touch (it should feel as dry as any other part of the body—like the tummy, for instance). If you smear cream or ointment when your baby's bottom is still a little damp, you'll be trapping in moisture, which sets the stage for irritation—exactly what you're trying to prevent.

Use a thick layer of diaper cream or ointment. Open that tube or tub of ointment or cream and spread a thick, protective layer all over your baby's tush. It'll create a barrier for your baby's skin, preventing chafing and relieving any rash. Experiment with different types and brands to find the one that works best for your babe's butt.

Give your baby some diaper-free time. Occasionally, place your baby on a protected surface and let his bum go free. Allowing the skin to breathe this way is helpful for preventing a rash, but especially great if your little one has redness or a rash in the diaper area already.

For a tough case, prescription cream may be necessary. If the rash doesn't clear up in a few days, if it starts to spread beyond the diaper area, or if it starts to look especially angry, call your pediatrician. A steroid or antifungal cream or ointment may be prescribed.

STIMULATING YOUR BABY IN THE THIRD MONTH

Offer rings and rattles for your baby to grab and play with

Change your baby's position and locations

Repeat your baby's coos and babbles and encourage her to imitate the sounds you make

Hang colorful toys on a toy bar and encourage your baby to bat at them

Put a mirror in front of your baby so she can "play" with "a friend"

PEEKABOO!

Play peekaboo

A CLOSER LOOK

Your baby's personality is beginning to shine through this month, and she'll be sharing a lot more smiles and even a few squeals with you each day! Here are some ideas to excite and entertain your baby in the third month.

Offer rings and rattles for your baby to grab and play with.
Your baby's fine motor skills are getting ready for some fine tuning. Though her fists are likely still clenched most of the time, her pudgy hands are becoming more coordinated, and she's

developed enough muscle strength and dexterity to get a grip on small objects you place in her hands. Rings and rattles are easy-to-grab toys, and if they make noise when shaken, even more fun!

Change your baby's position and locations. Tummy time will still be an important part of your baby's day—but so will time spent on her back and side and in every other position you can think of. The more opportunity your baby has to explore various positions, the more eager she'll be to roll over (and later to sit, crawl, pull up, cruise, and walk).

Introducing your baby to different locations is important, too. Her explorations shouldn't be confined to her play area alone. The kitchen, your bedroom, the park, the playground, the library, Grandma's house, the grocery store, and more will offer your little one varied environments to learn from, so be sure to bring your baby along for the ride whenever possible.

Repeat your baby's coos and babbles and encourage her to imitate the sounds you make. Your baby's sweet-sounding vocal exercises are a crucial step in language development, and you can help enrich her language environment by babbling right back at her. Before you know it, she'll be imitating the sounds you make, and you'll be participating in a back-and-forth—the first rung on the communication ladder. See page 113 for more on encouraging language development.

Hang colorful toys on a toy bar and encourage your baby to bat at them. One important skill that your baby will need to hone this first year is hand-eye coordination—matching the use of her hands to what she sees. The development of this skill will allow your baby to interact with and manipulate the world around her. As your baby's vision and dexterity improve, you can help sharpen this burgeoning ability by hanging colorful toys over your little one's play mat. Watch her follow the swaying objects with her eyes and use her hands to try to bat at the dangling toys.

Put a mirror in front of your baby so she can "play" with "a friend." Nothing is as enticing to your little babe as the faces she sees around her. Harness that excitement by introducing her to her own face. Using an infant-safe mirror, let your baby enjoy her smiles, frowns, blinks, coos, and movements. Sure, she won't know it's herself she's looking at . . . but that's not the point. Mirror gazing promotes social, physical, and emotional development. It's a playdate for one!

Play peekaboo. It's still too early for your baby to understand the concept of object permanence—the idea that even though you don't see something, it still exists. That understanding will come somewhere between four and eight months old. But it's never too early to start playing games that will help reinforce this important concept. Plus, peekaboo is a game that delights babies of all ages. Simply cover your face (use your hands, a burp cloth, a clean diaper, a lovey, anything!) and then uncover it, saying, "Peekaboo! I see you!" It's a perfect way to stimulate your little one's senses and boost her brain development.

FEELING CONFIDENT
AS A NEW PARENT

Follow your
instincts

Lower your
expectations

Avoid
comparisons

Listen to the advice of
one or two trusted people
and tune out the rest

Lose the guilt

Have fun with
your baby

A CLOSER LOOK

Becoming a parent is a huge transition . . . and it's not one that all moms and dads slip into with ease. In fact, most newbie parents feel as if they have no idea what they're doing at first—and that's perfectly normal. With time you'll become more self-assured and less stressed, making this whole parenting thing (hopefully) feel smoother. Here are some ways to feel more confident as a new parent.

Follow your instincts. There's nothing more powerful than a parent's gut feeling. You know your baby best, and if you feel something is right for your baby—or something is wrong with your baby—don't second-guess that instinct. Do what you feel is best for your little one, and follow your gut when you feel something about your baby needs a second look from a professional, even if that professional downplays your concerns. The more you trust your instincts, the more confident a parent you'll become.

Lower your expectations. You've heard this before, but it's worth repeating: Your life now probably bears little resemblance to your daydreams of a few months ago. Don't expect much more than making it through the day, and don't feel bad if you barely get through the first hour. You're doing the best you can! All your baby truly needs is your love and your presence—not a perfectly cleaned house and all-day parental entertainment. Give yourself a break, and when you do hit moments in your parenting journey that exceed your expectations, capture that celebratory feeling and revisit it when the less-than-perfect reality hits you again.

Avoid comparisons. Comparison is the thief of joy. No two parents are alike, no two families are alike, and no two babies are alike—which means there's no reason to compare yourself to another parent, your family to another family, or your baby to another baby. Every baby is on his own unique developmental journey, and with the range of normal as wide as it is, it makes no sense to waste time wondering why your baby only rolls one way while your friend's baby (who is two weeks younger) is already rolling both ways . . . or worrying that your baby weighs less than your sister's baby did at that age . . . or measuring your baby's sleeping habits against a social media baby's sleeping habits. Your baby is incomparable, so don't be tempted to compare.

Listen to the advice of one or two trusted people and tune out the rest. You'll get lots of unsolicited advice when it comes to parenting (see page 97). But you're better off choosing a few trusted advisors and then keeping all other opinions at arm's length. You're the expert on yourself and your baby, and the support system you choose (your baby's doctor, for instance, or your best friend or sister) will know you and your baby, too. Seek out and listen to their advice, but always remember that you're the final say when it comes to your little one.

Lose the guilt. Nothing screams parent more than feelings of guilt. Maybe you've decided your breastfeeding journey is over and can't help but wonder if that's best for your baby. Or perhaps you're headed back to work and feeling ambivalent about leaving your little one. Or maybe you asked your partner for a break so you can engage in some self-care and now are berating yourself for your "selfishness." Mom and dad guilt has a nasty way of putting a pit in your stomach that makes you feel like you're not doing enough for your child, not doing what's right, or making decisions that will "mess up" your little one. Remind yourself that there is truly no better parent for your baby than you—you're exactly the parent your baby needs. So, lose the guilt. Your baby will be fine no matter what you choose.

Have fun with your baby. Baby didn't have a blowout today? Celebrate it. Baby took a 22-minute nap (longest one yet)? Celebrate it. Baby blew raspberries for the first time? Celebrate it. You took your baby to the store on your own and neither of you cried? Celebrate it! It's often easier to focus on the challenges of parenting while losing sight of the wins. Of course, not every moment will be fun, but you can make this time with your little one more enjoyable by cheering the little wins and not sweating the small stuff.

LEARN MORE

Here are some other topics in the chapters to come that may be relevant this month:

- **Establishing healthy sleep habits (page 81)**
- **Pimples, cradle cap, and other common rashes (page 89)**
- **Spitting up (page 84)**
- **Baby massage (page 87)**
- **Rolling over (page 92)**
- **Communicating with your baby (page 113)**
- **Traveling with your baby (page 251)**

MONTH FOUR

Welcome to month four! The newborn days are behind you, and you're hopefully getting a little more sleep, leaving you a little less bleary-eyed and a lot better able to watch your baby with wonder. Your cutie is busy these days—learning about emotions and communication, watching your every facial expression, and listening to your every word. That social smile is getting plenty of practice, and you'll hopefully see a lot more of it (accompanied by lots of squeals and giggles, too) and a lot less fussiness now that your baby is a little more settled. On the agenda this month or next: rolling over, better head control, and the discovery of the greatest toys of all—those cute little fingers and toes. There's a lot of new things for you to learn, too, in the months to come, but a better understanding of who your baby is and more than three months of parenting under your belt will allow you to face them with confidence. There's no better guide for how to parent your little one than your own gut. Trust your instincts and enjoy the ride.

MONTH FOUR OVERVIEW

THREE TO FOUR MONTHS OLD

SLEEPING

14–16 HOURS
Total time your baby may sleep in a 24-hour day

2–4
Number of naps your baby may take each day

90–120 MINUTES
Time your baby may be awake between naps

EATING

6–7
Number of liquid meals your baby may have each day

24–36 OUNCES
Total amount of breast milk or formula your baby may drink each day

3–4 HOURS
Time between feedings

GROWING

10 LBS 2 OZ–16 LBS 5 OZ
22–25 IN
Average range of weight and height for a baby girl this age

11 LBS 4 OZ–17 LBS 7 OZ
22¾–25¾ IN
Average range of weight and height for a baby boy this age

A CLOSER LOOK

Your baby is a unique individual, on his or her own developmental timeline, growing at his or her own pace, with his or her own distinctive temperament, personality, desires, and needs. That means that how much (or how often) he sleeps, how many feedings she has, how tall he is, or how much she weighs will be unique to your little one.

This overview (and the other monthly overviews in this book) represents what a baby *might* be doing, eating, or gaining this month. But because every child is different, your baby won't necessarily fit perfectly into these averages. That's okay. Use these overviews as rough guides to help you gauge what might be happening with your baby each month, recognizing that the range of normal is wide. And then enjoy your baby wherever he or she happens to land.

MILESTONES CHECK-IN

Tracking milestones is a great way to keep on top of your baby's development. There's no reason to overthink the milestone charts (remember, every baby is on an individual timeline), but if your baby doesn't seem to be meeting any one of these milestones, mention it to your pediatrician. Also speak up about anything that your baby does or doesn't do that concerns you. You're the expert when it comes to your baby, and a parent's intuition is often a better indicator of developmental progress than any milestones checklist.

Seventy-five percent of babies will be able to do at least the following by the end of four months:

- Smile, move, look at you, or make sounds to get your attention
- Turn their heads toward the sound of a voice
- Coo (and coo back at you when you talk to them)
- Chuckle when you try to make them laugh (full-on laughing will come later!)
- Look at their hands with interest
- Bring their hands to their mouths
- Hold a toy that you put in their hands
- Swing or bat at toys
- Hold their heads steady when being held
- Push up on their forearms during tummy time

Don't forget to use your baby's adjusted age if he or she was born early!

ESTABLISHING HEALTHY SLEEP HABITS

Have a bedtime routine

Aim for a bedtime around 7 PM to 8 PM

Have your baby nap at regular intervals

Don't let your baby nap too long or too late in the day

Don't rush in at the first whimper

Be patient—good sleepers aren't made overnight

A CLOSER LOOK

As your baby matures, you'll probably see some sort of sleep pattern emerge (though it might not be a perfect pattern just yet—more likely far from it!—and that's okay). Laying the foundation for healthy sleep now will pay dividends later, when your baby is older and you're hoping for longer stretches of sleep (and maybe, fingers crossed, your baby sleeping through the night; see page 103). Here are some steps you can take now to help establish healthy sleep habits.

Have a bedtime routine. A consistent, nightly bedtime routine will become a cherished ritual for both you and your baby. The optimal length of a bedtime routine is no longer than 30 to 45 minutes. See page 58 for more on creating a bedtime routine.

Aim for a bedtime around 7 PM to 8 PM. Research shows that a baby's natural circadian rhythm, which starts to develop between three and five months old, will induce drowsiness between 7 PM and 8 PM. By putting your baby to sleep within or around that hour each evening, you'll be harnessing what your baby's body is already doing, making it easier for her to fall asleep, hopefully stay asleep, and ultimately get the right amount of sleep overnight.

A 7 PM or so bedtime when your baby is this young doesn't mean she'll automatically sleep through the night. Most babies this age won't, and many still need middle-of-the-night feedings. But an early bedtime will help set the stage for sleeping through the night when the time is right.

One other point: Keeping your baby up later in the evening won't help her sleep later in the morning. That same circadian rhythm will naturally rouse your baby early in the morning, and a late bedtime won't change that. Remember, overtired babies tend to sleep less well and for shorter lengths of time than well-rested babies. See page 191 for more on early wake-ups.

Have your baby nap at regular intervals. Naps are crucial for babies—they provide needed downtime from babies' very stimulating days and optimize babies' brain power during awake time. Naps are also linked to emotional regulation and physical development. Plus, a baby who naps well during the day will have an easier time falling asleep (and staying asleep) at night. Little ones who skip naps or who have very irregular nap schedules tend to be crankier and more irritable, are more likely to have trouble focusing during playtime, may have more difficulty feeding, and often have poor quality sleep at night. Try to get your baby down for naps at regular intervals during the day— based on sleep cues and wake windows, which are around 90 to 120 minutes long at this age—and (when possible) in the same location, ideally the crib. For more on naps, see pages 133, 237, and 265.

Don't let your baby nap too long or too late in the day. Yes, you've just learned that naps are critically important for overall sleep health. But your baby can get too much of a good thing. Naps that go on for too long (longer than 4 hours, for instance) or that come too late in the day can make it harder for your baby to fall asleep when it's bedtime. As a general rule, start by making sure your baby is getting enough sleep for her age during the day. If her night sleep is impacted, you'll need to tweak her schedule and shorten those extra-long naps until you get them just right.

Don't rush in at the first whimper. Babies are noisy and active sleepers. They'll grunt and grimace, stretch and call out, whimper, and even cry. But often, they'll be able to get cozy again and fall right back to sleep. And sometimes, a well-intentioned parent who rushes in to soothe at the first whimper wakes baby up when she would have settled back down on her own. The lesson here: No need to drop what you're doing the second you hear a noise coming through the baby monitor, especially if your little one hasn't slept for a long enough stretch (usually 30 to 45 minutes or longer at this age). Wait a minute or two before deciding whether your baby needs a helping hand to settle back down or that her nap is actually over.

Be patient—good sleepers aren't made overnight. Sleep deprivation in the early months is hard for parents, and there's nothing a new parent wants more than to get past that stage. But most babies need time to learn how to sleep well, how to consolidate sleep into longer stretches, and eventually, how to sleep through the night. Don't expect too much at this young age. For now, focus on consistency and regularity, and you'll be setting the stage for healthy sleep routines to come.

DEALING WITH A BABY WHO SPITS UP

Spitting up is normal and not a health issue as long as your baby is gaining weight

Spit-up amounts are smaller than they look

Spitting up can happen after feedings and/or at other times

You may notice an increase in spitting up at 2 to 4 months

Babies typically outgrow spitting when they start sitting

The introduction of solids also helps reduce spitting up

A CLOSER LOOK

Most babies spit up. Many babies spit up a lot . . . or all the time . . . which can cause a lot of anxiety in new parents. It's important to distinguish between spitting up, which is normal and not cause for concern, and vomiting and GERD (gastroesophageal reflux disease), both of which may warrant an evaluation by your pediatrician. Spitting up (called gastroesophageal reflux in the medical world) happens because the muscle between your baby's esophagus and stomach—called the sphincter—is immature, making it easy for the liquid diet your baby is consuming to come back up. Vomiting is more forceful and can occur when your baby is sick, if he has a food allergy, or if there's an issue like pyloric stenosis (when the opening between the stomach and the small intestine narrows, blocking food and causing vomiting). GERD is gastroesophageal reflux *disease*, and you can learn more about GERD in the box on page 86. Here's what you should know about spitting up.

Spitting up is normal. The majority of babies who spit up are referred to as "happy spitters"—meaning they might spit up often but don't lose weight or experience discomfort when spitting. So, grab those burp cloths and protect your clothes, but there's no need to worry as long as your baby is gaining weight—even if he's spitting up all the time.

Spit up amounts are smaller than they look. When your baby spits up, it often looks like he's bringing up his entire meal. The good news is, he's not—it's more likely closer to just a tablespoon of formula or breast milk along with some saliva. Not convinced? Try this experiment: Take one tablespoon of milk and spill it on your kitchen counter, letting it spread out. You'll see how much it appears to be . . . but you know it measures only a tablespoon. It's a helpful reminder that regular, normal spitting up is not going to interfere with your baby's nutritional intake or impact his weight.

Spitting up can happen after feedings and/or at other times. Some babies spit up with every burp. Other babies spit up after every meal. And still other babies spit up throughout the day. All those scenarios are normal. You can try to reduce spitting up by feeding your baby before he's crying frantically for a meal. If you wait too long for a feeding, your baby may gulp a lot of air along with the milk, increasing the potential for milk to come back up with any air bubbles. Overfeeding may also increase spitting up, so don't push your baby to take more than he needs. Feeding your baby in a more upright position, as well as burping mid-feed (see page 42), may lessen spitting up somewhat. If you're bottle feeding, a switch in the type of bottle may reduce spitting up by helping decrease the amount of air your baby swallows (though it usually does not). Or you might try all these tactics and your baby will still be a prolific spitter—that's normal, too.

You may notice an increase in spitting up at two to four months. Some babies spit up throughout the first year, but you may see the amount of spitting increase between two to four months old and peak at four to five months old.

Babies do outgrow spitting up. You'll likely notice a decrease in spitting when your baby starts sitting, around six to eight months old, with most babies seeing a complete resolution of spitting up by nine to twelve months. Starting solids (also around six months old) helps reduce spitting up as well, since your little one's meals won't be all liquid.

GERD

Occasionally, frequent and persistent spitting up, when accompanied by poor weight gain and other symptoms, is an indication that your baby has acid reflux, or GERD—gastroesophageal reflux disease.

GERD happens when the area between the esophagus and stomach is underdeveloped, allowing stomach acid to come back up into the esophagus. Common GERD symptoms include more than just frequent spitting up. During feedings, you'll hear gurgling, congested, or wheezing sounds and you might notice your baby arching his back. Your baby may be extra fussy or cry inconsolably after feedings, and may sleep poorly and have trouble gaining weight. If you see these signs in your baby, ask the doctor if it might be related to GERD.

Treatment is usually aimed at making your baby more comfortable—keeping him upright after a feeding (while still maintaining a flat, on-the-back position during sleep), feeding him small meals, burping him more often, and possibly giving him probiotics and medication.

GERD usually peaks at around four months old, and completely resolves between the ages of twelve and eighteen months.

MASSAGING YOUR BABY

Choose the
right time

Make it comfortable
for your baby

Use a baby-safe
massage oil or lotion

Stroke your baby's
chest and tummy in
gentle circles and
in long strokes

Knead and roll
your baby's arms,
legs, hands,
and feet

Turn your baby
tummy-down and stroke
her back from side to
side and up and down

A CLOSER LOOK

A baby massage can do wonders for your little one, helping to calm her, decrease stress hormones, boost her immune system, enhance her sleep, and even stimulate growth. This kind of gentle touching can also help the two of you bond. If you'd like to give baby massage a try, you can start whenever you want—and you can continue to massage into the toddler years or beyond, if your little spa-goer will stay still for it. Here are some tips on how.

Choose the right time. After a bath is often ideal, since your little one may be most relaxed then—and it'll help set the stage for a restful night. As your baby gets older, you can adapt the time and the setting. Maybe you'll do it before the bath, for instance, or while your baby is on your lap.

When you're first starting out, aim for just a few minutes of gentle caresses. If your baby is enjoying the massage, you can increase the amount of time you dedicate to the rubdown. Of course, if neither of you are in the mood, try the massage another time.

Make it comfortable for your baby. When you go to the spa for a massage, the soft music, dim lights, warm blankets, and perfect room temperature optimizes the experience for you. When possible, bring that same sort of atmosphere to your baby's massage treatment. No time for the full spa experience? No worries—your baby will still benefit from a massage even if the lights aren't dimmed and there's no piped in spa music (though using a soft voice and making sure it's not too cold in the room will be helpful in keeping your baby comfortable).

Use a baby-safe massage oil. Or a lavender-scented baby lotion, or a neutral food-grade oil—ask your pediatrician for a recommendation. If the oil or lotion is cold, warm it up between your hands first.

Stroke, knead, and roll. There are no rules for how to do the actual massage, so do what feels comfortable for you and your baby. You can start by stroking your baby's face and head in a circular motion or down and toward the sides of the face. Some babies love when the front and back of their ears are massaged. Rub your baby's chest and tummy in circles or with strokes from top to bottom or side to side. You can do the same motions on your baby's back. Then knead and roll your baby's arms, legs, hands, and feet. You can also start from the feet and work your way up. Baby's not in the mood for a full-service massage? No problem! Try just a back or foot massage.

COMMON BABY RASHES

Diaper rash:
Redness in the
diaper area

Eczema: Flaky,
patchy, crusty
eruptions

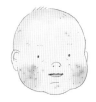

Baby acne or milia:
Red pimples or
whiteheads on the face

Cradle cap: Greasy,
yellow-brown
crusty scales
on the scalp

Heat rash:
Tiny red dots
on the face,
neck, or torso

Teething rash: Redness,
chapping, and chafing
on the skin triggered
by dripping saliva

A CLOSER LOOK

Your baby might have flawless skin . . . or more likely not. Babies are notorious for sporting rashes and skin blemishes of all kinds. Not to worry—most rashes are temporary and easily treatable, if necessary. Here's a look at some of the more common rashes you might notice on your baby and what you can do about them.

Diaper rash. You'll know your little one has a diaper rash when you see redness accompanied by small spots or bumps on your baby's diaper region. Most of the time, diaper rash is mild, though if left untreated it can spread all over your baby's genitals, bottom, and thighs. See page 69 for more on preventing and treating diaper rash.

Eczema. This (often hereditary) skin condition pops up as flaky, patchy, crusty, and itchy eruptions, most often on the cheeks, chin, forehead, and scalp in babies under six months old and on the inside of elbows and back of knees in babies older than six months. In light-skinned babies, the rash is typically pink or red. In infants with dark skin, it can be purple, gray, brown, or red.

Keeping your baby's skin well moisturized can help prevent and treat this rash, though a more stubborn case will likely need a hydrocortisone cream or ointment. Keep your baby's nails short to prevent him from scratching this itchy rash. You may have heard that short (or no) baths are best for babies with eczema, and that is true in some cases. However, the latest research indicates that longer baths (up to 15 to 20 minutes) in warm, not hot, water followed immediately by patting (not rubbing) dry and applying lotion to lock in moisture is ideal.

Baby acne or milia. Nearly half of all babies have red pimples or whiteheads on their faces in the first few months. Maternal hormones tend to stick around in a baby's body for a while after birth, and they in turn stimulate a baby's oil-producing glands, causing zits. Though it's disappointing for parents, especially if you were hoping for picture-perfect baby skin on your little one, the good news is that these baby pimples will go away on their own by the fourth month, no treatment needed. In the meantime, keep your baby's face clean by wiping it with water. You can also dab some breast milk on the acne—there's no research to prove it works, but anecdotal evidence points to its healing powers.

Cradle cap. If your baby has greasy, yellow-brown crusty scales on his scalp, forehead, and/or eyebrows, it could be cradle cap, a rash that affects up to 70 percent of infants. Its cause? It could be mom's still-circulating hormones revving up oil glands in the skin. To treat, simply wash your baby's hair with mild shampoo and massage your baby's scalp with a soft brush to loosen the scales. If the cradle cap is more than just a few scales, you can rub your baby's scalp with a small amount of baby oil, olive oil, white petroleum jelly, or other emollient before massaging his scalp with a soft brush, and then follow with a shampoo. Breast milk may also help heal the rash faster (at least according to anecdotal evidence). If your baby has an especially stubborn case, your doctor may prescribe a special shampoo or cream.

Heat rash. Appearing as tiny red dots on the face, neck, and/or torso (though the redness may be less obvious on darker skin), heat rash (or prickly heat) is caused by sweat buildup. Though heat rash will usually fade on its own, keeping your baby from getting overheated will help prevent and treat it.

Teething rash. Teething symptoms, including drooling, can show up well before that first tooth pops out of the gum (see page 119). A byproduct of all that dripping saliva is redness, chapping, and/or chafing on the chin. The best way to prevent and treat a teething rash is to keep the area dry, so be sure to gently pat away your baby's drool as soon as it starts dribbling down.

HELPING YOUR BABY LEARN TO ROLL OVER

Minimize the time your baby spends in seats and containers

Give your baby plenty of tummy time

Let your baby play on her back often

Encourage your baby to play on her side

Place a toy off to the side so your baby reaches for it—it may result in a roll

Gently nudge your baby over to show her how it's done

A CLOSER LOOK

One of the exciting early baby milestones to look forward to is rolling over. Many babies have enough upper body strength to flip over from the stomach to the back by four months old. And before six months rolls around, you can expect your baby to have also mastered the back-to-tummy flip. Remember, however, that babies hit developmental milestones on their own timelines. It may take weeks of practice (and failure) before your baby acrobat is able to roll over. Here are some tricks you can use if your baby needs a little nudge in the right (or left) direction.

Minimize the time your baby spends in seats and containers.
Too much time spent confined to containers (such as swings,
carriers, strollers, car seats, bouncers, and other confining seats)
means fewer opportunities for your baby to strengthen the
muscles needed for large motor skills (rolling over, sitting, and
crawling) and less practice time perfecting those skills. Try to limit
stints in these seats to no more than 15 to 30 minutes at a time,
once or twice a day.

Give your baby plenty of tummy time. You've heard this
before, but it bears repeating. Supervised tummy time every day
is the best way for your baby to strengthen her upper back and
core muscles—muscles needed for rolling over. For ways to make
tummy time more fun, check out pages 21–22.

Let your baby play on her back and side often. Yes, tummy
time is important, but so is back time and side time. Think of it
this way: Your baby needs to experience and get used to every
position on the floor in order to learn how to maneuver into
those positions. Rolling over from tummy to back is, for some
babies, easier than back to tummy, and with lots of tummy time,
your baby will learn how to push up and flip over. But it will take
playtime on the back and side, too, before your baby perfects the
art of tucking her arm in and heaving over onto her tummy. (Keep
in mind that for some babies, rolling from back to tummy comes
before the tummy to back flip. Every baby is different!)

Place a toy off to the side. When helping your baby learn
how to roll over, think about enticement. Place your baby on
an activity mat and add some tempting toys off to the side to
encourage her to reach for them. A roll to the side may be the
first step, but eventually a full flip is sure to happen. Offer lots of
praise and encouragement as motivation.

Gently nudge your baby over to show her how it's done.
Does your little one need a little extra help? You can position
your cutie on her side and gently rock her from side to side,
help her tuck her arm in, or even softly nudge her over so she
rolls completely. She might be startled at first, but with repeated
extra assists from you, she'll eventually realize she can do it on
her own.

ROLLING OVER DURING SLEEP

Once your baby starts rolling over, she might roll onto her tummy during sleep. But here's news that may ease some parental anxiety: While you should always place your baby in the crib on her back, don't worry if she flips positions during the night. Once your little one is strong enough to manage the back-to-tummy flip, she's also strong enough to get herself out of any position that might compromise her breathing, which means tummy sleeping is less dangerous. And a repeat reminder: As soon as your baby is showing signs of rolling, you'll need to stop using a swaddle.

STIMULATING YOUR BABY IN THE FOURTH MONTH

Encourage rolling

PEEKABOO!

Hide a toy and encourage your baby to find it

Lift your baby up in the air and back down again

Give your baby objects of different shapes, sizes, and textures to explore

Run a scarf from your baby's toes to his nose

Provide your baby with toys that make sounds

A CLOSER LOOK

Spoiler alert: This stage—when your baby begins working on (or reaching) some major physical and developmental milestones and craving social interaction—is loads of fun. Be on the lookout in the next few months for rolling, reaching, grabbing, babbling, and your baby's greater awareness of everything that's happening around him. Thanks to these emerging developmental feats, you'll find plenty of ways to interact with your cutie this month.

Encourage rolling. Rolling, as you've just read, is a new (or developing) skill that your little one will love to practice. Further encourage your baby's new trick by placing toys just off to his side and cheering as he reaches for them and (possibly) flips over.

Hide a toy and encourage your baby to find it. Object permanence—the understanding that when something disappears from sight it isn't gone forever—typically starts to develop between ages four and eight months. Help jumpstart this developmental milestone by hiding a toy behind or under a small blanket and then lifting it up with a "peekaboo!"

Lift your baby up in the air and back down again. Thanks to improving head and neck control, your little gymnast may be ready for some gentle "flying" in your arms (if your baby's head is still wobbly, save this activity for another month). This simple movement (with your baby securely in your hands) will give him a new perspective on the world . . . plus elicit plenty of smiles. Bonus: You'll get a good laugh, not to mention an arm workout!

Give your baby objects of different shapes, sizes, and textures to explore. Your baby does lots of learning through touch, so offer up varied tactile experiences. Think stuffed animals, toys of all shapes and (safe) sizes, fabrics and surfaces (from velvet, faux fur, and terry to carpets and hardwood), and safe household items like clean sponges, plastic cups, and silicone serving utensils. This not only helps your baby learn about his surroundings, but also helps with sensory development.

Run a scarf from your baby's toes to his nose. This activity marries visual excitement to tactile exploration. Your baby will have fun following the colorful scarf as it trails up and down his body, and the sensory input will help him build brain connections.

Provide your baby with toys that make sounds. Hearing is what helps babies learn about language, cadence, rhythm, and feelings. Expose your baby to all types of sounds, including toys that play tunes or make animal sounds (though be sure they are kept at a safe volume—under eighty decibels). Music has been shown to help boost brain development and social skills, while soothing music and lullabies can help calm your baby down.

DEALING WITH UNSOLICITED ADVICE

Start by listening instead of being defensive

Explore if there might be something of value in the advice

Smile and say, "Interesting!"—then disregard if the advice doesn't work for you

Quote your doctor: "I hear you, but I'm going to follow my pediatrician's advice"

Learn about your parenting choices— knowledge is power

Trust your gut

A CLOSER LOOK

Nothing seems to bring out unsolicited advice more than seeing a new baby (and the new parents accompanying her). From your mom to your mother-in-law, close friends to "friends" on social media (or random shoppers you run into at the grocery store), you'll find yourself on the receiving end of plenty of unsolicited advice. These advice-givers mean well (even your mother-in-law), and they're usually not judging your parenting abilities (okay . . . maybe your mother-in-law is a little), but regardless of where these words of "wisdom" come from, the bombardment of parenting advice can get overwhelming and frustrating. Here are ways to handle unsolicited advice.

Start by listening instead of being defensive. You're exhausted, you're feeling vulnerable, you may be questioning your own parenting choices, and then *bam!*—someone swoops in to tell you about the way they parented and what their recommendations would be. It's easy to get defensive when this happens. But take a breath and a step back, and let your guard down long enough to listen to what they have to say. Often, they aren't being critical or judging you as a parent or for your parenting choices; rather, they see an opening to dole out tips or advice that may be helpful. Before you get upset by someone offering their suggestions, take a minute to listen to what they have to say.

Explore if there might be something valuable in the advice. As you're listening to someone's advice, you may hear a tidbit that you find interesting, a small nugget that gets you thinking more deeply, or something that may actually help you in your own parenting journey. While you may not have been seeking the advice (or perhaps you were put off by the fact that it was offered in the first place), you may be able to leave with something helpful.

Smile and say, "Interesting!"—then disregard the advice if it doesn't work for you. You're not required to follow even the most well-meaning guidance. Remember, you know what will work best for you and your child, and if someone's tips or tricks aren't a good fit (or are unwise, unsafe, or old-fashioned), just ignore it. A simple way to end a conversation is to flash a sincere smile, say, "Interesting!" or, "Wow, so glad that worked well for you!"—and move on to a new topic.

Quote your doctor: "I hear you, but I'm going to follow my pediatrician's advice." When in doubt, quote the expert. Most people offering opinions you didn't ask for will back down if you mention your doctor's recommendations on the subject. Bringing in a pediatrician's advice is a polite way of letting someone know that you've already consulted with a trusted individual and you're on top of it.

Learn about your parenting choices—knowledge is power.
The best thing that you can do when you don't know a lot
about a topic is educate yourself. Luckily, there are loads of
resources that can help you learn the ins and outs of parenting
and find answers on any topic you're interested in. And the more
you know, the more confident you'll feel as a parent, and the
better able you'll be to deflect any advice that's unwanted (or,
frankly, wrong).

Information overload has you overwhelmed? Don't go
overboard seeking information. Stick with just a few trusted
sources: reliable books like this one, websites, social media
accounts, podcasts, online courses, and/or expert coaching.

Trust your gut. Once you've done the research, spoken to (and
learned from) a few experts, and test run a parenting option or
two, have faith in your choices. Ultimately, the best way to parent
your little one is to parent in the way that feels right for you. Trust
that you're doing the best for you and your baby—because guess
what? You are!

LEARN MORE

Here are some other topics in the chapters to come
that may be relevant this month:

- Helping your baby sleep through the night (page 103)
- Short naps (page 133)
- Sleep regressions (page 215)
- Dropping night feedings (page 165)
- Readiness for solids (page 109)
- Communicating with your baby (page 113)
- Reading to your baby (page 153)
- Sitting (page 116)
- Teething (page 119)
- Traveling with your baby (page 251)

MONTH FIVE

It's month five—one of the most delightful times in your baby's first year. Your baby will likely be all (or mostly) smiles and laughs this month—interactive and expressive, yet still not on the move, which makes your life as a parent fun and a little easier (at least compared to what was and what is to come). Watch as your baby brings out his or her inner entertainer, enchanting you and random passersby with his or her super-cute antics, giggles, smiles, babbles, and winning personality. Your baby's playing skills are improving, too, as refinements in motor development allow your little one to pick up toys of all shapes, manipulate them, and bring them to the mouth. Play—even oral play—is the way your baby learns about his or her world, so let the exploration happen. And remember, every interaction, hug, and conversation you have with your cutie is helping to promote important development. Your baby may also be on a more predictable schedule and possibly even sleeping longer stretches during the night. Now that's something to celebrate!

MONTH FIVE OVERVIEW

FOUR TO FIVE MONTHS OLD

SLEEPING

14–15 HOURS
Total time your baby may sleep in a 24-hour day

3
Number of naps your baby may take each day

90–120 MINUTES
Time your baby may be awake between naps

EATING

5–6
Number of liquid meals your baby may have each day

24–32 OUNCES
Total amount of breast milk or formula your baby may drink each day

0–1
Number of solid meals

GROWING

11 LBS 4 OZ–17 LBS 14 OZ
22¾–26 IN
Average range of weight and height for a baby girl this age

12 LBS 6 OZ–18 LBS 15 OZ
23½–26¾ IN
Average range of weight and height for a baby boy this age

A CLOSER LOOK

Your baby is a unique individual, on his or her own developmental timeline, growing at his or her own pace, with his or her own distinctive temperament, personality, desires, and needs. That means that how much (or how often) he sleeps, how many feedings she has, how tall he is, or how much she weighs will be unique to your little one.

This overview (and the other monthly overviews in this book) represents what a baby *might* be doing, eating, or gaining this month. But because every child is different, your baby won't necessarily fit perfectly into these averages. That's okay. Use these overviews as rough guides to help you gauge what might be happening with your baby each month, recognizing that the range of normal is wide. And then enjoy your baby wherever he or she happens to land.

HELPING YOUR BABY SLEEP THROUGH THE NIGHT

Figure out if your baby is waking from hunger or habit

Consider what external sleep associations your baby has

Put your baby in the crib before he's sound asleep

Choose a sleep teaching method you're comfortable with

Pick the right time

Commit to being consistent so your baby doesn't get mixed messages

A CLOSER LOOK

Sleeping through the night is a baby milestone most parents look forward to, but it's not always one that comes easily. For most babies, sleeping well and for long stretches is a skill that needs to be learned—much like walking, chewing food, riding a bike, and tying a shoe. Helping your baby learn how to fall asleep independently and sleep through the night may take a lot of effort and commitment on your part, but the result will be a well-rested baby and a better-rested you.

Sleeping through the night is technically defined as your baby sleeping for a 6- to 8-hour stretch overnight. Just over half of all babies will sleep through the night by six months old, and up to 80 percent do so by nine months. Lots of parents hope for more, though, aiming for that magical 12 hours of sleep each night. And, happily, many six-plus monthers are able to achieve that goal (perhaps with a few wake-ups here and there, but with the ability to settle back to sleep as they learn to consolidate sleep cycles).

Not all parents feel comfortable leaving a baby to fall asleep independently, and if you're content feeding or rocking your baby to sleep and repeating those steps multiple times overnight, there's nothing wrong with that (and you can just skip this section). If, however, you're looking for tips on how to help your baby learn to sleep through the night mostly independently, read on.

Figure out if your baby is waking from hunger or habit.
According to the AAP, by the time your baby reaches twelve to fourteen pounds (or around twice his birthweight), he no longer *needs* a middle-of-the-night feeding from a strictly metabolic perspective and can meet all his nutritional requirements with daytime feedings. That doesn't mean your little one won't wake up and eat if you offer the breast or bottle, of course. But it's good to know what's possible, to help calibrate your expectations. If your baby continues to wake up every 3 hours for a feeding beyond the fifth or sixth month (whether he's breastfed or formula fed), it's unlikely he's waking because of a nutritional need and more likely he's waking because he's become used to being fed throughout the night.

It's not always easy to determine if your baby is waking in the night because he's actually hungry—especially if he eagerly laps up the offered liquid meal. But there are some clues to look for to help figure out whether it's hunger or habit that's keeping your baby from sleeping through the night. For instance, if your baby wakes for a feed after a long stretch of sleep, or nighttime feeds last as long as (and your baby drinks as much milk as) during the day, those nighttime wake-up calls may be because of hunger. But if your baby demands to be fed every few hours throughout the night, or feeds for only a few minutes and then falls right back asleep, it's likely habit—and possibly a sleep association (see below)—rather than a nutritional need. See page 165 for more about dropping night feedings, which many babies are able to do around four to six months old.

Consider what external sleep associations your baby has. A sleep association is any action that helps your baby fall asleep. We all have sleep associations, whether we're aware of them or not. An adult might need to read a little before turning in, or have a blanket tucked under an arm in just the right way. A baby might need a pacifier, rocking, nursing or a bottle, or white noise to fall asleep.

Sleep experts will usually differentiate between positive (or internal) sleep associations and negative (or external) sleep associations based on who is carrying out the action that helps your baby fall asleep. Positive sleep associations are things that a baby can do himself to fall asleep without any help: sucking his thumb, rubbing his face on the sheet, babbling, banging his feet against the crib slats, and so on. Negative sleep associations require somebody else to do something for the baby, like rocking or feeding him until he falls asleep. The downside to an external sleep association is that when your baby wakes in the middle of the night, he may not be able to get back to sleep on his own. That's not an issue if you're content to always be on call for rocking or feeding. But if you're not, it'll be smart to help your baby replace negative sleep associations with new, positive ones.

The ideal age to start removing negative sleep associations is around the time your baby is able to sleep through the night without a feed, around four to six months old. It's also a lot easier to break sleep associations at this age compared to when your baby is older and more set in his ways.

Put your baby in the crib before he's sound asleep. The best way to start teaching your baby to fall asleep without external sleep associations is to put your baby in the crib when he's sleepy but not fully asleep (and that means being attuned to your baby's tiredness cues; see page 55). If you rock your baby fully to sleep in your arms before placing him down in the crib, then when he wakes a few minutes or hours later, he may not be able to put himself back to sleep without the rocking—not to mention he may be surprised to find himself waking up somewhere other than where he fell asleep. If, instead, he's been rocked only until he's drowsy before being put in the crib, he is putting *himself* to sleep, not the rocking. So, when he wakes up, he'll know how to put himself back to sleep on his own—at least in theory. In practice, it will take consistency on your part and repetition for your baby to learn this.

Your baby's ability to return to sleep independently is especially important because babies, like adults, wake multiple times during the night—usually between sleep cycles. Adults have learned how to connect their sleep cycles, so they tend to fall right back to sleep in between without even being aware they've woken up. Babies need to learn this skill, and if they're only taught how to fall asleep while being fed or rocked, they'll have a harder time getting back to sleep on their own.

Choose a sleep teaching method you're comfortable with. You've likely heard the phrase "sleep training" to describe techniques that can help your baby learn to sleep through the night. Unfortunately, the term sometimes gets a bad rap from parents who fear it's all about leaving a baby to cry for hours on end. "Sleep teaching" might be a better way of putting it, since these techniques all have a shared goal: to *teach* your baby how to fall asleep on his own and stay asleep throughout the night. This can involve a little crying, but certainly not endless amounts.

There's no rule that says you must sleep teach your baby. Most children eventually learn to sleep through the night even without parental guidance, and if you're more comfortable feeding on demand throughout the night, responding to each wake-up with holding and rocking and/or bed sharing, that's fine (remember, your baby, your way!). But sleep teaching can be an incredibly helpful tool, especially if you have a clear idea of your goal. When parents are consistent with sleep teaching, most babies learn how to fall asleep and put themselves back to sleep on their own within a few days to a few weeks.

There are multiple sleep teaching methods. It's best to choose the one that matches your baby's specific needs and temperament—and yours.

One effective method is called timed intervals. It involves settling your baby in his crib, then leaving him to fall asleep on his own. If he starts to whimper or cry when you lay him down and/or leave the room (a likely scenario), choose an amount of time that you'll let him try to settle back down on his own (say, 5 minutes—or whatever length of time you're comfortable with), and return to comfort him when that time has elapsed. When you return, stay for only a minute or so, and don't take your baby out of his crib, since it's important for him to learn that he stays in his crib at night. Soothe him by patting his tummy, stroking his cheek, whispering "shhh," or singing a short lullaby. Then remind him that it's time to sleep, say you love him, let him know you'll see him in the morning, and leave. If he cries after you leave, wait another short period (of whatever length of time you've chosen) before returning and repeating the soothing process as many times as necessary. You're being responsive, but without creating a new negative sleep association or reinforcing old ones.

There are other methods of sleep teaching, too. For example, in the "pick up, put down" method, you pick up your crying baby, soothe him for a minute or two in your arms until he stops crying but not until he falls asleep, and then return him to his crib to fall asleep on his own, repeating as often as needed. There's also the approach where you soothe your baby in the crib without picking him up for as long as it takes for him to settle down completely (even if that means an hour!), and then stay a shorter amount of time soothing him by his side each night. Or the method where you stay next to the crib until he completely falls asleep, then, after a few nights, stay in the room but not next to the crib, and then, after a few more nights, stay near the door, continuing to move farther away until he's able to get to sleep without your presence. This technique usually works better for older babies than young ones.

Pick the right time. Only begin sleep teaching when the time is right. Not when there's been a major change or stress in your baby's life. Not when you're going back to work for the first time, or your baby has a cold or ear infection. Not when your family is at Grandma's house for the weekend, or your partner is on a business trip, leaving you solo. Wait until things have settled down before starting sleep teaching.

Commit to being consistent so your baby doesn't get mixed messages. Whatever method you choose, whether it is responsive timed check-ins or by-the-crib soothing, full crying it out or no crying at all, your baby needs to receive consistent responses from you to learn this new skill of falling asleep independently. If your baby gets a different response each night or at each wake-up, he'll be confused. Once you choose a method, it's crucial that you stick with it for at least two to three weeks before deciding whether or not it's working. Consistency is key.

IS SLEEP TEACHING HARMFUL?

Parents often wonder if sleep teaching of any type is harmful to their baby. It's a worry you can put to rest. In randomized controlled longitudinal studies, which are considered the gold standard in science, researchers found no long-term differences between children who were sleep trained as babies and those who weren't. Plus, researchers found that sleep training leaves no harmful short- or long-term effects on children's sleep patterns, behavior, or attachment to their parents.

SIGNS YOUR BABY IS READY TO START SOLIDS

Your baby is close to or at 6 months of age

Your baby has good head and neck control

Your baby can sit well

Your baby is eager to participate in mealtime and intently watches you eat

Your baby leans forward for food

Your baby is able to bring objects to her mouth

A CLOSER LOOK

You may be eager to transition your baby from an all-liquid diet to a liquid-plus-solid eating plan, but it's best to wait to serve solid food until your baby shows certain signs of readiness. That said, even if your baby shows a number of readiness signs, there's still no need to rush to start solids. Breast milk or formula is the only source of nutrition your baby requires during the first six months of life. Even once solids are introduced, food will still take a back seat to breast milk or formula until later in the first year. The bonus of not rushing to start solids: You'll get to postpone the hassles of high chair meals. It's much easier to breastfeed or bottle feed alone than it is to also pull out the feeding seat and prepare baby meals multiple times a day.

Here's what to look for when deciding whether your baby is ready for solids.

Your baby is close to or at six months of age. You might have heard that you can start feeding you baby solids when she's between four and six months old. But closer to six months is better (and what's recommended by the AAP and WHO), not only because babies are more developmentally ready for solids at that age, but also because introducing solid foods too early can cause babies to miss out on important nutrients that come from breast milk and formula. What's more, if you're planning to begin solids using the baby-led weaning method (BLW, a.k.a. finger foods instead of purees; see page 140), you'll need to wait until your baby is six months old for safety reasons. Starting at six months gives you the flexibility to choose right from the start if you'll be serving purees, finger foods, or a mix of both.

There is a caveat to this recommendation. If there's a family history of food allergies or if you have a strong suspicion that your baby will have them (because she has severe eczema, for instance), the AAP recommends serving allergenic foods (with medical guidance) as early as four months old. Research shows that the early introduction of certain allergens significantly decreases the chances your higher-risk baby will develop food allergies. Your doctor will recommend a feeding schedule based on your baby's unique risk level. See page 168 for more on serving allergens.

Something else to keep in mind: It's not a good idea to wait too long before starting solids, since an older baby (an eight-month-old, for example) may be less willing to learn how to chew and swallow than a six-month-old. Waiting too long after the six-month mark to serve solids may also prevent your baby from getting enough daily calories.

Your baby has good head and neck control. Safety comes first when you're feeding your baby, and it's definitely not safe for a baby who isn't able to hold up her head to eat solids. Imagine how difficult, never mind dangerous, it would be for you to swallow food with a wobbly head that's slumped forward or to the side. It's the same for your little one. Your baby also needs to have enough head control to communicate with you—to turn her head to the side to let you know she's full, for instance.

Your baby can sit well. Sitting well (meaning, when placed in a seated position on the floor, staying that way without immediately toppling over) is a great indication your baby can eat safely without choking. A baby who doesn't have adequate trunk control may end up with a compromised airway. The importance of being able to sit well is about more than just safety, though. Physical therapists suggest that good postural control and stability (a.k.a. sitting well) is the first step in a baby's ability to bring food to the mouth and coordinate those all-important chewing skills.

Your baby is eager to participate in mealtime and leans forward for food. Does your baby watch you eat with big open eyes? Reach for your spoon or that slice of mango you're munching on? Lean forward with excited anticipation when she catches a glimpse of you putting fork to mouth? Such eagerness may be a sign your baby is ready for solids.

Keep in mind, however, that most babies around four to six months old naturally start showing curiosity and enthusiasm about everything around them. What you may be interpreting as an interest in solid foods may simply be your little one's excitement about her environment—which is why it's smart to view this sign of enthusiasm not in a vacuum but as one piece of the readiness package.

Your baby can bring objects to her mouth. It makes sense that a baby who can bring objects to her mouth will be more successful at eating solids, especially if you'll be starting with finger foods or encouraging self-feeding, so look for this sign, too, when deciding whether your baby is ready.

Conventional wisdom has long suggested that you should wait to start solids until after a baby's tongue thrust reflex (in which a baby pushes or thrusts her tongue out when something touches her lips) fades. And this makes sense if you're spoon-feeding purees, since your baby's tongue will push out the pureed food as soon as the spoon touches her tongue, impeding the feeding process. But if you're serving finger foods right from the start, as with BLW, there's no need to wait for the tongue thrust to disappear. That reflex will actually help your baby explore food by licking it, moving it around the mouth, and doing exactly what is needed to navigate finger foods. The tongue thrust fades for most babies at around four to six months old, though some stubborn ones hold on to it until later in the first year.

COMMUNICATING
WITH YOUR BABY

Make eye contact so your baby can watch you vocalize

Narrate your actions

Repeat your baby's babbles to encourage back-and-forth sounds

Interpret your baby's babbles

Ask questions and wait for answers, modeling the art of conversation

Watch for nonverbal communication

Read to your baby often

Sing songs and listen to music

A CLOSER LOOK

Your baby's babbles and coos may not sound like much to you, but they're important building blocks for communication, language skills, and social interactions. Here are ways you can communicate with your baby, helping boost language development to come.

Make eye contact so your baby can watch you vocalize.
While language development is certainly about listening, it's also

about watching. When you make eye contact with your baby, your little one is able to watch the movements of your mouth as the sounds come out. For an added learning boost, exaggerate certain words. Your baby will be able to feel each word from the puff of air it makes.

Narrate your actions. The richer your baby's language environment, the richer his language skills—so let your baby hear lots of words. Tell your baby what's happening as it happens ("It's time to walk to the park . . . look at the squirrel . . . see that green leaf . . . let's take off your coat . . ."). Speak slowly so your baby can pick out discrete words, and try to be animated when articulating, with lots of facial expressions. If you find yourself slipping into "parentese"—that exaggerated, higher-pitched voice and elongated vowels parents often use when speaking to their babies—you're doing great! That's the best way to capture your little one's attention.

Repeat your baby's babbles to encourage back-and-forth sounds. Babies are born mimics (even newborns will stick out their tongue to copy an adult doing the same), and they get a kick out of an adult copying them. So, when your babe babbles, repeat what you've heard . . . and then encourage him to vocalize the babble again in return. Or start with a few babbles of your own, like "bababa" or "dadada" and wait for your little talker to respond. This copying and interacting (also known as "serve and return") presents a wonderful language learning opportunity for your baby: Research shows that mimicking or returning those baby babbles teaches your baby that his words are a form of communication.

Interpret your baby's babbles. Turn your little one's babbles into real words so that they become meaningful. Hold a ball in your hands and say, "Ba-ba-ball." And later, as your baby get older, interpret his babbles—say, "Yes, rabbit!" when he says, "Wawawa" or, "Yes, grandma!" when he says, "Ama-ama."

Ask questions and wait for answers, modeling the art of conversation. Always give your baby the opportunity to respond to your babbles or words. By waiting a few seconds after you say something, you're opening the door for your baby to fill the space with some words or babbles of his own. This give-and-take helps to teach back-and-forth conversation.

Watch for nonverbal communication. Your baby is communicating plenty, even without using words. Watch for your baby's nonverbal communication—hand movements, baby signs (see page 180), facial expressions—and name what he's trying to communicate ("Looks like you're hungry" or "Charlie is feeling sad"). Responding verbally will boost your little one's receptive and expressive language skills.

Read to your baby often. Books introduce your baby to new words and teach that speech is made up of complex sounds. Reading together can start as early as you want it to, and those reading sessions will become treasured times for both you and your baby. Read more about why reading is so important on page 153.

Sing songs and listen to music. Consider the way you remember the words to a song you haven't heard in years, but struggle to remember your best friend's phone number. That's because music helps us retain words, thanks to the rhythm and repetitive patterns within the melody. Nursery rhymes, lullabies, and finger games (like *Itsy Bitsy Spider* or *Open Shut Them*) are repetitive, engaging, and tailor-made to help young children learn all about words, speech pronunciation, and communication skills. It doesn't matter if you can't carry a tune—your baby will benefit regardless!

HELPING YOUR BABY LEARN TO SIT INDEPENDENTLY

Wait until your baby can hold up her head well

Prop your baby on an incline in her stroller or infant seat for short bursts of time

Hold your baby on your lap in an inclined position

Help your baby balance in a seated position on the floor

Place a toy in front of your baby so she can reach for it

Expect wobbling— it's how your baby learns

A CLOSER LOOK

By the fifth month, your little lounger may be ready for a different perspective on her environment. Sitting independently offers your baby a new way to explore her toys, her favorite people, and her surroundings—plus it's the beginning of milestones to come, from eating solids to crawling, pulling up, cruising, and walking. Of course, you should never push your little one to sit before she's ready. But once you notice signs of readiness (rolling over, good head control when upright, and being able to use her arms to lift her head and chest off the floor when in tummy time—

all of which can happen anywhere from four to seven months old), there's plenty you can do to help your little one progress toward sitting.

Wait until your baby can hold up her head well. Before your baby can sit well, she'll need to have adequate core strength. But since a baby's muscles strengthen from top to bottom—or more accurately, head to toe—the first step in sitting is strong head and neck muscles. If your baby's head is still wobbly, she's not yet ready for sitting. You can help her strengthen her neck, shoulder, stomach, back, and hip muscles through lots of tummy time and time on the floor rolling from side to side. Once your baby in tummy time is lifting her head off the floor with open palms and straight elbows to look across the room and is able to move her head from side to side in that position, she's on her way to gaining the skills needed for sitting.

Prop your baby (or hold her on your lap) in an inclined position for short bursts of time. Your baby will need to learn balance in order to sit alone. Gently propping her at an incline (always with supervision) in her stroller, an infant seat, with pillows, and on your lap will help your little one strengthen her trunk muscles. When she's securely on your lap you can also rock back and forth gently to help her learn the skill of balancing.

Never force your baby into an inclined position or keep her there for too long, especially if she doesn't seem ready for it, but if your baby seems amenable, you can work up to a few minutes at a time a few times a day.

Wondering about structured seats that keep young babies upright? It's never a good idea from a developmental perspective to place a nonsitting baby in a seat that artificially keeps her in a seated, as opposed to an inclined, position.

Help your baby balance in a seated position. As your baby gets stronger, she'll be able to balance for a few seconds in a seated position. You'll notice that your newbie sitter starts in a tripod position, with one or both hands in front of her on the floor, to help with balance and hold up her body weight. As she gets stronger and more adventurous, she'll lift her hands off the floor.

Place a toy in front of your baby so she can reach for it. You can encourage your sitting baby to further strengthen her core and back muscles by placing a toy just within arm's length. Let her reach for the toy on her own or lift it to entice her to extend her arm(s) toward it.

Expect wobbling—it's how your baby learns. Though you should never push your baby to sit before she's ready, don't prevent her from trying. Your baby will learn through opportunity and practice. Don't worry about her falling over—just stay within arm's distance so you can catch her when she tumbles, and cushion the landing with soft blankets and pillows. But let her learn what it feels like to "fail" so she can learn what it means to succeed. Practice makes progress!

Remember, don't keep your baby in any type of container or seat for longer than 15 to 30 minutes at a time and no more than twice a day (transportation in a stroller or car seat aside).

TEETHING SIGNS AND SOOTHING TIPS

TEETHING SIGNS

Drooling, face rash, or coughing

Ear pulling and/or cheek rubbing

Biting

Crankiness and feeding/sleeping disruptions

SOOTHING TEETHING PAIN

Offer something for counterpressure

Give extra comfort

Ask your pediatrician about pain relievers

Avoid numbing gels and teething necklaces

A CLOSER LOOK

Precisely when teething begins will vary from baby to baby, with some little ones showing symptoms months before the first tooth arrives, and others never showing any symptoms at all.

On average, the first tooth (usually one of the lower central incisors) makes its appearance when your baby is around six months old, followed quickly by the second, with another batch of teeth (usually the upper center teeth) popping out after eight months old. But those are just averages. Plenty of babies don't cut any teeth until much later, and others have their chompers show up even earlier. Don't worry if your baby doesn't get any teeth in the first year—that's not unusual—but do speak to your pediatrician or a dentist if no teeth have erupted by eighteen months old.

Also not consistent from baby to baby are the accompanying symptoms. Some babies have every symptom in the book, while others have none. Some need lots of help getting through the teething process, while others sail through it without needing any extra comfort. Here are teething signs that you might notice (they can show up two to three months before the first tooth shows up!).

Drooling, face rash, and coughing. Drool happens in most babies, and it doesn't always herald teething. Even pre-teething babies drool, a sign that the digestive system is up and running and that the swallowing muscles are still immature. But teething often increases the production of saliva, resulting in yet more drool, skin irritation, and a rash around the mouth (check out page 91 for more about teething rashes). Excess saliva from teething can also lead to coughing and gagging (remember those immature swallowing muscles?).

Ear pulling and/or cheek rubbing. Gum soreness where the molars are located can lead a baby to pull his ear or rub his cheek. Ear pulling can also be a sign of tiredness (see page 55), so do your best to interpret this sign appropriately.

Biting. Counterpressure on sore gums can help relieve some of the pain your baby feels, so you might notice an increase in biting (your shoulder, the bottle nipple, your own nipple) when your baby is teething. (See page 297 for tips on what to do if your baby is biting out of aggression or playfulness instead of teething.)

Crankiness and feeding/sleeping disruptions. An uncomfortable baby is often a cranky baby—and one who struggles with eating and sleeping. Inflammation in the gums can make it harder for your baby to suck, chew, or sleep comfortably, causing feeding and sleeping disruptions. Though it's not uncommon for a baby to wake up from teething pain, sleep disruptions due to teething usually don't last longer than a week, so if your baby is having difficulties sleeping for weeks on end, teething is unlikely to blame.

It's important to know that a high fever (over 101°F) and diarrhea are *not* signs of teething (despite what your grandmother or social media may have told you). Both are more likely caused by an infection, a cold, or an upset stomach, so be sure to mention either symptom to your pediatrician should you notice it in your baby.

Here are some ways to help ease teething discomfort.

Offer something for counterpressure. Biting down on something—a teething toy, your finger, a cold washcloth (soaked in chamomile for extra soothing), a feeder bag with frozen formula/breast milk (or fruit, if your baby has already started solids)—can relieve the ache from teething. Using something cold provides bonus numbing for sore gums.

Give extra comfort. You know that the pain from teething is temporary (and usually retreats as soon as the tooth pops through the gum), but your baby doesn't. Extra comfort—in the form of soothing hugs, warm cuddles, and a little extra sympathy—can go a long way toward easing your baby's pain.

Ask your pediatrician about pain relievers. If the teething toys, counterpressure, and cold washcloths aren't working well enough to ease the ache, your pediatrician might recommend a dose or two of acetaminophen (if your baby is over two months old) or ibuprofen (if your baby is over six months old).

Avoid numbing gels and teething necklaces. Numbing gels containing benzocaine, rubbing alcohol, or lidocaine are dangerous and should be avoided completely. Pediatricians also recommend that parents avoid herbal and homeopathic teething remedies or gels (especially ones containing belladonna), since they, too, could be dangerous (plus, none have been proven to work).

Also in the to-avoid category: amber teething necklaces and bracelets. Not only is there zero medical evidence to suggest they ease teething pain, they also pose a choking or strangulation risk. Ditto for necklaces made of wood or silicone.

MONTH 5

STIMULATING YOUR BABY IN THE FIFTH MONTH

Offer toys of various shapes and sizes

Teach with texture

Sing songs with finger movements

Blow bubbles and let your baby try to grab them

Bounce your baby on a medicine ball

Find your baby's ticklish spots and bring on the giggles

A CLOSER LOOK

Your little baby has been making some big developmental strides over the last few months. Here are some ways you can continue to boost your baby's physical, emotional, and mental growth this month.

Offer toys of various shapes and sizes. Last month your baby was super fascinated by her little hands. This month she realizes those hands can do a lot! Let her use them to explore objects of various shapes and sizes: square blocks, round balls, rectangular books. In a few months she'll be transferring objects from one hand to the other—so anything she gets her hands on these days will help develop her muscle dexterity and hand-eye coordination. Let her taste all those (safe) objects as well. Oral exploration is crucial at this age, so no need to stop it. Just be sure that the toys you're handing over aren't small enough to be choking hazards (if the toy can fit through the inside of a toilet paper tube, it's too small). Check out page 278 for guidance on the best types of toys for your baby.

Teach with texture. Never underestimate the power of touch as a learning tool. Exposing your baby to a diversity of textures hones her observational skills and strengthens motor skills; she'll learn about pressure and dexterity as she grips and squeezes differently textured objects. Touch also offers a pathway to more descriptive language ("That flower has silky petals," "The rubber duck is slippery when it's in the water"). Introducing varied textures also allows your little one to explore and learn about different tactile sensations, helping to prevent sensory sensitivities later on. While your baby has certainly been enjoying the soft blankets and stuffed animals you've let her feel so far, broaden her touch horizons with exposure to other textures as well: a hardwood floor, a nubby carpet, a hard metal bowl, a rubbery ball, a spiky pinecone, slippery water, or a velvety flower.

Sing songs with finger movements. You've noticed that your baby loves to listen to all types of sounds and music. Ramp up her music selection by adding songs with hand motions and actions. Fan favorites include *This Little Piggy* or *Itsy Bitsy Spider*. Your fingers will be doing all the work at first, but in a few months your baby will be singing and repeating the motions back to you!

Blow bubbles and let your baby try to grab them. Your cutie's recent antics likely include blowing bubbles (or more accurately, raspberries) with her own mouth. Show her you can join in the fun by blowing (soap and water) bubbles and letting her reach out and try to grab them! This little game helps your baby's visual perception and is a great activity to combine with time outdoors.

Bounce your baby on a medicine ball. Put that exercise ball to good use by taking your baby for a ride! Whether your little one is soothed by the repetitive movement of soft, gentle bouncing, or ready to show off her new motor skills and strength, there's plenty to love about bouncing up and down.

Find your baby's ticklish spots and bring on the giggles. Your baby has graduated from little squeals to full-on giggles, which means it's time to start taking your tickling role seriously (just kidding—have fun with it!). Laughing together isn't only a source of joy for both of you, it also helps your baby develop her social, emotional, and sensory skills. One caveat: Not all babies enjoy being tickled, and too much tickling can irritate even a baby who does laugh, so break out the tickle monster sparingly.

YOU'RE STILL A GOOD PARENT IF . . .

You feel overwhelmed by daily decisions

You feel uncomfortable in your post-baby body

You're rethinking your back-to-work or stay-at-home decision

You decide to stop (or never started) breastfeeding

You let the house get messy

You feel frustrated when you don't know why your baby is crying

A CLOSER LOOK

Worried you're not a perfect parent? Of course you're not—there's no such thing! But you *are* a great parent . . . the perfect one for your baby, even if (or when) moments of self-doubt creep in and consume your thoughts. Remind yourself every day that you're still a good parent (an amazing one!) even if. . .

You feel overwhelmed by daily decisions. As a new parent you're constantly faced with decisions: What formula should you supplement with? Should you sleep teach? How will you introduce solids? Should you go back to the office or stay at home? What baby products should you buy? Let's be honest—you're beyond overwhelmed. Take a deep breath and trust yourself. Whatever you decide for you and your baby is the right choice.

You feel uncomfortable in your post-baby body. If you've carried and delivered your baby, it's okay (and natural) to feel insecure and unsure about your new post-baby body. But while you're busy pulling up those high-waisted leggings and adjusting that oversized sweatshirt, know this: Your baby loves you no matter what you look like and sees only the person who brought him into this world, and who loves him, cares for him, and would do anything for him. Ditto for your partner. The people who love you will love you for what's inside, and whatever you might be feeling insecure about right now likely doesn't faze them at all.

You're rethinking your back-to-work or stay-at-home decision. Perhaps you had a generous parental leave and have only recently returned to the office, but with some ambivalence. Or maybe you've been back at work for a while and something feels off. Or maybe you chose to leave your job to be a full-time stay-at-home parent and now you're not sure it's working for you. Questioning what makes sense career-wise is normal after having a baby, so don't feel bad about feeling unsure. Some parents have trouble getting back into the groove of their full-time office job and feel uneasy leaving their baby with a caregiver every day. Others crave their time in the office and feel they're a better parent because they work outside the home. Still others are thrilled to make the choice to stay home. And if you're like many parents these days and have no choice in the matter, your feelings may be all over the place. There's no one-size-fits-all when it comes to your outside job, and whatever decision you make about your work situation will be the right decision for you . . . even if you change your mind a few times.

You decide to stop (or never started) breastfeeding. The AAP recommends that you breastfeed for as long as you and your baby would like to, for the first two years or beyond—though any amount of breast milk your little one gets is beneficial. But breastfeeding is hard, and for some, impossible. If you've never breastfed, or choose at any time to stop nursing or pumping, you're not a failure. Far from it! Fed is best, and if you're ready to turn the page on this chapter in your motherhood journey, there's no reason to feel guilty about it. By the way, if you're loving breastfeeding and have no intention of stopping any time soon, that's also great, and not something you should feel pressured to give up.

You let the house get messy. Wondering how someone so small can create so much chaos? While it's true that babies themselves don't make much of a mess (poop blowouts notwithstanding), the amount of paraphernalia that accompanies them can feel overwhelming. From bottles and pump parts to burp cloths, dirty clothes, and toys (oh my!), your floors and countertops have never looked as cluttered as they do now. Though you might feel the constant need to straighten up, the mess can wait until you've given yourself some "me time." Refresh yourself by doing something for you . . . and then clean up later (or at the end of the week).

You feel frustrated when you don't know why your baby is crying. You've been a parent for a whole five months now, so you're probably thinking you've got the whole thing figured out. Not so fast! Just when you thought you knew what your baby needed throughout the day, he switches up his schedule and demands. You may need lots of trial and error before you figure out if your fussy baby wants his favorite toy, a nursing session, some cuddles, a little rocking, a walk outdoors, or something else. It's okay to feel frustrated when your baby is crying and you're not sure how to fix it. That's to be expected—you're only human, after all. You're still an excellent parent even if you join your baby for a quick cry every now and then—and hey, it might make you feel better, too!

LEARN MORE

Here are some other topics in the chapters to come that may be relevant this month:

- Short naps (page 133)
- Sleep regressions (page 215)
- Dropping naps (page 265)
- Dropping night feedings (page 165)
- Starting solids (page 136 and page 140)
- Serving allergenic foods (page 168)
- Reading to your baby (page 153)
- Baby sign language (page 180)
- Traveling with your baby (page 251)
- Baby toys (page 278)

MONTH SIX

It's month six (halfway to the first birthday!) and there are lots of transitions on the horizon for your baby. From starting solids to sitting solo, recognizing his or her name to getting his or her first tooth, stringing vowels and consonants together to raking objects (and finger foods) in his or her palm, your baby will be hitting milestones and learning new skills every day in the coming months. Get ready for the beginning of mobility—your energetic baby may be rolling across the room or even trying to scooch along the floor. Pretty soon you won't be able to put your baby down in one place and have him or her stay put, so enjoy the quiet before the storm. Before you know it, you'll have a real mover and shaker on your hands!

FIVE TO SIX MONTHS OLD

SLEEPING

13–15 HOURS
Total time your baby may sleep in a 24-hour day

2–3
Number of naps your baby may take each day

90–120 MINUTES
Time your baby may be awake between naps

EATING

4–5
Number of liquid meals your baby may have each day

24–32 OUNCES
Total amount of breast milk or formula your baby may drink each day

0–2
Number of solid meals

GROWING

12 LBS 2 OZ–19 LBS 3 OZ
23½–27 IN
Average range of weight and height for a baby girl this age

13 LBS 7 OZ–20 LBS 5 OZ
24½–27½ IN
Average range of weight and height for a baby boy this age

Your baby is a unique individual, on his or her own developmental timeline, growing at his or her own pace, with his or her own distinctive temperament, personality, desires, and needs. That means that how much (or how often) he sleeps, how many feedings she has, how tall he is, or how much she weighs will be unique to your little one.

This overview (and the other monthly overviews in this book) represents what a baby *might* be doing, eating, or gaining this month. But because every child is different, your baby won't necessarily fit perfectly into these averages. That's okay. Use these overviews as rough guides to help you gauge what might be happening with your baby each month, recognizing that the range of normal is wide. And then enjoy your baby wherever he or she happens to land.

MILESTONES CHECK-IN

Time for another milestone check-in, though remember, every child is different and on his or her own unique developmental timeline. Some babies may be faster to reach some milestones and slower to reach others, and that's okay. But if your baby doesn't seem to be meeting any of these milestones, mention it to your pediatrician. Also speak up about anything your baby does or doesn't do that concerns you, or if your baby seems to have lost a skill completely.

Seventy-five percent of babies will be able to do at least the following by the end of six months:

- Laugh out loud
- Recognize familiar faces
- Enjoy looking at themselves in the mirror
- Blow raspberries and squeal
- Make back-and-forth sounds with you
- Reach for toys
- Explore objects and toys with their mouths
- Shut their mouths to indicate they don't want food anymore
- Roll over
- Push up with straight arms during tummy time
- Sit in a tripod position (leaning on hands to support themselves)

Don't forget to use your baby's adjusted age if he or she was born early!

SOLUTIONS FOR YOUR BABY'S SHORT NAPS

Watch for sleep cues and respond when your baby is sleepy

Make sure your baby is tired before attempting a nap

Keep your baby active between naps so sleep pressure builds up

Create an environment conducive to sleep

Have a nap routine

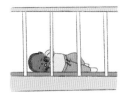

Offer opportunities for your baby to learn the skill of falling asleep on her own

A CLOSER LOOK

One of the most frustrating aspects of baby sleep (and there are many) is short naps. Naps that are too short aren't only disruptive to your to-do list, they're also not great for your baby.

A sleep cycle in a baby older than four or so months lasts around 45 to 60 minutes, which means that your baby will do best with naps that last longer than 45 minutes. Anything less, and your baby may end up overtired. What's more, there's research that links short naps to increased fussiness, tantrums, inability to regulate emotions, and more. Here are some tips that can help if your baby over six months old is taking naps that are just too brief.

Watch for sleep cues and respond when your baby is sleepy. It seems counterintuitive, but an overtired baby will sleep less well. What that means is that waiting too long to put your sleepyhead to sleep (in other words, when your baby is already overtired) can result in naps that are too short. Need a refresher on what sleep cues look like? Check out page 55.

Make sure your baby is tired and sleep pressure has built up. Not only should you not wait until your baby is overtired to put her in for a nap, you also want to ensure your cutie is tired enough before you put her down. Good napping comes only after enough sleep pressure (a.k.a. the biological "need to sleep") has built up between naps. So, keep your baby active between sleep times: Offer plenty of opportunities for active play, stimulation (say, with a walk outside exploring the neighborhood), and physical activity (rolling, getting into a sitting position, attempting to crawl). If you think your baby is taking short naps because she's not tired enough, try to lengthen the time between naps (a.k.a. her wake windows) by 10 to 15 minutes to see if that makes a difference in nap length.

Create an environment conducive to sleep. Some older babies have a hard time sleeping when there's noise or light. Once a baby is past the newborn stage and has learned the difference between night and day (see page 34), it's best to create a nap environment that's as conducive to sleep as possible. That could mean blocking out the light with blackout shades and/ or using white noise in the room (though be sure to keep the machine away from the crib and at a low volume to protect your baby's ears).

Another important tip: Try to keep your baby's nap location consistent—the crib is best—instead of letting your little one nap on the go in the car seat or stroller. While being tethered to the house is, of course, not always possible, making a habit out of your baby sleeping in the car seat or stroller for nap time will not only result in short naps (your baby will wake when you get back home or the car stops, and the quality of sleep isn't as good when she's being jostled around), but it will also create more sleep difficulties overall—your baby will resist being put to sleep in the crib at night.

Have a nap routine. Just as you have a routine for bedtime (see page 58), you'll find it helpful to have an abridged version of that routine at nap time as well. A short 10-minute nap routine will help ease your baby into a restful sleep.

Offer opportunities for your baby to learn the skill of falling asleep on her own. Waking during sleep is something we all do, even as adults. But being able to turn over, straighten our blankets (in the case of an adult, not a baby, of course), and go back to sleep is a skill we have learned. A baby this age is capable of learning that skill as well. And teaching it starts with allowing your baby to fall asleep on her own, even during nap times. Sure, you can rock her to sleep, nurse her to sleep, or put her in the stroller for a walk around the block in the hope it'll get her to sleep, but if she wakes too early in her nap or sleep cycle, she won't have the skills to put herself back to sleep on her own, and will need the rocking, the nursing, or the strolling. See page 105 for more.

STARTING SOLIDS USING PUREES

Start with a small amount on the spoon

Feed your baby . . .

. . . or preload the spoon and let your baby self-feed

Serve up a wide variety of flavors

Offer the spoon until your baby indicates he's done

Once your baby becomes proficient in thin purees, move on to chunkier ones

A CLOSER LOOK

Moving from an all-liquid diet to purees will likely be an easy transition for your little one. If you choose to start with purees (rather than, or along with, finger foods; see page 140), here's a quick primer on how to do it.

Start with a small amount on the spoon. Especially for those first feedings (which you can begin after four months old, though closer to six months old is better; see page 110), you'll want to start with small amounts of puree on a baby-sized spoon so as not to overwhelm your newbie eater. What food to choose? Check out some options on page 145.

Feed your baby . . . Start by placing the spoon on the tip of your baby's tongue and allowing him to explore its contents. Assuming your baby is enjoying the new experience, continue the meal by moving the spoon slightly further back into his mouth. Watch your baby lick or suck the food off the spoon, let him swallow, and wait for him to open his little mouth for more before feeding the next spoonful. Never push more food than he wants to eat.

Expect that more food will come out of your baby's mouth at first than goes in. That's normal! Your baby is learning to move the food from the front of his mouth to the back for swallowing. No need to wipe his mouth between each spoonful, even if there's food dribbling down his chin. You don't want him to equate food exploration with being "dirty," since that could create a negative association with food and feeding. In fact, making a mess while eating is an important learning experience for your baby, so let him touch the food, squish it between his fingers, smear it across the high chair tray, or rub it into his hair (see page 220 for why).

. . . or preload the spoon and let your baby self-feed. Just because you're feeding purees doesn't mean feedings must be parent-led. Giving your new eater practice self-feeding with a spoon is an excellent way to let him hone his fine motor skills and hand-eye coordination, and it's a perfect middle ground between purees and baby-led weaning. It's worth noting, too, that even if you're doing the bulk of the feeding, there's no rule that says you can't also offer your baby a spoon to self-feed at the same time.

Start by choosing a small soft spoon that your baby can easily grab and maneuver into his eager mouth. Dip the spoon into the food and hand the spoon vertically to your baby to grab onto. While he's munching on the first pre-loaded spoon, get a second one ready to go. Your baby will likely drop the first spoon and reach for the second for his next bite. You can also let him dip (or shove) his hands into the bowl of puree and suck the food off his fingers. Sure, it's not the epitome of manners, but eating is not just about nutrition—it's also about skill building.

Allowing your baby the independence to self-feed is an excellent way to encourage responsive eating, which is when a baby is allowed to eat as much or as little as he'd like based on his own hunger and satiety cues. Responsive feeding and eating supports your baby's natural responses to his appetite signals, and by letting your baby take charge of feeding (instead of pushing the spoon into his mouth to get him to finish the contents of the baby food jar), you're giving your baby the chance to listen to, respond to, and trust what his body is telling him. Ignoring those hunger and fullness signs, or encouraging food intake beyond his appetite, will only train your baby to overeat.

Serve up a wide variety of flavors. Food does not have to be bland, even when feeding purees. Indeed, the more flavor varieties you serve up, the more adventurous an eater your baby will become. So, reach for a wide variety of different foods (see page 145 for some suggestions), don't be afraid to add herbs and spices (but not extra salt; see page 174), and consider mixing a few flavors together (squeeze some lime into mashed-up avocado, for instance).

Wondering if you need to pause a few days between new foods? Unless your pediatrician has specified otherwise, you don't have to wait—as long as the new food is *nonallergenic* (see page 169 for a list of the most common allergenic foods). Go ahead and serve multiple new nonallergenic foods on the same day (or at the same meal) if you'd like. Waiting days between new foods will only mean it takes longer to expose your baby to a wider variety of flavors, and the more foods and flavors your baby encounters in the first year, the more likely it is that he'll become an adventurous eater (instead of a picky one) in the toddler years.

Offer the spoon until your baby indicates he's done. Watch for "all done" cues—turning his head away, pursing his lips tightly, getting cranky, leaning back in the high chair, or pushing the spoon away. Listen to what your baby is telling you, and never force-feed an unwilling eater by trying to shove the spoon into his mouth—even if the bowl is still half full. Doing so will set you up for future food fights, since your baby will come to view mealtime as an unpleasant experience.

Once your baby becomes proficient in thin purees, move on to chunkier ones. When your baby has mastered eating thin purees (something that usually happens quickly), offer thicker purees, then purees with lumps, and then those with even more texture. You can do this by mashing soft foods instead of pureeing them, and/or by slowly increasing the size and amount of "solids" (grains, meat, poultry, mashed beans, vegetables, or fruit) you put into the puree.

You're best off moving to chunkier purees by seven or so months old. Waiting too long (say, until after nine months) to offer lumpier foods can lead to reduced food acceptance and diminished oral-motor-sensory skills later in childhood. And remember, you'll be offering finger foods starting at around eight to nine months anyway, so it's a good idea to get your puree-eating baby used to chunkier foods sooner rather than later.

CHOOSING BOTH PUREES AND FINGER FOODS

The good news is that you don't have to choose between serving only purees or only finger foods (a.k.a. baby-led weaning or BLW). As long as your baby is already six months old, you can offer both at the same time, right from the start. And in fact, serving both purees and finger foods provides your baby with the widest variety of textures from the beginning—a worthy goal. You also don't have to stop offering purees once your baby has moved on to finger foods. Even adults eat purees—applesauce, soups, guacamole, yogurt, humus, and more—so there's nothing wrong with serving both purees and finger foods at your baby's meals.

Something else to know: Feeding is more about practice and skill building than nutrition at first, so don't worry about how much your baby eats in the beginning. Focus instead on the learning your baby is doing, from exploring tastes and textures to honing oral-motor skills—which he'll be able to do no matter which method, purees or BLW, you choose to use.

STARTING SOLIDS USING BABY-LED WEANING

BLW is a feeding method that emphasizes finger food (instead of purees) right from the start

BLW exposes babies to varied textures and tastes and encourages independent self-feeding

BLW should be started after age 6 months—finger foods before 6 months can be dangerous

The younger the baby, the bigger the pieces of food should be to avoid choking risk

For ages 6 to 9 months, cut foods the length of an adult finger and the width of 2 adult fingers

Give food a "handle" or some texture so your baby can easily grab and hold on to it

Food can be cut into smaller pieces once your baby develops the pincer grasp (around 9 months old)

Offer food that is soft and easy to gum

Let your baby self-feed

If you're not interested in feeding your baby purees (or at least not all the time), there's another option you can try. Called baby-led weaning or BLW (though it may be more accurate to call it baby-led eating), this approach is one that you can implement as soon as you start feeding your baby solids at six months.

With BLW, you skip (or minimize) purees and start with finger foods—and while BLW may seem like a new way of feeding solids, it's how parents fed their babies for generations, long before baby food jars, pouches, blenders, and spoons were invented. This method of feeding solids, where your baby is an active participant in the feeding process from the get-go rather than a passive recipient (as with parent-led spoon-feeding), helps promote oral-motor development, hand-eye coordination, and general motor skills, and may possibly lead to less fussiness around foods. You can opt for all BLW all the time (defined as your baby self-feeding 90 percent of the time, with 10 percent or less involving purees by spoon), or you can do a combo of BLW and purees (either parent- or self-fed).

Here's a deeper dive into BLW.

BLW should only be started after six months—finger foods before six months can be dangerous. When it comes to BLW, you'll need to wait until your baby is six months old, since that's when the vast majority of babies are developmentally able to self-feed and chew, making eating finger foods safer.

Offer finger foods of varied textures and tastes. With BLW, instead of mashing avocado and serving it as a puree, you coat a wedge of avocado with breadcrumbs or ground pistachios and let your baby munch on it. Instead of blending banana into a fine goo, you hand your baby a finger length piece of the sweet fruit. Instead of feeding from a bowl of baby cereal, you hand your baby a piece of toasted whole grain bread topped with thinly spread peanut butter or mashed beans. Instead of mushing meat into a paste to mix with fruit, you offer your baby a rib (yes . . . a big hunk of meat!) so she can suck off the iron-rich juices. This increased exposure to flavors, textures, and tastes with BLW, as

MONTH 6

compared to traditional single-ingredient purees, may reduce picky eating later (though research is mixed). Keep in mind that nuts, peanut butter, and wheat are allergens, so you'll want to introduce these foods with care. See page 168 for more on serving allergens to your baby.

You can serve safe finger foods of all kinds—even adult foods. A benefit to BLW is that you and your baby can eat from the same menu. If your dinner consists of salmon, sweet potato, and broccoli, your baby's dinner can be exactly the same. If your go-to snack is a ripe mango, there's no reason not to serve the same to your little one. Omelet for breakfast, anyone? As long as the food you're serving is safe (see page 172 for off-limit foods in the first year) and served in the right size (see below), your baby can eat the same foods you are (and with the same spices and other flavorings as well!).

The younger the baby, the bigger the pieces of food should be to avoid choking risk. Though common sense would dictate the opposite, the bigger the size of the food, the better for babies ages six to nine months. That's because it's hard for new eaters to move small pieces of food around in their mouths. Plus, it's easier for a baby to choke on a small piece of food than on a large one (the small size means it can fit into a baby's airway). Also, your baby is unlikely to even attempt to swallow an extra-large piece of food—she'll either chew it to turn the food into a more manageable size or spit it out. (You can teach your baby how to spit by sticking out your own tongue in an exaggerated way and modeling how to push food out with the tongue.)

Never stick your finger in your baby's mouth to remove food or put food directly into her mouth. Both can push food too deep in the mouth, causing choking. Worried about gagging? Turn to page 150 for reassurance.

For ages six to nine months, cut foods the length of an adult finger and the width of two adult fingers. The ideal length and width for food is *at least* the length of an adult finger and the width of two adult fingers (about four inches in length and one and a half inches across). That's because, at this age, your baby will be using her palm, not her fingers, to pick up food. In order for her to be able to grab the food and bring it to her mouth on her own (something that's very important, because self-feeding reduces the risk of choking), it needs to be big enough to grasp with her entire hand and long enough that part of the food will stick out beyond your baby's closed fist. Plus, as you've just learned, bigger is better for babies this age.

Give food a "handle" or some texture so your baby can easily grab and hold on to it. Keeping a handle on the food (a broccoli stalk or rib bone, for instance) will aid your little one as she grabs for it. For slippery fruits, coating them with something textured (such as breadcrumbs, hemp hearts, or finely chopped nuts) can help.

Food can be cut into smaller pieces once your baby develops the pincer grasp (around nine months old). As you've learned, self-feeding reduces the risk of choking, so it's important, at first, to offer large pieces of food that your six- to nine-month-old baby is able to palm and bring to her mouth on her own. But once your baby develops the pincer grasp (using the thumb and pointer finger to pick up small objects) at around nine months old, she'll be able to grab and feed herself smaller pieces, and that means you can begin cutting foods into smaller sizes, serving them shredded, thinly sliced, or diced. You can also continue to offer bigger pieces of food for extra biting and chewing practice.

Offer food that is soft and easy to gum. Your new eater doesn't need teeth to eat finger foods, but you'll still want to serve food that is soft enough for your baby to mash with her gums or against the roof of her mouth with her tongue (if it squishes easily between your fingers, you're good to go!). You can also safely offer food that is tough enough that small pieces can't be broken off (strips of meat, for instance). Avoid food that forms a large crumb or soggy ball in your baby's mouth, such as bread that hasn't been toasted. A toasted whole grain bagel or the crusty end of a loaf of country bread are better options.

Let your baby self-feed. With BLW, babies are in charge of their eating—there's no adult leading the feeding or pushing "just one more bite." You choose what foods to offer and when, and your baby decides what and how much of the food to eat. It still requires parental involvement, but it's less parent-controlled.

This is your baby's show. Let her self-feed without pressure, get messy, and eat whatever amount she wants. But also keep safety in mind. Even though your baby will be leading the feeding, never leave her alone when she's eating. Limit distractions (no TV in the background) and make sure your baby is upright in the high chair (one with a footrest is ideal because it helps stabilize your baby, keeping her hips at 90 degrees).

Keep in mind that new eaters don't necessarily know what to do with finger food when you offer it. So, model what you want your baby to do. With your baby watching, pick up a piece of food and eat it—your baby will likely follow your lead. See page 196 for more on teaching your baby how to chew. And check out page 240 for tips on what to do if your baby refuses solids entirely.

FOODS TO FEED YOUR BABY

Broccoli

Green beans

Sweet potato

Carrot

Squash

Cauliflower

Avocado

Ripe melon

Ripe peach

Ripe mango

Ripe plum

Ripe pear

Berries

Banana

Beans and lentils

Beef

Fish

Poultry

Eggs

Tofu

Yogurt

Whole grain pasta

Baby cereal (oat, wheat, quinoa, barley, possibly rice)

Whole grain bread, toasted

A CLOSER LOOK

While you can stick with traditional baby food jars when feeding your new eater, you can—even should!—also offer your baby what you're eating to expose him to a wide variety of tastes, textures, and flavors. The AAP recommends iron-rich foods (iron-fortified cereal, lentils, beans, beef, tofu), energy-rich foods (banana, beans, sweet potato, avocado, eggs), and fruits and vegetables (those high in vitamin C will help with iron absorption) as good first foods. Here is just a small sample of the many food options to consider when feeding your baby in the first year. Most of the foods on this list can be given to a baby beginning at six months.

Vegetables. There's a bounty of vegetables out there that you can serve to your baby. Choose from broccoli, green beans, potatoes, squash, cauliflower, carrots, asparagus, beets, parsnips, zucchini, eggplant, peppers, and more. These wholesome veggies, full of vitamins, can be served well-cooked as purees or as finger foods. When serving as finger foods to babies between six and nine months old (or before your baby has developed the pincer grasp), cut vegetables into strips the length and width of two adult fingers or larger (remember, the younger the baby, the bigger the food should be). Once the pincer grasp has developed, you can cut foods into smaller pieces. Be sure vegetables are cooked soft enough to be mashed between your baby's gums.

By the way, you may have heard that you should introduce vegetables before fruit so that your baby doesn't get used to sweet flavors and end up rejecting the sharper taste of vegetables. That's a myth. Your little one was born with a preference for sweet stuff and has been tasting sweet breast milk and formula from day one. Offering vegetables before introducing fruit is a fine choice, but it won't make your baby more likely to eat vegetables in the long run. In other words, there's no need to introduce solids in a specific order. Serve up whatever foods you want in whatever order you prefer. Remember, the best way to make your baby a well-rounded eater is to offer a wide variety of foods, flavors, and textures.

Fruits. A cornucopia of fruit awaits your new eater. From ripe mango, plum, peach, pear, and melon, to avocado, banana, berries, and more, the choices are endless. Fruit can be served cooked and mashed, pureed, or as finger food. Only serve uncooked fruits if they are very soft when they're ripe (a peach fits the bill; an apple shouldn't be served raw until your baby is older, though cooked is fine). If you're serving a fruit as a finger food, cut it into pieces no smaller than the length and width of two adult fingers. Or hand your baby an entire ripe mango pit with a little flesh left on and let him gnaw away. Once the pincer grasp is developed, smaller pieces of super-ripe or cooked fruit are safe for your baby to eat, though you can continue to offer larger pieces, too.

Since fruits as finger foods can be slippery to hold, coat them with a dusting of wheat germ, hemp seeds, finely ground nuts, breadcrumbs, or finely ground Cheerios. Another option: leaving a handle for easier gripping. For example, leave the lower half of the banana peel on so your baby can chew on the flesh while holding onto the peel "handle" (though make sure to wash the peel first in case your baby samples the peel side as well).

You can hand your baby a whole large strawberry (the bigger the better), but be sure to smash and flatten blueberries or raspberries before letting your baby at them. Your baby can also suck on citrus fruits that have been cut into large wedges (wash and keep the peel on and check to make sure there are no seeds). Alternatively, you can section an orange by cutting away the membrane and handing your baby a segment to munch on. Kiwis can be mashed into a puree or quartered and skinned so your little one can suck on the fruit.

Beef, poultry, fish, and eggs. Never thought of handing your six-month-old a rib? Maybe it's time to think about it! The AAP considers meat a perfect first food for your baby thanks to its high iron and protein content. You can puree meats to a fine consistency and serve them mixed with fruits or vegetables. Or you can serve small pieces of ground beef mixed with mashed potatoes, for instance. But you can also (if you're going the BLW route) hand your baby an entire rib or lamb chop for him to suck on. He won't be able to bite off the flesh, but he will be able to net some of the iron-rich juices—and iron is important, especially in breastfed babies, since breast milk doesn't contain enough of that mineral for babies over six months old.

Poultry is another great source of protein. You can hand your baby an entire skinned and well-cooked chicken leg (after six months), shredded or thinly sliced chicken (after nine months), or pureed chicken mixed with fruit or vegetables (at any age once feeding solids has begun).

Mashed flakes of soft, well-cooked fish (check carefully for bones) can be mixed with vegetables, or you can serve fish in pieces the length and width of two adult fingers or diced (after the pincer grasp has developed).

Eggs are *egg*cellent for new eaters. Offer strips of fully cooked omelet (throw in some chopped spinach or kale while cooking for a green, iron-rich bonus!). You can also mash hard-boiled eggs and mix with vegetables or spread thinly on strips of whole grain toast. Once your baby's pincer grasp has developed you can cut omelets into bite-sized pieces or offer hard-boiled eggs, quartered.

Keep in mind that fish and eggs are allergens, so introduce them slowly. See page 168 for a how-to.

Nuts and legumes. Also allergenic but important to introduce early in your baby's food journey are nuts and peanuts. While you obviously can't, for safety's sake, offer whole nuts or peanuts, you can offer thinly spread nut butters on fruit or on whole grain toast strips, thinned nut butter mixed into cereals or yogurts, finely ground or powdered nuts mixed into or coating other foods, or peanut butter puffs.

In the legume department, turn to beans and lentils, though start slowly and with small amounts so your baby's tummy doesn't protest. Beans should be well cooked, then pureed and turned into a paste that can be spread on toast or thin rice cakes or (for older babies) smashed before serving. Lentils can be mashed into a textured puree and served on a spoon (hand it pre-loaded to your baby to self-feed). Hummus can be spread just like nut butters. Firm tofu can be cut into large strips and given to babies over six months old. When the pincer grasp develops, you can cut tofu into cubes for easy grabbing.

Dairy. While you shouldn't serve cow's milk as a drink until your baby reaches his first birthday (see the box on page 270), dairy products can be introduced as early as six months old. Keep in mind that dairy allergies are common, so you'll want to start with small portions and watch your baby carefully for any signs of allergy if this is his first exposure (if he's been on cow's milk–based formula without any signs of allergies, you don't have to worry).

Full-fat yogurt (such as unsweetened Greek yogurt) can be served on its own or mixed with pureed fruit or nut butters. Spoon feed it to your little one, or let him self-feed, either with a preloaded spoon or by hand. Soft cheese options include mascarpone, which can be mixed into mashed vegetables or spread thinly on rice cakes or toast, and fresh, soft ricotta or low-sodium cottage cheese mixed with fruit purees or nut butters. While strips of soft, fresh mozzarella are fine to serve early on, hard cheeses can wait until after the first birthday, both because of choking risk and because of their high sodium content, though an occasional dusting of parmesan on food can give your baby a calcium boost. If you think your baby can handle it, you can offer a large thin slice (not chunks) of a low-sodium cheese such as Swiss to your baby after nine months old.

Grains. Fortified baby cereals are a great way to get grains in—and making them whole grain boosts the nutrients your baby will get. Try the standard oatmeal, but also consider cereal made from amaranth, barley, buckwheat, bulgur, or millet. Quinoa is another great cereal option, and you can also serve this superfood in little oven-baked patties. Rice (and rice cereal) should be served only occasionally because of its trace arsenic content, but you can sometimes offer extra-thin brown rice cakes spread with avocado, thinned nut butter, or soft cheeses. Even polenta (cooked cornmeal) is a good option and can offer more whole grain variety.

Because pasta can get sticky and be hard to chew, you may decide to wait to offer it until your baby is nine months old, when you can serve small pieces of it. However, there's no reason to wait if your baby seems capable, especially with long tubular-type pastas. And if you're going to serve bread, make sure it's whole grain and toasted. Untoasted bread (especially white bread) can get gummy in a baby's mouth, leading to gagging or even choking. You can also turn bread into French toast sticks. And parents, rejoice: Once your baby's pincer grasp has developed, you can offer plain Cheerios!

WHEN YOUR BABY GAGS

Gagging is a protective reflex designed to prevent choking

A baby's gag reflex is located toward the front of the tongue

You'll hear gurgling or coughing sounds and you'll see a red face, watery eyes, an open mouth, and the tongue thrusting forward

When your baby gags, stay calm, since overreacting can frighten a baby into choking

Let your baby work the food forward on her own

Get lower than your baby and put your hand under her mouth to encourage her to spit out the food

A CLOSER LOOK

The inevitable gagging your baby will do when she's learning how to navigate solids is undeniably the hardest part of baby-led weaning—or starting solids in general, since gagging can happen even with purees. Though it's normal and not unsafe, many parents get nervous, mistaking gagging for choking. Choking is rare (and happily, studies show that the BLW method of feeding solids doesn't lead to a higher risk). Knowing the difference between gagging and choking (see below and the box on page 152) can help you feed your baby without fear.

Gagging is a protective reflex designed to prevent choking. As scary as it looks the first (or second, or tenth) time you see it, gagging is not something to be frightened of—it's a protective reflex. Gagging means your baby's body is doing exactly what it needs to do to prevent choking: using its built-in safety mechanisms to prevent food from getting too close to your baby's airway.

A baby's gag reflex is located toward the front of the tongue. While an adult's gag reflex is located far back on the tongue, a baby's gag reflex is much closer to the tip, which makes it easily triggered by even small amounts of food. This reflex is completely normal—it's just the way babies learn how to eat—plus, babies are rarely fazed by it. Your little one should outgrow her gag reflex as she gets older and learns to handle the challenge of solids. Do check in with your pediatrician, however, if your baby gags or vomits at every meal past the first month or so of eating solids, just to rule out any underlying issues.

What gagging looks like. When your baby gags, you'll hear gurgling, retching, or coughing sounds and you'll see her open her mouth and thrust her tongue forward. Her eyes may water, and her face may turn red. Read the box on page 152 to learn how choking looks and sounds very different from gagging.

An excellent way to learn what to expect when your baby gags is to watch videos online of other babies gagging—and to do so before you start feeding solids to your baby. This way, the first time you see it in your little one, you'll know what's happening and you'll remember to stay calm.

What to do when your baby gags. As difficult as it might be to sit back and let your baby handle it on her own, that's exactly what's called for when your baby gags. Jumping out of your seat and yelling, "Oh my god!" can alarm your baby, upping the chances of her choking. Sticking your finger in her mouth to remove the food she's gagging on can push it further back, also raising the risk of choking. Instead, stay calm—just as you (hopefully) do when your newbie sitter topples, or when your new walker will fall on her bottom—and observe quietly. Let your baby work the food toward the front of her mouth. If doing something will make you feel better, you can calmly say, "Push it forward . . . spit it out." Model for your baby how to spit out food that's too big by sticking out your tongue and saying "aaahhh." Getting lower than your baby's seat and holding your hand under her chin so she leans forward to push the food out and into your hand can help as well.

CHOKING

The best way to minimize the risk of choking when feeding finger foods to your baby is to always follow safety recommendations: Never leave your baby alone when eating, ensure that your baby is sitting up straight (at 90 degrees), offer your baby soft, properly sized food that is easily mashable (nothing that's hard, round, or coin-shaped), and let your baby bring the food to her mouth at her own pace. Eliminating distractions during mealtime is also important (no TV in the background).

True choking is when your baby has trouble breathing because her airway is obstructed. When that happens, your baby won't be able to make any sounds, or will only be able to make a high-pitched wheezing sound, because her airway is blocked. In other words, if your baby is crying or making sounds, she's not choking. Other signs of choking include blue or purple lips due to lack of oxygen, and a panicked look or blank stare. Remember, gagging (which is a thrusting outward motion) isn't choking (which is a sucking inward motion).

If you suspect your baby is choking, immediate action is required. You'll need to administer infant choking first aid—remove your baby from the high chair, position her face down on your forearm with her head lower than her body, and alternate between five back blows and five chest thrusts (you'll turn her over to administer the chest thrusts)—while someone calls 911.

WHY YOU SHOULD READ TO YOUR BABY

Reading is a great bonding experience

Reading builds listening skills

Reading improves language skills

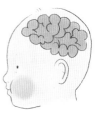

Reading builds memory skills

Reading encourages social development

Reading helps babies see and hear more of the world around them

A CLOSER LOOK

Reading to your baby doesn't have to wait until your little one understands the words on the page. You can (and should) start reading together early in the first year—even right from those first few weeks. Sure, your baby won't pay much attention in the beginning, and he might do more nibbling on the book than looking at it, but don't let that stop you from story time. Establishing a practice of reading to your baby each day (say, as part of your bedtime routine) can be comforting for your little one. Plus, reading has plenty of other benefits.

Reading is a great bonding experience. When you snuggle together to read a book, it reinforces your emotional connection and makes your baby feel safe. Not only does spending book time together teach your baby that reading is important, but the one-on-one attention also shows your baby that he's important to you.

Reading builds listening skills. The sound of your voice, whether you're singing a song, reciting a nursery rhyme, chatting with your baby, or reading a book, offers your baby an opportunity to sharpen his listening skills. Sure, your little one may resist sitting for longer than a page (especially at this age), and his listening skills won't necessarily be strong right from the start, but with time, your baby will come to treasure your story sessions. Lower your standards: Reading doesn't have to be a perfect, quiet, page-by-page experience just yet. Even drooling on a book or looking at it upside down is considered "reading" at this age. What you're doing now is setting the stage for a lifelong love of reading.

Reading improves language skills. Every time you read aloud, your baby hears words, rhymes, rhythms, and cadence—the building blocks of language. And the more you read to him, the more words he's introduced to. Reading also introduces your baby to concepts such as letters, numbers, colors, patterns, and shapes—important basics that lay the foundation for more advanced learning to come.

Reading builds memory skills. Reading helps build brain connections, and hearing the same book again and again (as much as it drives you nuts) strengthens those neural links. Every time your baby copies the sound the duck in the book makes, a word that's repeated in the story, or your facial expression, he's building all-important memory skills.

Reading encourages social development. Books aren't just vehicles for words and language development. They also teach about expressions, feelings, and social skills. Through books your baby will be exposed to emotions like happiness, sadness, fear, playfulness, and frustration. Your baby will also learn about smiling and frowning, sharing and friendship—important foundational skills for socialization.

Reading helps babies see and hear more of the world around them. Reading exposes your baby to sights, sounds, and experiences beyond his environment. He'll learn about safari animals even if you live in a city. He'll discover subways even if your standard mode of transportation is a car. He'll be exposed to chickens and airplanes and bicycles and clowns, even if he hasn't yet had the opportunity to encounter any of these things in his daily life. Books offer a window to objects, ideas, and experiences beyond your baby's immediate surroundings, expanding his horizons.

CHOOSING BOOKS FOR YOUR BABY

Here are some features to look for when choosing from the wide world of baby books:

- Books with high-contrast, brightly colored, and/or black and white illustrations and patterns are great for young babies. As your baby gets older, focus on books with simple illustrations or photos, especially of the human face, which babies love. Books with mirrors, textures, flaps, and pop-ups are great for older babies who are ready to interact and explore.
- Rhymes and phrases that repeat will catch your baby's attention and hone his listening and memory skills.
- When your baby is old enough to respond to the story— usually sometime after nine months—turn to books that depict familiar objects (toys, bottles, stuffed animals), people (parents, siblings, doctors), and activities (bath time, sleep time, playing with friends), as well as books that offer a window into parts of the world he hasn't yet encountered (trains, farm animals, skyscrapers).
- Look for books with just a few words per page and those that use simple language. But remember that you're not locked into reading the sentences on the page word for word. Make reading interactive by asking questions, pointing out pictures, simplifying language when necessary, and pausing to see if your baby will finish the sentence (it'll happen before you know it!).

STIMULATING YOUR BABY IN THE SIXTH MONTH

Gently pull your baby into sit ups

Stack cups and let your baby knock them down

Play a game of copycat

Turn off the lights and use a flashlight to give a mini light show

Bounce your baby up and down and side to side on your legs

Play clapping games

A CLOSER LOOK

Happy (almost) half-birthday to your sweet little one! And congrats to you . . . you've made it nearly six whole months entertaining your baby. Now is when things really get exciting because your baby is starting to understand the concept of play and self-entertainment. Here are a few activities to make your baby's day fun.

Gently pull your baby into sit ups. If your baby isn't already sitting up unassisted, she's likely getting close. Place your baby tummy-up on your lap, let her grab your hands, and encourage her to pull herself up to a seated position. This simple activity helps with head control, motor skills, and muscle strength.

Stack cups and let your baby knock them down. Believe it or not, that little baby slobbering on your floor is starting to learn some big life lessons, and one of them is the concept of cause and effect. Letting her knock over that tower you've created is more than just her making a mess. It's an amazing brain-stimulating activity that helps her learn that her actions (the cause) can have an impact (the effect).

Play a game of copycat. They say imitation is the sincerest form of flattery, and that's especially true when your little mini me tries to be just like you! While you and your baby are facing each other, make different facial expressions, stick out your tongue, or make different sounds, like ba-ba, da-da, and ma-ma, and see if you can get your cutie to copy you. You'll be delighted every time your baby matches your movements, and she'll love seeing your response.

Turn off the lights and use a flashlight to give a mini light show. Give your baby's more mature visual capabilities something new and exciting to look at. Turn off the lights, grab a flashlight or two, and shine the beams on the walls, ceiling, and floor to enhance your baby's visual perception and tracking. Watch her eyes widen and light up at this new experience!

Bounce your baby up and down and side to side on your legs. Your baby, who was once content with lying and sitting still, can use a little movement these days. Put her on your lap, hold onto her belly, and tell her to saddle up! Move your legs from side to side and up and down, gently bouncing her to give that little body a big thrill. The giggles and squeals coming from your baby will let you know how much she's enjoying this horsey game.

Play clapping games. While your baby is too young to clap on her own (that'll come around or after nine months), she'll still delight in watching and hearing you clap along to songs or nursery rhymes. You can even bring your baby along for the ride by taking her hands in your own and clapping them together. Teaching clapping can help her learn imitation and how different things, objects, or body parts can make sounds.

DON'T COMPARE . . .

Your baby's feeding schedule to another baby's feeding schedule

Your baby's growth to another baby's growth (just to your baby's own growth curve)

Your baby's milestones to another baby's milestones

Your baby's method of starting solids to another baby's method of starting solids

Your baby's sleep habits to another baby's sleep habits

Remember, your baby is unique and should only be compared to himself

A CLOSER LOOK

Being a parent is hard, especially when there are other parents (and babies) all around that serve as points of comparison. That baby is already crawling and mine barely sits! *What am I doing wrong?* She's so much bigger than my baby! *What am I doing wrong?* My baby is sleeping so much less that that baby! *What am I doing wrong?* Comparisons like these lead to doubt and worry—two things a parent doesn't need more of. So, try a new perspective. Instead of comparing your baby to others, pay attention to (and celebrate) him as the unique individual he is.

Don't compare your baby's feeding schedule to another baby's feeding schedule. Maybe you're still nursing around the clock, and your friend isn't. Or perhaps your sweet little one just dropped his nighttime feed for the first time, and your sister's baby did it months ago. Or maybe your baby isn't taking to solids yet, and his older sib ate like a champ from bite one. Take a deep breath because all these feeding permutations are fine. Your baby will settle into a feeding schedule and pattern all his own when the time is right, so it doesn't matter what another baby's feeding routine looks like.

Don't compare your baby's growth to another baby's growth (just to your baby's own growth curve). Babies come in all shapes and sizes, and the only thing that matters when it comes to your little one's shape or size is whether he's progressing along his own growth curve. If your pediatrician isn't concerned about your baby's growth, you shouldn't be either, even if you see a similar-age baby (or, *gasp*—a younger baby) who is taller or chunkier (or shorter or skinnier) than your baby.

Don't compare your baby's milestones to another baby's milestones. Remind yourself that there is an extremely wide range of normal when it comes to developmental milestones, and that each child is a unique individual on a unique developmental timeline. You may panic if a baby younger than yours is sitting already, but maybe that baby doesn't sleep through the night and yours does. Every baby develops differently. Your baby's development is part of what makes him uniquely yours. (Of course, if you think your baby is lagging behind, bring up those concerns to your pediatrician or seek a consultation with a specialist.)

Don't compare your baby's method of starting solids to another baby's. Thinking about doing BLW at six months only to second guess your choice when your BFF tells you she's been feeding her baby purees since he was four months old? Don't go there. Whether you're the baby-led weaning family, the family packing baby food jars for day care, the homemade puree family, or the family with the baby who refuses to use a spoon, it just doesn't matter. It's your baby, your way, which means there's no reason to compare how you've started solids to how some other parent started solids. And remember, one day you and your friend will be sitting next to each other at a birthday party, watching both of your children eat cake with their fingers.

Don't compare your baby's sleep habits to another baby's sleep habits. Sleep comparisons can be enough to drive you crazy in the first year of your baby's life. Some babies are great sleepers and nappers, and their parents rave about how well rested their family is. Other babies, well, they need a little extra work. It doesn't matter if you've decided to continue letting your baby nap in your arms while your playgroup buddy decided to sleep teach. Both options work if they work for each of your babies. And both your babies will still need to be woken up for school when they're teenagers!

Remember, your baby is unique and should only be compared to himself. You love your baby because he is so uniquely himself. He has a tiny personality and quirks that are fitting for him. And he will develop on a timeline that is also uniquely his. As you go through this first year of your little one's life, watch as he grows, develops, and changes each month. Instead of only looking at what your baby isn't doing yet, feel proud of all the great strides he's already made. Let yourself be amazed by all he's learned and what he's accomplished so far—and don't give those other babies a second glance.

LEARN MORE

Here are some other topics in the chapters to come that may be relevant this month:

- Sleep regressions (page 215)
- Dropping night feedings (page 165)
- Early wake-ups (page 191)
- Dropping naps (page 265)
- Serving allergenic foods (page 168)
- Foods to avoid (page 172)
- Introducing a cup (page 175)
- Serving water (page 194)
- Messy eating (page 220)
- Baby sign language (page 180)
- Baby won't stay still for diaper changes (page 223)
- Baby is unhappy in the car seat (page 225)
- Traveling with your baby (page 251)
- Baby toys (page 278)
- Weaning from the breast (page 294)

MONTH SEVEN

As your baby enters the second half of the first year, chances are your cutie is sitting—perhaps well or perhaps with some wobbles—and likely able to bear weight on his or her legs when held in a standing position. These new large motor skills will soon be accompanied by small motor skill leaps as well—your baby will be ready to start practicing stacking toys and passing an object between his or her hands. And listen to that adorable babbling! Your baby is probably combining vowels and consonant sounds, showing just how far his or her intellectual development is progressing.

As you beam with pride over your baby's new tricks, be sure to also take a moment to marvel at this and all the other wonderful parts of being a parent. It's easy to get caught up in the overwhelming moments (and there will be plenty—the sleepless nights, the unexplained crying, the feeding challenges, the stuffy noses), but taking a step back every now and then can help remind you of how many moments of happiness you've experienced so far as a parent . . . with plenty more to come.

MONTH SEVEN OVERVIEW

SIX TO SEVEN MONTHS OLD

SLEEPING

12–15 HOURS
Total time your baby may sleep in a 24-hour day

2–3
Number of naps your baby may take each day

2–3 HOURS
Time your baby may be awake between naps

EATING

4–5
Number of liquid meals your baby may have each day

24–32 OUNCES
Total amount of breast milk or formula your baby may drink each day

1–3
Number of solid meals

GROWING

12 LBS 13 OZ–20 LBS 5 OZ
24¼–27½ IN
Average range of weight and height for a baby girl this age

14 LBS 2 OZ–21 LBS 6 OZ
25–28¼ IN
Average range of weight and height for a baby boy this age

A CLOSER LOOK

Your baby is a unique individual, on his or her own developmental timeline, growing at his or her own pace, with his or her own distinctive temperament, personality, desires, and needs. That means that how much (or how often) he sleeps, how many feedings she has, how tall he is, or how much she weighs will be unique to your little one.

This overview (and the other monthly overviews in this book) represents what a baby *might* be doing, eating, or gaining this month. But because every child is different, your baby won't necessarily fit perfectly into these averages. That's okay. Use these overviews as rough guides to help you gauge what might be happening with your baby each month, recognizing that the range of normal is wide. And then enjoy your baby wherever he or she happens to land.

DROPPING NIGHT FEEDINGS

Make sure your baby is getting enough to eat during the day

Confirm the night feeds are due to habit, not hunger

If nursing, gradually shorten the length of each night feed

If bottle feeding, gradually reduce the amount of formula or breast milk in the bottle

Cut out night feeds one at a time

Have someone other than the nursing parent comfort your baby at night

A CLOSER LOOK

Now that your baby is over six months old and likely more than twice his birth weight, he no longer *needs* night feedings—at least from a metabolic and nutritional perspective. He's now capable of meeting all his caloric and nutritional requirements during the day. But your baby might not have gotten that message yet, and he may still be waking up multiple times throughout the night for feedings. It's not necessary to phase out night feedings if you're comfortable with them (maybe you like the comfort it offers your little one, especially if you're nursing), but if you're ready to transition from all-night nibbling to a full night's sleep for you and your baby, here are a few strategies to try.

Make sure your baby is getting enough to eat during the day. Sometimes, when babies are still eating throughout the night, they tend to eat less during the day because they know the buffet is open 24 hours. As you transition slowly away from night feedings, make sure your baby is getting the right number of ounces of formula or breast milk for his age during daylight hours. While any solids at this age add to your baby's calorie count, they won't be an important part of his overall caloric intake until later in the first year. Your baby should also get a steady dose of daytime cuddles to help compensate for any snuggle time lost when night feedings are dropped.

Confirm the night feeds are due to habit, not hunger. If your baby's night feeds last for only a few minutes before he falls back asleep, if your baby demands to feed every hour or two throughout the night, if your baby needs to eat to fall asleep, or if your baby has a hard time falling back to sleep after a night feed, there's a good chance your baby is eating at night because he's used to it, not because he's hungry. On the other hand, if the night feeds last as long as (and consist of a similar amount of breast milk or formula as) daytime feeds or if your baby is waking for a feed after a long stretch of sleep, there's a greater chance he's waking out of hunger. Shifting more of your baby's calorie intake to the day can combat hunger wake-ups. If the wake-ups are due to habit, read on.

If nursing, gradually shorten the length of each night feed. If your baby usually nurses for 20 minutes, reduce the length of each feed by a few minutes every night over the course of a week, until the feeds are 3 to 5 minutes long or less.

If bottle feeding, gradually reduce the amount of formula or breast milk in the bottle. Slowly reduce the amount of fluids you put in the bottle by an ounce or two each night over the course of a week, until there's only a little in the bottle.

Cut out night feeds one at a time. Once they are just a few minutes long or just an ounce or two, drop the feeds one at a time so it's not jarring for your baby (or your breasts).

Have someone other than the nursing parent comfort your baby at night. It's a tease for a nursing baby to have mom (and her boobs) so close yet off-limits. During the night weaning process, have the non-nursing partner take on the lion's share of the night comforts. If there's one parent that's usually in charge of the night bottles, have the other parent step in for night comfort during the weaning process.

SERVING ALLERGENIC FOODS

Know which foods are allergenic

Know your baby's allergy risk profile—eczema, for instance, increases the risk of food allergies

Start introducing allergenic foods as early as 4 months old

Make the first introduction in the morning at home

Serve allergenic foods one at a time, waiting a few days before serving the next allergenic food

Know the signs of an allergic reaction

A CLOSER LOOK

Most children—more than 90 percent of babies—won't be allergic to any foods. Still, introducing common food allergens to your baby can be stressful, especially if there's a history of allergies in your family. Knowing the best way to serve up common allergens and being able to spot allergic reactions if they occur can make the whole process less confusing and scary.

Know which foods are allergenic. There are over one hundred and sixty foods that can cause allergies, but the major food allergens—the ones responsible for 90 percent of the serious allergic reactions in babies in the US—are dairy, eggs, wheat, soy, sesame, fish, shellfish, peanuts, and tree nuts. Knowing what they are can help you safely introduce them into your baby's diet. Experts now know that delaying the introduction of some of these allergenic foods beyond a year could increase your baby's chance of developing an allergy to them, so don't hold back.

Know your baby's allergy risk profile. Before you start feeding any solids, it's a good idea to assess your baby's allergy profile to see if she's at elevated risk of developing food allergies. Babies who have eczema, a family history of allergies (for example, parents or siblings with severe food allergies), or a demonstrated sensitivity or allergy to food (such as an allergic reaction to cow's milk–based formula) are at a higher risk of developing food allergies. If you know your baby is at increased risk, it's best to work with your pediatrician to develop a plan before you begin feeding solids. You may be advised to have your baby tested for allergies first or to give the first feeding in the doctor's office.

Start introducing allergenic foods as early as four months old. While waiting until six months to feed solids is best, pediatricians and nutritionists have learned that in some cases the earlier an allergenic food is introduced, the lower the risk a baby has of developing an allergy to that food and of developing other allergic conditions like asthma or eczema generally. In fact, waiting too long to introduce certain common allergens may increase the chances that your baby will develop allergies— which is why the AAP (and most international pediatric medical authorities) recommends the following: For babies at higher risk of developing food allergies, begin solids and the introduction of allergenic foods as early as four months old (with monitoring by your doctor). For all babies, regardless of allergy risk, expose them to all types of foods, even allergenic ones, in the first year, beginning at six months old. What that means for you and your baby is that no food is off-limits after six months old (other than choking hazards or unsafe foods; see page 172), and that there is no reason to hold off serving any allergenic foods, including the major ones (see above).

There are plenty of products on the market these days to help you with this introduction (like powders or puffs), but don't feel compelled to use those. Offering foods you already have in the house, adapted to your baby's age, may be the best tactic. For instance, you can mix any type of nut butter thinned with water or breast milk/formula into your baby's cereal, yogurt, or purees. Or spread a small amount of the thinned nut butter on a stick of toasted bread or slice of soft fruit. Cooked eggs are easy to serve as strips of omelet or (if using hard-boiled eggs) mashed into small pieces. You can feed your baby dairy in the form of yogurt or soft cheese. Firm tofu strips are a great way to serve soy, while wheat cereal or other wheat-based grains and breads can become fast favorites. Serve well-cooked low-mercury fish or certain low-sodium shellfish in small quantities blended into purees or as finger food.

Make the first introduction in the morning at home. It's always best to introduce allergenic foods in your house—not at day care, at a restaurant, or when you're traveling. This way your full attention will be on your baby, and you'll be able to monitor for any reactions to the food for the next hour or two. Start with half a teaspoon or an even smaller amount of the allergenic food and offer it at the first meal of the day. You'll want to start small, since the greater the amount of allergenic food eaten, the more severe your baby's reaction will be, should she be allergic.

If there's no allergic reaction, you can very gradually increase the amount of that food until you're serving it in amounts and with a frequency consistent with the other nonallergenic foods you offer your baby. Keep in mind that some babies with allergies will react to a food on a second or subsequent exposure, which is why keeping serving sizes small in the beginning is a smart tactic before you work your way up to larger quantities.

Serve one at a time. There's no need to wait a few days between introducing *nonallergenic* foods. But the rules are different when it comes to allergenic foods. Instead of introducing five allergenic foods in the same week, for instance, start with just one at a time, waiting two to three days of feeding that allergen before offering another type of allergenic food. Doing it this way will enable you to pinpoint exactly which food is causing a reaction should one occur. But don't wait too long between even allergenic foods. You'll want to establish a good pace of food introduction so your baby is exposed to a wide variety before her first birthday. And be sure to continue to offer allergenic foods (once you've established your little one isn't allergic) throughout the first year so your baby gets regular exposure to them.

Know the signs of an allergic reaction. Food allergies affect up to 8 percent of babies under age two. They happen when a child's immune system overreacts to a food, thinking it's a threat. The body then develops histamines and antibodies to fight it, resulting in telltale symptoms. Note that the symptoms of food allergies will often show up within minutes of eating the offending food, and almost always within 2 hours.

The most common symptoms of an allergic reaction to food in babies are a runny nose/nasal congestion, sneezing, swelling of the eyes, hives, and vomiting; all are considered mild reactions. Diarrhea is another common sign of food allergy, and red blood in a baby's stool can be a sign of a milk allergy. If your baby has a mild allergic reaction, call your pediatrician. Depending on the symptoms, your doctor might suggest treating with an antihistamine. If your child has mild symptoms in two areas (say, hives and eye swelling), medical attention may be warranted, so don't wait to make that phone call. And because a severe allergic reaction can be fatal, you'll need to act quickly if your baby is having trouble breathing or is wheezing, has severe swelling of the face, has obstructive swelling of the lips, tongue, or throat, or develops severe vomiting. Call 911 without delay.

FOODS AND DRINKS TO AVOID IN YOUR BABY'S FIRST YEAR

Honey

Choking hazards

Chunks of hard raw fruits and vegetables

Added sugar

Cow's milk (as a drink)

Juice

A CLOSER LOOK

Yes, your baby can eat nearly anything in your kitchen during the first year—with the operative word in that sentence being "nearly." Here's a rundown of the foods (and drinks) that are off-limits for your under-one-year-old.

Honey. It seems innocuous, but honey can be dangerous for babies under a year old. The reason is *Clostridium botulinum*, a type of bacteria found in honey. This bacteria is not a problem for adults and big kids with more mature digestive tracts, but in babies, the bacteria spores can cause botulism, an illness that affects nerve function, leading to "floppiness," lethargy, and other dangerous symptoms. The no-honey rule includes both raw and cooked honey (the spores are heat-resistant), so that means no honey graham crackers, foods cooked with honey, or breads or other products sweetened with honey until after your baby turns one.

Choking hazards. It's best to avoid giving your baby any food that is hard and round or coin-shaped, that can't be mashed by your little one's gums (other than resistive foods used for chewing practice; see page 197), or that doesn't dissolve in his mouth. These off-limits foods include popcorn, hot dogs, whole grapes, uncooked raisins, uncut grape or cherry tomatoes, whole nuts, hard crackers or chips, chunks of meat or hard cheese, and anything else that can be sucked into the windpipe because of its shape (a melon ball, for instance). Note that you may need to hold off on most of these foods, in these forms, until age four. See pages 147–149 for ways to safely serve meats and hard cheeses.

Chunks of hard raw fruit or vegetables. Avoid serving your baby round, hard pieces of certain raw fruits and vegetables, even those that you can safely serve when cooked. For instance, carrots and peppers are safe if cooked until soft, but they're choking hazards for babies when served raw in sizes and shapes that could easily cover or get lodged in your baby's windpipe (which is around the diameter of a drinking straw). Chunks of raw apples and unripe pears fall into this category, too, during the first year. Note that you can serve hard, raw fruits and vegetables in shredded form after nine months old.

Added sugar. It makes good sense—and it's part of national dietary guidelines—for babies and toddlers under age two to avoid all foods that contain added sugars. The reason? Too much sugar in the diet dulls the appetite for more nutrient-dense foods, increasing the risk of nutritional inadequacies. It also increases the chances of too much weight gain (even in a baby), and can impact long-term health and contribute to cavities in those emerging teeth. Your baby will get plenty of sweet-tasting goodness from natural sugars found in fruits (which happily come packaged with incredible vitamins and nutrients) and in formula and breast milk (which also contains immune-boosting antibodies and plenty of other healthy components), so no need to offer up cookies, desserts, and other sweetened foods. Watch for added sugars in yogurt and bread, and check labels of processed foods that you might be serving your baby to avoid or limit those that list added sugar in the ingredients. Brown sugar, corn sweetener, corn syrup, dextrose, fructose, glucose, and lactose are all sugars to watch out for in ingredient lists.

Cow's milk as a drink. The best drink for your baby—and the only drink he needs, in the first year—is breast milk or formula. Cow's milk as a beverage doesn't contain all the nutrients your little one needs to grow and develop, so wait until the first birthday before offering it up (see the box on page 270). Dairy products (like yogurt or soft cheese) or milk in food products, however, are perfectly fine once your baby begins solids—and, in fact, should be served to your baby to help reduce the risk of allergies (see page 148–149).

Juice. Also on the drinks-to-avoid-in-the-first-year list are fruit juices. Little more than sugar water, juice provides few of the nutrients that babies need in their first year, while delivering too many calories and too much sugar (leading to too much weight gain plus an increased risk of cavities and diarrhea). What's more, drinking juice can decrease a baby's appetite for much-needed breast milk or formula. That's why the AAP recommends that babies under twelve months old not drink any fruit juice at all (and that, in the toddler years, juice intake be limited to less than 4 ounces per day). Some pediatricians will okay small amounts (1 to 2 ounces) of apple or pear juice if your baby is constipated, though it's still preferable to offer solid foods that help with constipation (like beans, lentils, chickpeas, berries, kiwi, chia, flax, whole grains, oatmeal, avocado, or ripe fruit) after six months.

By the way, no need to completely avoid salt, but try to limit the amount of high-sodium foods you serve your baby, and skip the salt shaker for now when preparing foods for your little one.

TEACHING YOUR BABY HOW TO DRINK FROM A CUP

Introduce a cup at meals at 6 months old

Model cup drinking

Choose the right cup—an open cup or a straw cup are the best options

Experiment with cups of different styles

Fill the cup with a small amount of liquid

TEACHING OPEN CUP USE

Guide the open cup to your baby's mouth and tilt it

Hold the cup to promote lip closure

TEACHING STRAW CUP USE

Close your finger on the straw and release in your baby's mouth

Or use a squeezecup

A CLOSER LOOK

As with all new skills your baby is tackling in the first year, cup drinking will take a lot of practice before you'll notice progress. The more opportunities your baby has with open and straw cups, the better. So let your baby at it with the cup and don't worry about the mess—it's how she learns! With time, and with your guidance and modeling, your baby will turn into a cup pro. Here are some ways to make the process easier.

Introduce a cup at meals at six months old. Experts recommend that you introduce a cup to your baby as soon as she starts solids—around six months old. The earlier in the first year that you introduce a cup, the better. This way, when you wean from the bottle at around twelve months, your baby will already be proficient with the cup.

Offer a cup at each meal, after your baby has eaten some solid food. While you can also give occasional sips from the cup outside of mealtimes, it's better to offer the cup only when your baby is sitting so she doesn't get used to carrying it around all day long—something that's not good for her teeth and oral development. As with a bottle, never give your baby a cup in the crib—not only might that cause your baby to associate food with sleep, but doing so could also lead to choking and (if the cup is filled with milk) cavities.

Model cup drinking. Babies love to copy their moms and dads. So, show off your own drinking skills by bringing a cup to your mouth with exaggerated motions, sipping from a straw with extra dramatic flair, and encouraging your baby to be a little mimic.

Choose the right cup. The best first cup for your baby is an open cup or a straw cup.

Most pediatricians, dentists, speech-language pathologists, and developmental experts recommend the open cup over any other variety because it has the fewest downsides (yes, it's messy) with plenty of upsides. An open cup helps your baby develop important oral motor skills (and it does so better than any other cup style), teaches your baby how to seal her lips around the sides of a cup, and promotes independence. Choose a small open cup at first so that your little one can hold it on her own when learning independent drinking. Then, as your baby gets older, you can transition to some of the larger tot-sized cups.

There are also plenty of pros to a straw cup, which is why it's the second-best type of baby cup to introduce. Some styles are spill proof, so if you're worried about a mess, especially on the go, it's a great option. A straw cup helps build lip, cheek, and tongue strength, and it also helps a baby learn how to pull her tongue to the back of her mouth, a skill needed for speech development and proper swallowing patterns. And if you think about it, those straw drinking muscles are the same ones babies use to manipulate food around their mouths, so working out those muscles helps set the stage for excellent eating abilities as well. Some babies can master drinking from a straw as early as six months old, while most don't have the coordination needed for proficiency with a straw until closer to eight or nine months or later.

Wondering about a sippy cup? Sure, it's spill-proof, but most experts recommend against a sippy cup because it doesn't teach anything about sipping, nor does it promote oral motor development. As with a bottle, a baby forms a seal on the sippy cup spout by placing her tongue at the front of the mouth and then sucks (as opposed to sips) out the liquid. What's more, prolonged use of a sippy cup into the toddler years has been shown to delay oral motor development, impact speech development, and lead to tooth decay (because of pooled liquids in the mouth). It also limits the development of a mature swallowing pattern, plus can end up being used as a comfort object much in the way a bottle might, causing too much liquid intake and a reduced appetite for solid foods. Using one occasionally is fine, especially when you're out and about, but it's better to opt for an open or straw cup as your go-to style.

Experiment with cups of different styles. Eventually your little one will want to hold the cup herself. This is the goal! While any cup will work, some babies find that cups with handles are easier to maneuver. Other babies, especially those with less core stability, may do better with non-handled cups. (Handles force your baby's hands wider apart, which may make body stabilization harder.) Experiment with a few styles until you find the one (or two) that works for your baby. Consider that the style that works better when out and about may be different from the one you use at home.

Fill the cup with a small amount of liquid. Your baby's cup adventures will be messy in the beginning. So, to minimize waste, you can start by filling the cup with water (see page 194 for information about serving water to your baby) before moving on to formula or breast milk. However, because water is very thin, there may be more sputtering and spilling when your baby drinks water, so you might consider filling the cup with the slightly-thicker breast milk or formula right from the start. There's no right answer—do what works for you. That said, getting your baby used to using a cup for formula or breast milk will be especially important the closer she is to her first birthday, since it's best to stop using a bottle around twelve months old (see page 268).

Teaching open cup use. When starting with the open cup, you'll need to be the driver at first. Bring the cup to your baby's mouth, let the rim touch her lips, and then tilt the cup just enough to allow a tiny amount of fluid to trickle into her mouth. Don't be shocked if your baby is surprised—it's something new and unexpected! After a few tries your baby will learn that a cup holds fluids.

Hold the cup in position for a few seconds so your baby has time to close her lips on the rim. Keeping that lip seal while swallowing is a new skill she'll have to learn, and it could take time for her to make headway. After a while, your baby will start to lean forward to put her lips on the cup and hold the cup herself. Pretty soon she'll be able to pick up the cup on her own and drink with proficiency.

Teaching straw cup use. Learning the art of drinking from a straw takes babies longer than learning to drink from an open cup. That's because your little one must figure out both how to seal her lips around the small straw and then how to draw out the liquid.

You can just offer a straw as a trial, but it's unlikely the first introduction will net any liquid for your baby. Instead, fill a cup with water, put a straw in the cup, and cover the straw's opening with your finger. This traps some liquid inside the straw. Slowly lift the straw out of the cup, keeping the vacuum seal so the water stays inside, then place the bottom of the straw in your baby's mouth and wait until your baby's lips close automatically around it. You'll then remove your finger from the top of the straw to allow a little water to drip into your baby's mouth. Try this a few times, until your baby seals her lips on the straw and begins to suck. With time she'll learn how to suck fluids through a straw on her own.

Another option is to use a squeezable straw cup. Place the straw in your baby's mouth and gently squeeze the cup to shoot a small amount of liquid inside. She'll catch on quickly and learn to suck on the straw herself.

Some babies tend to suck and swallow very quickly from a straw, sputtering, coughing, and even choking on the liquid. If this seems to happen every time your baby drinks from a straw, it might be a good idea to shelve the straw cup for a while in favor of an open cup—at least until your baby's swallowing skills improve.

SIGN LANGUAGE WITH YOUR BABY

Start early

Don't expect your baby to sign back until 9 to 12 months old

Continue to talk to your baby along with signing

Start with commonly used words: *bottle*, *more*, *up*, *sleep*

Say the word along with the sign and repeat it again and again

Be patient and keep at it—one day your baby will sign back!

A CLOSER LOOK

Your baby won't be able to say his first word until sometime after eight to twelve months old. But even before that first word is spoken, he's able to understand and communicate plenty—through crying, babbles, and gestures. You can steer your baby's gestures toward becoming more intentional through baby signs, giving your little one an extra method of early communication.

Signing with your baby won't prevent or slow language development. On the contrary, researchers have discovered that babies who are taught to sign may have a larger vocabulary at twelve months than those who aren't (signs, by the way, count as words!). No need to sign up for any formal classes, however. Just follow these tips.

Start early. The earlier you start teaching your baby signs, the better. It will take a while for your little one to catch on, so the longer he's exposed to signs, the more likely he'll end up using them. Watch for when your baby starts paying attention to his hands, using them to bring objects to his mouth, or playing with them—at around four to seven months old. This is a great time to start introducing signs.

Don't expect your baby to sign back until nine to twelve months old. Babies begin to connect the sounds of words to their meanings at around six to eight months of age. But the ability to sign to express needs or wants doesn't develop until nine months at the earliest.

Continue to talk to your baby along with signing. Every time you use a sign, be sure to say the word out loud as well. This will help your baby associate the sign with its corresponding word. This is important because it ensures that signing acts as a bridge to verbal language instead of taking its place.

Start with commonly used words. Since the idea behind signing is to get your baby on the path to communication, it makes sense to start with signs that allow him to communicate everyday needs. You can follow your baby's interests and let that guide you when choosing signs to teach. Great signs to start with might include a sign for "up" when he wants to be picked up, a sign for "bottle" or "hungry" when he wants to eat, a sign for "tired" when he's ready for a nap, or a sign for "more" when he wants to play or eat more. "Milk" and "all done" are also helpful early signs. You can make up your own signs or use the more formalized signs from a language like ASL.

Say the word along with the sign and repeat it again and again. Children learn through repetition and the more consistently you use a sign, the more likely your baby will learn it and eventually use it. Repeating a sign with the actual word ("Do you want some *milk*?" "Are you thirsty for *milk*?" "Are you ready for *milk* in your cup?") will help your little one connect the sign with the word and learn both.

Be patient and keep at it—one day your baby will sign back.
Patience and consistency are key when signing with your baby. As your baby gets older, continue to build his signing vocabulary, and one day you'll be rewarded by seeing those signs back. That's when you'll get a mind-blowing window into your cutie's mind! Eventually this rudimentary sign language will stimulate your little one's desire to learn other methods of communication, like talking.

By the way, if you prefer not to use signs with your baby, that's perfectly fine. It's not a must do; your baby will learn to talk and communicate with or without it.

STIMULATING YOUR BABY IN THE SEVENTH MONTH

Use a water mat during tummy time

Hold your baby on her belly on top of a medicine or beach ball

Sing nursery rhymes using finger puppets, different voices, and movements to entertain your baby

Go on a sensory walk with your baby and let her touch different things in nature

Play a game of "Who Called Baby's Name?"

Let your baby get messy

MONTH 7

A CLOSER LOOK

Get ready for some serious baby exploration! Here are some fun ways to keep your little one entertained in the seventh month.

Use a water mat during tummy time. Even though your baby is probably a master roller by now, tummy time is still an important activity, especially with crawling on the horizon. To keep your little one entertained on her belly, try offering a water mat filled with fun shapes or sea creatures. Not only will she love looking at all these new friends, the texture and squishiness of the water mat will help her learn through touch.

Hold your baby on her belly on top of a medicine or beach ball. Using a large ball during tummy time will be sure to excite your little one. Take things up a notch by rolling the ball back and forth gently. This balance-building activity helps improve your baby's upper body strength, getting her ready for crawling.

Sing nursery rhymes using finger puppets, different voices, and movements to entertain your baby. Ramp up nursery rhymes and songs by adding finger puppets, different voices, and movements to your regular routine. Use different voices to play the roles of parent and doctor for *Five Little Monkeys* or break out some finger puppets for *Old McDonald* to give your baby a front row seat to a brand-new show. Rhymes and repetition are key to your baby's language and cognitive learning—and with these added sensory experiences, you're taking your baby's development to a new level.

Go on a sensory walk with your baby and let her touch different things in nature. What once was a newborn fascinated by a rattle is now a baby who needs to see (and touch) everything. So, expand your baby's horizons and get outdoors. Stimulate her senses by narrating your journey and pointing out new sights to see and things to touch (but stay alert—stuff will inevitably go towards her mouth).

Play a game of "Who Called Baby's Name?" Your baby may begin to recognize her name this month, so use it to stimulate her listening skills with this mix between Marco Polo and hide-and-seek. Have a partner hide around the house calling your baby's name while you and your baby search for the source of the noise.

Let your baby get messy. Play is how babies learn, and messy play is where creativity gets unleashed. Messy play encourages exploration, stimulates the imagination, and boosts sensory development. Whether during mealtime (see page 220) or play, embrace the mess (and just throw your baby in the bath later for cleanup). Messy sensory play allows your little one to hone fine motor skills, learn about cause and effect, and practice other important cognitive skills. So, sit back while she splashes water in the tub, smears yogurt in her hair, and knocks down towers again and again. It's all in the name of learning!

HOW PARENTS CAN MAKE TIME FOR EACH OTHER

Pick a new show to binge-watch together

Plan a date night

Rekindle the passion in the bedroom

Have phone-free time

Treat weekends like vacations

Send romantic texts to each other

A CLOSER LOOK

If you feel like your relationship with your significant other has changed since your baby arrived on the scene, you're not alone. These days, your nights are less about which restaurant to visit and more about whose turn it is to get up for that 3 AM wake-up. Your whispers of sweet nothings have been replaced with resentful, sleep-deprived mumblings under your breath. The reality is, most parents have to make some adjustments after the birth of a baby. Here are a few tips to help you transition to this new stage in your relationship and reclaim some of what you had pre-baby.

Pick a new show to binge-watch together. While it may seem counterintuitive to sit in silence and stream a show together, there are a lot of benefits to this shared social experience. For one, it allows you the opportunity to talk about something other than your baby. Share theories about the plotline or what you think might happen to the characters, and involve friends who are also tuning in. It'll remind you what it's like to have adult conversations.

Plan a date night. A date night might seem like a lot of work, but it'll be worth it in the end. Hire a babysitter, get dressed up (or just get dressed!), and hit the town. Or try something a little less glamorous: Skip the childcare and be creative at home. Wait until your baby is asleep (hopefully for the night, or at least for a few hours), order your favorite takeout, pop a bottle of vino, light some candles, and play some good music.

Rekindle the passion in the bedroom. Sex may be the last thing on your mind these days. Many parents don't find themselves in the mood, with intimacy feeling like another chore on the never-ending to-do list. But for many couples, passion in the bedroom is important. Fortunately, even if you're not up for sex, there are still ways you can enjoy each other. Turn down the lights, start with a sensual massage, and see where the night takes you. Hang up your parent role for a bit, and enjoy this time as a couple.

Have phone-free time. When the end of the day rolls around, exhausted moms and dads often turn to their phones for mindless scrolling. While social media can be a great outlet, phone-free time is important for your relationship. So set aside time each week to put your phones down and focus just on each other.

Treat weekends like vacations. While weekends are often the best time to get things done (such as everything you've been pushing off during the week), too many chores will leave you exhausted for the week ahead—and without time for a relationship recharge. So, don't fill every weekend with household projects and to-dos. Schedule in some family or couple fun to make memories and embrace those few days off. Treating your weekend like a vacation gives you a needed break from daily stressors and helps you remember why you like your partner as much as you do.

Send romantic texts to each other. Remember the flirty texts you used to send to each other when you were first dating? Fire up your texting fingers and send your partner some short romantic messages (a heart emoji, an "I love you," something flirty but safe for work). These middle-of-the-day moments of connection can help maintain your bond.

LEARN MORE

Here are some other topics in the chapters to come that may be relevant this month:

MONTH EIGHT

It's month eight, and your little one may be on the verge of (or already) crawling clear across the room. (Don't worry if he or she isn't yet. Remember, every baby is on a unique developmental timeline, and yours will likely start crawling in the months to come.) More important than crawling perfectly at this age is the ability to get moving. So, offer toys that encourage your baby to reach, push, pull, rock, or roll, and plenty of floor time to practice large motor skills of all types on the path toward crawling, pulling up, cruising, and eventually walking. Keeping a baby cooped up in a jumper, bouncer, activity center, or swing is never a good idea, so resist the urge to do so.

Talking and singing to your baby will continue to be important this month. The more you engage verbally with your little one, the more he or she will attempt to babble, blabber, and otherwise communicate—all important rungs on the language milestones ladder. Be sure, too, to listen for (and do things that bring on) your little one's adorable giggles. Finding the humor in even the littlest of things is the name of the game for a baby this age, so enjoy the laughter-filled days to come.

MONTH EIGHT OVERVIEW
SEVEN TO EIGHT MONTHS OLD

SLEEPING

12–15 HOURS
Total time your baby may sleep in a 24-hour day

2–3
Number of naps your baby may take each day

2–3 HOURS
Time your baby may be awake between naps

EATING

3–5
Number of liquid meals your baby may have each day

24–30 OUNCES
Total amount of breast milk or formula your baby may drink each day

2–3
Number of solid meals

GROWING

13 LBS 7 OZ–21 LBS 3 OZ
24¾–28¼ IN
Average range of weight and height for a baby girl this age

14 LBS 12 OZ–22 LBS 8 OZ
25½–28¾ IN
Average range of weight and height for a baby boy this age

A CLOSER LOOK

Your baby is a unique individual, on his or her own developmental timeline, growing at his or her own pace, with his or her own distinctive temperament, personality, desires, and needs. That means that how much (or how often) he sleeps, how many feedings she has, how tall he is, or how much she weighs will be unique to your little one.

This overview (and the other monthly overviews in this book) represents what a baby *might* be doing, eating, or gaining this month. But because every child is different, your baby won't necessarily fit perfectly into these averages. That's okay. Use these overviews as rough guides to help you gauge what might be happening with your baby each month, recognizing that the range of normal is wide. And then enjoy your baby wherever he or she happens to land.

DEALING WITH EARLY WAKE-UPS

Don't put your baby to bed too early or too late

Adjust the number of daytime sleep hours

Make sure your baby's first nap of the day isn't too close to wake-up time

Don't rush to take your baby from the crib the moment you hear her

Block out the morning sun and monitor the sound level in your baby's room

Don't feed your baby immediately upon waking

A CLOSER LOOK

You may be thrilled that your baby is finally sleeping through the night (or at the very least, sleeping for longer stretches), but there's often a rude awakening that accompanies this sleeping milestone: 5 AM wake-up calls. Though early rising is fairly typical for babies this age, there are some strategies you can try that may encourage your little one to wake up a little bit later.

Don't put your baby to bed too early or too late. A bedtime that's too early in the evening can result in a too-early wake-up. A bedtime that's too late can also, surprisingly, result in an early wake-up (remember, overtired babies don't sleep as well!). Search for the bedtime sweet spot by moving it 10 minutes earlier or later each night. Most babies do best with a bedtime of around 7 PM to 7:30 PM.

Adjust the number of daytime sleep hours. Babies who sleep too much during the day may wake early because they're already well rested and therefore need fewer nighttime sleep hours. Babies who sleep too few hours during the day will be overtired at night, resulting in sleep difficulties and too-early wake-ups. Log how many hours your little one is sleeping during the day and adjust to a more age-appropriate amount as needed.

Make sure your baby's first nap of the day isn't too close to wake-up time. Having a nap that comes too soon after wake-up time may encourage early morning risings. That's because your baby may consider the first nap to be a continuation of the night—and her early wake-up to be just another night wake-up—creating a habit of waking up at the crack of dawn with the knowledge that she'll be able to continue sleeping shortly after rising. If your baby's first daytime snooze is too close to her morning wake-up, push off the nap by a few minutes every day until you hit the right balance.

Additionally, make sure your baby's last nap of the day isn't too close to bedtime. A too-late-in-the-day snooze may cause difficulty going to sleep because she won't be tired enough at bedtime. That will result in a shorter overnight sleep span, which in turn can trigger overtiredness. And because overtired babies don't sleep well, there's a greater chance of a too-early wake-up. You may need to rejigger your baby's entire schedule until you get it just right.

Don't rush to take your baby from the crib the moment you hear her. Your baby may be testing the water to see if the household is ready to wake up, and if she sees it's not time yet, she may fall back to sleep on her own.

Block out the morning sun and monitor the sound level in your baby's room. Once the sun comes up and daylight starts streaming in, it's hard to convince a baby it's not really morning. Block out the morning sun with blinds or blackout shades. Similarly, if your baby hears the outside world stirring, she may think it's a wake-up call. Keep outside noises muffled by closing the windows and/or using a white noise machine.

Don't feed your baby immediately upon waking. Pushing off breakfast (or the bottle or nursing session) so it's not the first thing that happens upon waking may help keep your baby sleeping longer. She'll soon come to realize it doesn't make sense to wake up early, since there isn't any food immediately at the ready.

SERVING WATER TO YOUR BABY

Water in the first year is optional

Breast milk and formula offer plenty of hydration

Don't offer water in a bottle

Use water for cup practice beginning at 6 months old

Between 6 and 12 months old, offer no more than 4 to 8 oz of water per day

Don't worry if your baby coughs or dribbles when drinking water at first

A CLOSER LOOK

Chugging ounces of water from your sports bottle might be a regular part of *your* day, but drinking water doesn't need to be part of your baby's. In fact, babies under age one don't need any water at all. Here's what you should know about serving water to your baby.

Water in the first year is optional. Breast milk and formula consist mostly of water and therefore provide all the hydration your little one needs. In fact, drinking too much water in the first year can be problematic for a baby, as it can dampen his appetite for more nutritious formula or breast milk and, after six months old, for solid food. Water in large amounts can also cause an imbalance of electrolytes or lead to weight loss. Which is why water is not a must-drink in the first year—even when it's hot out. The only exception to the water-is-not-needed rule? If your pediatrician has specifically recommended that your little one drink a few ounces of water to ease constipation.

Don't offer water in a bottle. Because babies tend to drink a lot of liquid when it comes from a bottle, and because too much water in the first year is not recommended (see above), it's never a good idea to serve water in a bottle.

Use water for cup practice beginning at six months old. Water won't be a regular part of your baby's day, but learning how to drink from a cup will be (see page 175). Filling your baby's cup with small amounts of water at first, especially since there's a significant likelihood of spilling, makes good sense.

Between six and twelve months old, offer no more than 4 to 8 ounces of water per day. The AAP recommends that your baby drink no more than 8 ounces of water per day in the first year. Hitting that many ounces each day is not a must do—it's just the upper limit. In fact, it's probably best for your six-month-plus baby to get no more than 4 to 6 ounces of water per day.

Don't worry if your baby coughs or dribbles when drinking water at first. Your baby is mastering the art of swallowing water—an unfamiliar liquid for him. Prepare for lots of mess and coughing as he learns.

TEACHING YOUR BABY HOW TO CHEW FOOD

Let your baby chew on teethers and toys

Model biting and chewing

Let your baby self-feed

Offer long pieces of food and guide your baby to put them towards the sides of her mouth

Offer foods that mash easily between your baby's gums

Stay calm, even if your baby gags

A CLOSER LOOK

If you haven't yet introduced your baby to finger foods (a.k.a. non-purees), now's the time! If you wait any longer, your baby might be reluctant to try new and different textures, leading to food resistance and picky eating. Hesitant to serve up finger foods because you're worried your little one won't know how to chew? Worry not. Babies are born to chew—and they don't even need teeth to do it. Their gums are strong enough on their own to break down food. Here are some tips that will help your baby figure out how to chew.

Let your baby chew on teethers and toys. You've watched your baby bring everything from toys to fingers to her mouth—an important part of oral exploration. Mouthing objects and chewing on teethers and toys helps your baby learn about different shapes and textures; how to use her hands to direct objects into her mouth; how to coordinate the movements of her tongue, lips, cheeks, and jaw; and what to do when she gags. Because mouthing is great preparation for chewing foods, there's no need to prevent your baby from exploring safe objects with her mouth, and plenty of reasons to encourage it when you see it happening.

Model biting and chewing. Babies are born mimics, so don't be shy. Model biting food into smaller pieces and chewing before swallowing. Exaggerate the chewing motions and do it with your mouth open (no one's going to tell your mother!) so your baby can learn by watching. If your baby bites off more than she can chew (literally), model for her how to spit out the too-large piece of food.

Let your baby self-feed. When you give your baby the opportunity to feed herself, she learns how to manipulate her tongue to move food around in her mouth and coordinate the movement of her cheeks and jaw—skills necessary for chewing. Plus, self-feeding, as opposed to being fed, reduces the risk of choking.

Offer long pieces of food and guide your baby to put them towards the sides of her mouth. Serving food "teethers," or long pieces of food that your baby can't bite into but can mouth on (like a whole fat carrot, a pineapple core, a long stalk of celery, or a chicken drumstick bone with most of the flesh removed), won't net your baby calories, but that's not the point. The idea behind serving these types of "resistive" foods is to teach your baby that chewing happens between the gums on the sides of the mouth. When offering resistive foods for chewing practice, let your baby grab them with her hands, and help direct them to the sides of her mouth if she doesn't get them there on her own. Remember, it's all about practice!

Too nervous to offer these types of foods (even though they aren't choking hazards)? Try a fruit feeder—a mesh or silicone bag with a piece of fruit inside—for your baby to chew. But use this only for a short amount of time, as a stepping-stone to eating finger foods without it. And keep in mind that if your baby is only using it to suck the fruit out of the bag instead of biting and chewing on it, it's not doing its job helping to teach chewing.

Offer foods that mash easily between your baby's gums. When choosing foods for your baby to actually eat (rather than just gnaw on), select soft foods that can be broken down easily by your baby's powerful gums, both for safety's sake and to help encourage chewing. A good place to start is the list of foods on page 145.

Stay calm, even if your baby gags. There's no doubt about it—your baby will gag, especially when finger foods are introduced (and even when eating purees). Remind yourself that gagging is a natural and protective reflex, and though it looks scary, staying calm is your best response. An overreaction may frighten your baby and even turn her off from trying new finger foods. See page 150 for more on gagging and what to do if it happens.

BRUSHING YOUR BABY'S TEETH

Start when your baby cuts the first tooth

Make brushing part of your baby's daily routine

Use a washcloth, gauze pad, finger brush, or very soft baby toothbrush

Use a rice-grain-sized amount of fluoride toothpaste

Take charge at first

Give your baby a chance to brush, but follow up with a thorough scrubbing

A CLOSER LOOK

Hello, baby teeth! Though your baby's first chompers will eventually be replaced by adult teeth, good dental hygiene is important from the beginning, since baby teeth will need to be healthy and cavity-free for years of biting and chewing ahead. Here's how to brush your baby's teeth.

Start when your baby cuts the first tooth. You'll want to start brushing your baby's teeth as soon as those teeth pop out. Most babies will get their first teeth between six and ten months old (see page page 119).

Make brushing part of your baby's daily routine. Actions that are routine and familiar become less scary for babies. So, make brushing a regular part of your baby's day (perhaps during the bedtime routine)—even if you're not actually doing any brushing at first. Merely letting your baby play with a toothbrush after dinner will help acclimate him to the idea that brushing is a part of the daily schedule. And the more consistent you are, the easier it'll be when brushing starts in earnest.

Use a washcloth, gauze pad, finger brush, or very soft baby toothbrush. Begin by wiping your baby's emerging teeth with a washcloth or gauze pad dipped in warm water. You can graduate to a finger brush as more teeth emerge, and then, once teeth are fully in and your baby builds a tolerance to oral sensations, you can switch to a toothbrush. When choosing a toothbrush, look for one with a small head, soft bristles, and a comfortable handle. Let your baby explore the toothbrush, play with it, and examine it at his own pace.

Use a rice-grain-sized amount of fluoride toothpaste. For babies this age, the AAP and the AAPD (American Academy of Pediatric Dentists) recommend using a small smear of fluoride toothpaste no larger than a grain of rice to help prevent cavities. Worried about your baby swallowing the toothpaste? It'll happen, but it's not dangerous in such a small quantity. If you're especially concerned (though you needn't be), you can always wipe your baby's teeth with a washcloth after the brushing (if your baby is cooperative) or use a fluoride-free toothpaste.

Take charge at first. When your baby is still young, without the dexterity needed for proficient brushing, you'll be doing the work. Brush in small gentle circles along all surfaces of the teeth. Try to squeeze in a few seconds per tooth, slowly building up your baby's tolerance for brushing. You may find that you won't be able to get a good brushing at one sitting, so do a little at a time—perhaps the lower teeth after lunch and the upper teeth after dinner, or half one day and the other half the next. Taking breaks between teeth can make it more palatable for your little one. If your baby balks at first, don't get frustrated. It will take time for brushing to become a welcomed (or at least tolerated) part of your daily routine—stick with it and be patient, but don't force it.

Some babies find the brushing experience enjoyable and don't put up much, if any, of a fight. Other babies are less cooperative, and if that's the case with your little one, try brushing with him on your lap, either sitting facing you or lying down. If your baby is extra squirmy, try this tactic: Reach from behind when he's seated, hug his head close to your body, and use your hand not holding the brush to both stabilize his head and retract his lips to reach those teeny baby teeth. Whatever position works best for you and your cutie, help ease the process by keeping your baby's hands occupied, maybe by giving him two other toothbrushes or a toy. Distracting your baby with a mirror or a song can help as well.

Give your baby a chance to brush, but follow up with a thorough scrubbing. When your little teether starts grabbing for the toothbrush, offer him one of his own. A wide, easy-grip toothbrush can be the perfect tool for your emerging self-brusher, encouraging independence. But because it will be many months (or years) before your baby will be skilled enough to really get the job done alone, be sure to follow up with a good brushing of your own.

By the way, the AAP, AAPD, and ADA (American Dental Association) all recommend that you take your baby for a first dental visit around age one (or about six months after the first tooth pokes through). Some pediatricians say it's okay to wait until your baby is a bit older. As always, do what feels right for you and your little one!

HELPING YOUR BABY LEARN TO CRAWL

Limit time spent in seats and containers

Give your baby plenty of tummy time

Encourage your baby to lift her hand out in front of her to strengthen those weight-shifting muscles

Place a favorite toy just out of reach during tummy time

Hold your baby in a crawling position by supporting her hips and abdomen

When your baby is on all fours, let her push off the palms of your hands with her feet

A CLOSER LOOK

The skills needed to crawl are complex. Babies must develop strength in their upper body and leg muscles and then coordinate their arms and legs in a reciprocal pattern to propel themselves forward. Babies learn to crawl, on average, somewhere between six and ten months old . . . but not all babies crawl. Some go straight to pulling up, cruising, and walking.

While most pediatricians say non-crawling is non-concerning as long as your baby is making some sort of effort to move, physical and occupational therapists disagree, calling crawling an important milestone that shouldn't be skipped. That's because moving across the floor on hands and knees practices and boosts important skills: bilateral coordination (coordinating both sides of the body), crossing the midline (the ability to move an arm or leg across the middle of the body to perform a task), depth perception, arm and leg strengthening in preparation for walking, and core strengthening. Here are some tips you can use to help your baby learn to crawl.

Limit time spent in seats and containers. A baby who spends much of the day in a seat (like a swing, activity center, jumper, infant seat, or stroller) will have little opportunity to learn to use her body. Your baby will obviously need to be in a stroller or car seat when you're on the go, but otherwise, be sure to let her loose on the floor, limiting time spent in seats to no more than 15 to 30 minutes at a time once or (at most) twice a day.

Give your baby plenty of tummy time. Floor time on the belly is crucial when it comes to learning how to crawl, and by this age, your baby has likely developed the strength to lift up on all fours—an important progression toward crawling. Placing her tummy-down on varied surfaces—carpets, pillows, hardwood or stone-tiled floors, and grass—can help boost balance, coordination, and body awareness, plus helps refine your baby's sense of touch.

Encourage your baby to lift her hand out in front of her to strengthen those weight-shifting muscles. Learning to bear weight on a single arm is a critical step on the path to crawling, since it helps strengthen the core and promotes shifting weight between sides of the body. You can help your baby practice this by holding something enticing just beyond an arm's length away during tummy time and encouraging your baby to reach for it. Encouraging your baby to play while in a high kneeling position is also great practice for eventual crawling.

Place a favorite toy just out of reach during tummy time. This not only helps with arm weight bearing (see above), but also stimulates your baby's desire to move toward the toy, encouraging forward travel.

Hold your baby in a crawling position by supporting her hips and abdomen. Your baby will need to learn how to get into and stay in the quadruped position—on hands and knees—to crawl properly. If your baby seems reluctant to get onto all fours, you can offer a helping hand. With your baby on her tummy, gently pull up on her hips and then move her bottom back, keeping your hands on the bony part of her pelvis. Once she's stable on hands and knees, you can add extra support by placing your hand or your thigh under your baby's chest. Your baby will need lots of core strength to hold this position (which is why plenty of floor time is encouraged). Give even more of a boost by helping her move one knee forward at a time. Pretty soon your baby will be on her way to a four-point crawl!

When your baby is on all fours, let her push off the palms of your hands with her feet. If your baby has mastered the quadruped position but isn't yet moving, you can place your hands behind her feet to give her something to push off of. It might just propel her forward.

Crawling isn't a skill that's mastered overnight. Instead, it's the result of a progression of skills developed over months and months. Stable sitting will come first, then getting up on all fours, then balancing on one hand, and finally propelling forward. That takes lots of strength, brain connections (baby needs to figure out how to use her right and left sides in reciprocal patterns), and practice. And while you don't *have* to do anything to get your baby to crawl—most babies will get there naturally—there's also nothing wrong with offering opportunities for it to happen.

Don't worry if during this natural progression your baby does the crab crawl (where she bends one knee and extends the opposite leg to scoot forward) or the commando crawl (where she drags herself forward on her tummy using her arms) or inchworms across the room. As long as your baby is making progress toward quadruped crawling, she's on the right path. If your baby isn't attempting the quadruped position by ten months or if your baby is using one of these nontypical methods of crawling for longer than a month, ask your pediatrician if a referral to a physical therapist would be helpful.

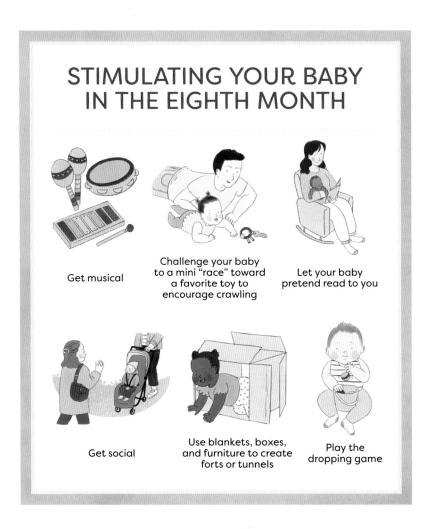

STIMULATING YOUR BABY IN THE EIGHTH MONTH

Get musical

Challenge your baby to a mini "race" toward a favorite toy to encourage crawling

Let your baby pretend read to you

Get social

Use blankets, boxes, and furniture to create forts or tunnels

Play the dropping game

A CLOSER LOOK

This month it's hard to know who has more on their to-do list— you or your busy baby bee! Your rarely sedentary and rarely quiet cutie is keeping you on your toes. Keep him on his toes in return with these fun activities.

Get musical. Let your little one bang on baby drums (homemade or store-bought), shake a tambourine, play with a xylophone, strum on a baby guitar, press the keys on a toy piano, or rub two rhythm sticks together. As you watch your little one-baby band perform, remind yourself that learning how instruments make sounds through play is great for his intellectual development, dexterity, and motor skills (though maybe not so great for your ears!).

Challenge your baby to a mini "race" toward a favorite toy to encourage crawling. Get in on the crawling fun by getting down to your baby's level. Mimic your baby's tummy-down or all fours position and challenge your mini-me to a mini "race": Place a favorite toy a few paces away on the floor and encourage your baby to beat you to it. Watch your baby reach the finish line and claim the prize! See page 202 for more about crawling.

Let your baby pretend to read to you. Sure, your baby can't read yet. But he loves to copy you, and you've been doing plenty of reading to him—which means he "knows" how to do it himself. Plus, with his verbal jabbers reaching new heights this month, there's plenty of positives to allowing him to occasionally take the lead at story time. Let him choose the book, turn the pages, and tell you the story. Babble away, baby!

Get social. Nurture your baby's natural social inclinations by giving him opportunities to interact with other adults and babies. Take him places—the supermarket, the playground, the zoo, a busy street. Expose him to people of all ages, ethnicities, races, and shapes and let him interact with them—smiling back at the stranger in the checkout line, "sharing" a toy with a fellow baby, babbling to a random person on the street. And start modeling social graces—waving bye-bye, blowing a kiss, clapping, saying thank you—to pave the way for years of socializing ahead. There's a bonus to all this mingling: It may help make stranger fear and separation anxiety (see page 275) a little less pronounced.

Use blankets, boxes, and furniture to create forts or tunnels. Upgrade your baby's emerging crawling skills with tunnels and forts for him to explore and crawl through. He'll love discovering new places and going from light to dark and back again, especially if you incorporate a game of peekaboo as he comes out the other side. These simple tunnels will help enhance your baby's physical skills and help him work on his coordination (crawling can be tricky!).

Play the dropping game. Hand over some toys and a bucket and encourage your playful baby to drop the toys into the pail. Get in on the fun by yelling, "Boom!" and pretending to be shocked by the loud noise. Your baby will love surprising you with each drop! This activity not only helps your baby finesse his fine motor skills, but also shows him how to pick up his toys and put them away. It's never too early to teach a baby to tidy up!

MONTH 8

WHY IT'S OKAY
TO ASK FOR HELP

You're not
superhuman

Everyone makes
mistakes sometimes

Parenting has a
learning curve

You may not
have a built-in
support system

Your partner can't
read your mind

Parenting
shouldn't be done
in a vacuum

A CLOSER LOOK

Why is it so hard asking for help? Maybe you worry it means
you're a failure. Perhaps you're concerned others will judge you.
Or maybe it makes you feel like you're not a good enough mom
or dad to your child. But there are plenty of reasons why asking
for help as a parent is important, and why you shouldn't hesitate
to accept when assistance is offered.

You're not superhuman. You can't be expected to do it all
yourself and do it all well. Nor should you feel like you must. All
parents are human, and all humans need a helping hand every

once in a while (or even all the time). Open yourself up to asking for and receiving help. There's no shame in it!

Everyone makes mistakes sometimes. Let's face it: You're going to dress your baby too warmly on some days and forget to bring enough diapers on your outing on others. You're going to get covered in spit up because you didn't reach for the burp cloth fast enough and your baby might even go a little hungry one afternoon because you didn't pack enough snacks. And that's okay. First, because you're not expected to be perfect (see above). And second, because making mistakes allows you to learn from them, building resilience. Not to mention that it's good for your child to see you making mistakes—it teaches her there's nothing scary about missteps. So instead of beating yourself up for those errors, spin them in a positive way, ask for help fixing them (ask another parent at the playground for an extra diaper, for instance, or ask your partner to load up on snacks at the grocery store when you forget), and treat each blunder as an opportunity for growth.

Parenting has a learning curve. The expectation that you should know what to do at every stage immediately, all on your own, is something to cast aside right now. Parenting is not something you're born knowing how to do. And while you can certainly learn on the job (or by reading books like this), there's often no better teacher than another trustworthy mom or dad who's already been there, done that. So, ask a more seasoned parent how they got their baby to sleep through the night or to help you with your picky eater. You'll learn a lot more that way than by just winging it yourself.

You may not have a built-in support system. Perhaps you hoped you'd be surrounded by family and friends who could swoop in and help you out whenever you needed it, but that didn't turn out to be the case. And maybe it worries you to have a stranger watching your baby, so you're choosing to figure it all out on your own instead of asking for help. But everyone needs a supportive network, and "strangers" often become family when you find the right fit. Don't hesitate to create your own support system if you don't have one ready-made—it'll pay off in the end.

Your partner can't read your mind. As much as we want our partners to be able to jump in with just the right assistance at just the right time, they aren't mind readers. Your partner won't know that you had an especially hard day and need him to take over night duty unless you ask him to do it. She won't know that you ran out of diaper rash cream and need her to buy more unless you make that request. Sharing what you need versus hoping your partner just figures it out on his or her own will do amazing things for your mental health and take the strain off your relationship, easing the frustration that comes from differing expectations. You are a partnership, and asking for help is part of the deal.

Parenting shouldn't be done in a vacuum. You wouldn't think twice about asking for help in most other areas of your life—asking colleagues at work for their help on a project, calling a plumber to help fix the running toilet, using a grocery delivery service to help with the shopping. Parenting is one of the hardest jobs there is. So, why second guess yourself when you need a bit of help?

LEARN MORE

Here are some other topics in the chapters to come that may be relevant this month:

- **Sleep regressions (page 215)**
- **Nap resistance (page 237)**
- **Dropping naps (page 265)**
- **Sleep hygiene (page 291)**
- **Messy eating (page 220)**
- **Eating with your baby (page 218)**
- **Food resistance (page 240)**
- **Food amounts (page 243)**
- **Baby won't stay still for diaper changes (page 223)**
- **Dealing with a clingy baby (page 245)**
- **Separation anxiety (page 275)**
- **Baby fears (page 248)**
- **Baby is unhappy in the car seat (page 225)**
- **Biting, hitting, hair pulling (page 297)**
- **Traveling with your baby (page 251)**
- **Baby toys (page 278)**
- **Language development (page 301)**
- **Weaning from the breast (page 294)**

MONTH NINE

Get ready for some exciting big and small motor milestones this month—crawling, pulling to stand, and the emerging pincer grasp. What these advances mean for you is that it's a great time to step up the babyproofing—keep all toys or objects small enough to fit through a toilet paper tube well out of reach of your adventurous baby, cushion pointy edges on furniture, and bracket heavy bookshelves, dressers, and TVs to the wall. At the same time, give your on-the-move baby plenty of opportunity for independent play and exploration. Trial and error (and falls and face-plants) will be how your baby learns, so resist the urge to swoop in and do everything for your cutie.

Your baby is also working hard these days to get your attention and make his or her needs known, from pointing and gesturing to laughing and screeching. Now's the time to ramp up your "conversations" with your little pre-talker, narrating the daily goings-on even more, repeating words, and introducing more complex rhyming books.

MONTH NINE OVERVIEW

EIGHT TO NINE MONTHS OLD

SLEEPING

12–15 HOURS
Total time your
baby may sleep
in a 24-hour day

2–3
Number of naps
your baby may
take each day

3–4 HOURS
Time your baby
may be awake
between naps

EATING

3–4
Number of
liquid meals
your baby may
have each day

24–30 OUNCES
Total amount
of breast milk
or formula your
baby may drink
each day

2–3
Number of
solid meals

GROWING

**13 LBS 14 OZ–22 LBS
25¼–28¾ IN**
Average range of weight and
height for a baby girl this age

**15 LBS 7 OZ–23 LBS 2 OZ
26¼–29½ IN**
Average range of weight and
height for a baby boy this age

A CLOSER LOOK

Your baby is a unique individual, on his or her own developmental timeline, growing at his or her own pace, with his or her own distinctive temperament, personality, desires, and needs. That means that how much (or how often) he sleeps, how many feedings she has, how tall he is, or how much she weighs will be unique to your little one.

This overview (and the other monthly overviews in this book) represents what a baby *might* be doing, eating, or gaining this month. But because every child is different, your baby won't necessarily fit perfectly into these averages. That's okay. Use these overviews as rough guides to help you gauge what might be happening with your baby each month, recognizing that the range of normal is wide. And then enjoy your baby wherever he or she happens to land.

MILESTONES CHECK-IN

Remember, your unique baby is on his or her own unique milestone timeline. Your little one may be miles ahead when it comes to milestones or on the slow side—and both those scenarios are fine. But if your baby doesn't seem to be meeting any one of the following milestones, mention it to your pediatrician. Also speak up about anything that your baby does or doesn't do that concerns you, or if your baby seems to have lost a skill completely.

Seventy-five percent of babies will be able to do at least the following by the end of nine months:

- Look when you call their name
- Communicate emotions like happy, sad, angry, and surprised with facial expressions
- Lift arms up to be picked up
- Cry or reach for you when you leave
- Act shy or clingy around strangers
- Smile or laugh when playing peekaboo
- Babble (make sounds like "mamamama" or "babababababa")
- Look for objects that have dropped out of sight
- Bang two items together
- Move things from one hand to the other
- Use fingers to "rake" food toward them
- Get into a sitting position by themselves
- Sit without support

Don't forget to use your baby's adjusted age if he or she was born early!

HANDLING YOUR BABY'S SLEEP REGRESSIONS

Sleep regressions often happen when babies master new skills

Watch for your baby's sleep cues and get her to bed before overtiredness kicks in

Spend more time winding down during the bedtime routine

Keep naps on schedule to avoid an overtired baby

Respond to wakings consistently

Sleep regressions usually last only a few weeks and typically fade on their own

A CLOSER LOOK

Oh no . . . the dreaded sleep regression—when your baby who used to sleep well suddenly becomes a nightmare when it's time to snooze. Not all sleep issues can be blamed on a sleep regression—there are plenty of reasons why your baby might not be sleeping well, after all (including that some babies are just wakeful babies)—but sometimes there are things going on in your baby's life and stage of development that can wreak havoc on her sleeping schedule. Here's how to handle this normal hazard of babyhood.

Sleep regressions often happen when babies master new skills. Your baby will be going through lots of developmental progressions in the first year—teething, rolling over, sitting, crawling, pulling up, walking, and more. These developmental advances are often accompanied by sleep regressions because your baby is too excited to sleep as she works to master new skills. Sleep regressions tend to happen around months four to five and nine to ten, though they can happen anytime in the first year and beyond. They can also appear after there's been a change in your baby's routine, when she's going through a growth spurt, or if she's experiencing separation anxiety.

Keep in mind that not all babies experience sleep regressions. If your baby doesn't go through them, consider yourself lucky!

Watch for your baby's sleep cues and get her to bed before overtiredness kicks in. As always, overtiredness is the enemy of good sleep. Especially during a sleep regression, it'll be important to put your baby to bed before overtiredness sets in. Watch your baby for sleep cues (see page 55) and respond accordingly.

Spend more time winding down during the bedtime routine. Settling down for sleep can be a challenge for babies who are learning to master a new skill. Help make the transition from awake to asleep a little smoother by tacking on an extra 10 to 15 minutes to your baby's bedtime routine for more comfort, unwinding, and relaxation.

Keep naps on schedule to avoid an overtired baby. Your little one might be resisting her naps during sleep regressions, but when night sleep is disrupted, those daytime breaks are more important than ever. Sticking to your baby's nap schedule will help make up for any loss of sleep at night as well as keep her from getting fussy during the day. See page 237 for some nap refusal tips.

Respond to wakings consistently. The good news: As long as you stay consistent with your sleep routines and comfort techniques, sleep regressions should last for only a short period—

your little sleeper will get back to being a dream sleeper in no time. Lean on whatever sleep teaching technique(s) you used when you first helped your baby get on a good sleep trajectory (see page 106) and stick closely to those responses. If your baby cries in the middle of the night, a few extra minutes of comfort (more than your typical response) may help, but don't let a brand-new response (rocking your baby to sleep, for instance, when in the past you would comfort your baby in the crib) turn into a new habit or expectation. If you start responding differently than in the way to which your baby has become accustomed, you may end up undoing all your sleep teaching efforts and have to start again.

Sleep regressions usually last only a few weeks and typically fade on their own. Happily, by the time your baby gets used to the new skill or routine disrupting her rest, the sleep regression ends—usually after two to four weeks. If your baby seems to be experiencing sleep disturbances that last longer than a month, it's more likely due to another cause.

WHY YOU SHOULD EAT WITH YOUR BABY

Babies are curious and observant

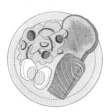

Eating together teaches about new foods

Eating together promotes social interactions

Babies learn table manners early

Parents can model how to use utensils

Family meals build a healthy relationship with food

A CLOSER LOOK

It might seem easier to feed your baby his dinner first and then eat by yourself later. And that's certainly okay some of the time. But there are lots of excellent reasons to eat meals together with your child. Bringing your baby's high chair to the family table can have a long-term positive impact on your little one's food preferences, eating habits, and even his socialization skills. It's never too early to get this healthy eating routine started. Here's why.

Babies are curious and observant. Babies are fascinated by watching adults eat, closely tracking every move and expressing interest in what they are partaking in. Use this to your advantage to make meals a learning experience for your new eater.

Eating together teaches about new foods. Even if you'll be serving your little one something different from what's on the adult menu (and remember, you don't have to do that; see page 142), your baby will still be exposed to the sights and smells of the food you're eating. The larger the variety of foods your baby sees, the more knowledgeable he will become about food and the more amenable he'll be when you eventually do offer him adult fare.

Eating together promotes social interactions. Sure, meals are about nutrition. But they're also about socializing, running through the day's events, and creating family bonds. Starting this tradition early is a great way to make the family dinner a welcome routine for years to come. Eating together also makes for richer table conversation, giving your little one a vocabulary boost and an introduction to back-and-forth conversation.

Babies learn early table manners. It's unlikely your baby will be Mr. Manners for years to come, but giving him a chance to see how adults do it (from chewing with your mouth closed to waiting until all the food is served before digging in) will acclimate him to your family's etiquette expectations.

Parents can model how to use utensils. Your baby may do more food flinging with his spoon than eating for now, but it's never too early to begin informal lessons in cutlery. Giving your baby the opportunity to watch you cut pieces of chicken, stab slices of fruit with your fork, and carefully bring spoonfuls of soup to your mouth will reap benefits as he learns to use utensils of his own.

Family meals build a healthy relationship with food. When it comes to feeding solids in the first year, your goal is to help your baby learn healthy eating habits. Partaking in family mealtime can help turn your baby into a more adventurous and more nutritious eater. Research shows that children will more readily try foods they've seen other people, particularly their parents, eat. Plus, they'll enjoy their food more, which makes family mealtime a win-win for everyone involved.

WHY MESSY EATING IS OKAY

It promotes
self-feeding
and autonomy

It leads to
a greater
acceptance
of food

It makes your
baby more
tolerant of
textures

It encourages
hand-eye
coordination

It keeps mealtime
positive

It's a type of
sensory play

It helps develop
fine motor skills

A CLOSER LOOK

Who's smashing, smooshing, finger painting, and decorating the floor, her hair, her face, and the walls with her food? Your baby is—and it's something you shouldn't try to prevent. Resist the urge to immediately wipe food off your baby's face and don't clean the flung food off the floor right away (you can do it when the meal is over), even if it drives you nuts. Lay out a splat mat and stand back. Your baby is an untidy eater by nature—and allowing for messy eating gives her the chance to perfect important skills and learn crucial lessons. Here's why you shouldn't stress about the mess and should embrace it instead.

It promotes self-feeding and autonomy. If you signal to your baby that messy eating makes you uncomfortable (you always say, "Oh no, you made a mess!" for instance, or wipe her hands between each bite), it could potentially stymie her desire to self-feed—something you want to be encouraging, not discouraging. So let your baby take the lead at the table and get as messy as she needs to. Her feeding autonomy is promoting a healthy relationship with food for the long term.

It leads to a greater acceptance of food. For a baby, touching a food, squishing it between her fingers, smearing it in her hair and on her face, and rubbing it across the high chair tray fosters a closer relationship to the food, making eating a more pleasurable experience in general and increasing the likelihood your little one will accept that particular food. Think of messy eating as making friends with the food she's about to eat.

It makes your baby more tolerant of textures. A baby who learns there's nothing wrong with messy play with a variety of textures will be open to all types of textures during mealtime—a smooth mango, a rough slice of beef, a bumpy broccoli floret, a slippery peach, a scratchy slice of toast, a slimy kiwi, a mushy bowl of oatmeal. And openness to new textures means openness to new flavors, too.

It encourages hand-eye coordination. Sure, if you take charge of the feeding you'll be able to keep things neat. But standing back and letting your baby use her hands to pick up food and bring it to her mouth strengthens her hand-eye coordination, an important skill for so many things to come, from playing games and drawing to tying shoelaces and catching a ball.

It keeps mealtime positive. Fighting with your baby over a spoon or trying to keep her clean with continuous face wiping can create a negative association with mealtime and food, potentially setting you up for future mealtime battles. Meals should be enjoyable, and letting your baby control how much food to eat and how that food is eaten will, in turn, set her up for a positive relationship with food. You also don't want to send the message that there's something wrong with exploring.

It's a type of sensory play. Play is how babies learn . . . and tactile sensory play is one of the best kinds of learning experiences. The more a baby is able to touch, feel, and explore objects with her hands, the more she'll learn about her environment. As your baby squishes a banana between her fingers, she learns that objects can change shape. When she throws her chicken on the floor she learns about gravity. When she smears ricotta cheese across the tray she learns about cause and effect. Blueberry puree that lands on her cheeks and chin is a sensory cue that teaches her to try something different next time to ensure the food makes it into her mouth instead.

It helps develop fine motor skills. When your baby practices using her hands to rake food into her fist (the palmar grasp), she's developing fine motor skills. When your cutie is given the opportunity to use her fingers to take food on her own (even if it makes a mess), she's developing even finer motor skills like the pincer grasp. And these fine motor skills are the building blocks of other skills to come.

WHEN YOUR BABY WON'T STAY STILL FOR DIAPER CHANGES

Have everything you need at hand

Act fast

Try a different location for the change

Change your baby only when he takes a break from playing

Keep your baby distracted while you change

Engage your baby by narrating what you're doing

A CLOSER LOOK

Once your baby becomes mobile, the last thing he'll want to do is stay still—especially for a boring diaper change. Here's how you can handle this very common challenge.

Have everything you need at hand. Make sure the wipes, diaper, diaper cream, and anything else you may need are within reach. There won't be time to gather all the diapering paraphernalia when your baby is trying to wiggle away.

Act fast. Make speed your game—just wipe, dry, apply cream, and fasten. Some days the do-it-as-fast-as-you-can method will be needed, while other days diaper changing can be a more mindful process. You'll have to gauge your little one's mood at each change to figure out the best approach.

Try a different location for the change. Maybe your baby attempts escape as soon as he spies his usual changing location. Change things up by changing him where he is (maybe it's the playroom floor on a changing mat instead of the changing table in his room)—a new location may minimize the protests. As your baby gets older and even more mobile, you'll find you need to be even more creative to get the deed done, such as changing the diaper while he's standing!

Change your baby only when he takes a break from playing. If you change your baby's diaper on his schedule, instead of when it's convenient only for you, it may make him more cooperative.

Keep your baby distracted while you change. Bring on the toys, songs, finger games—anything to keep your little one occupied while you're diapering.

Engage your baby by narrating what you're doing. Tell your baby what you're doing (wiping, rubbing, unfolding, sticking). Being included in the process may get your baby more interested and less resistant.

WHEN YOUR BABY IS UNHAPPY IN THE CAR SEAT

Make sure the seat is comfortable

Dress your baby with temperature and safety in mind

Do practice runs in the seat

Make it fun

Give your baby a seatmate when possible

Empathize, but be firm

Stay calm

A CLOSER LOOK

Does this scenario sound familiar? You need to go somewhere in the car (day care, the grocery store, Grandma's house), your baby is all dressed, her diaper is changed, and she's ready to go, but the minute you place her in the car seat, she starts screaming . . . and doesn't stop until you get to your destination. This predicament, which is beyond stressful, is fairly typical—you're not the only parent struggling with baby's unhappiness in the car seat. Here are some tricks you can try to make things a little easier for your little one and you.

Make sure the seat is comfortable. You'd also be miserable if the seat you were locked into had straps that dug into you, wasn't well cushioned, or felt too snug. It's the same for your baby. Make sure your baby's car seat is the right size for her weight and that there isn't anything sharp or extra tight that could be causing discomfort. Your baby might also be fussing if the sun is shining on her face. Use a sunshade on the car window if the sun's rays are too bright. Check, too, to make sure her clothes aren't bunching up, causing discomfort.

Dress your baby with temperature and safety in mind. Consider what your baby is wearing and adjust as needed for the weather and comfort. For instance, your baby might be struggling in the car seat because she's too warm. Try not to overdress her before strapping her in. Also keep safety in mind—bulky layers (including thick sweaters and down-filled coats) between your child and the car seat straps can be unsafe, preventing you from adequately tightening the straps and allowing for unsafe movement (and even your baby being ejected from the car seat) in the event of a crash. Remove bulky layers, harness your baby, and tighten the straps, then place a blanket or coat over the car seat. Don't use any aftermarket covers unless the car seat manufacturer says it's safe for that particular seat.

Do practice runs. Help your baby become friends with the car seat so strapping her in is less of a struggle. Bring the car seat into the house and let your baby play with or in it while it's on the floor. Or do a practice run in the car without any keys in the ignition. Sit in the back seat with your baby, strap her in, and play with her for a little bit.

Make it fun. On car rides, sing songs, pipe in a playlist of your baby's favorite tunes, have special (and safe, soft) toys that are used only in the car—anything that creates a positive association with being in the car. Opening a window so your baby gets a light breeze can be helpful, too. If your baby takes a pacifier, you can opt to offer one in the car (though try to limit pacifier use, even in the car, after six months old).

Does your rear-facing baby hate not being able see you? A mirror might help, but know that many safety experts recommend against using them, since they could become unsafe projectiles in the event of a car accident. If you nevertheless opt for one, make sure the mirror is lightweight, made of soft-edged plastic, and securely attached to the back seat head restraints. And be careful that you don't get distracted while driving by using it to check in on your baby.

Give your baby a seatmate when possible. If your baby has an older sibling or if you're driving with another adult, having them sit next to your baby in the back seat can help keep her entertained and happier on the road.

Empathize, but be firm. It can be hard for your baby to understand that life has limits, but it's an important lesson for her to learn. Car safety is one area where there is no wiggle room when it comes to limits. But you can help decrease the intensity of her resistance by showing some empathy when laying down the rules—saying, "I know you don't want to be strapped in, but this is the only way we can drive," even if your baby is too young to understand.

Stay calm. It's heartbreaking when your baby is screaming at the top of her lungs in the back seat, facing away from you. You're stressed and worried and out of sorts. But it can also drive you to distraction, and that can be extremely dangerous when you're the one behind the wheel. Which is why using every ounce of strength you have to remain calm will be important. Take some deep breaths, remind yourself that it's not an emergency (and if it is, you can pull over and address it), and stay as zen as possible. Keep in mind that keeping your cool can help calm your baby, too—if she sees that you're all worked up, she might match your mood and ramp up the struggling.

By the way, it can be tempting to turn your baby's car seat around too early in hopes it will make it easier to deal with your screaming baby. But remember, the safest position for your baby is rear-facing for as long as possible (and at least until age two).

STIMULATING YOUR BABY IN THE NINTH MONTH

Play a game of "catch"

Introduce a shape sorter toy

Create a homemade shaking toy

Let your baby paint with water

Introduce an activity table

Let your baby play with a push toy

A CLOSER LOOK

These days your little one barely stops moving for a minute, which means you'll need to ramp up your creativity (and your babyproofing) when it comes to play. Here are some ideas to keep your baby entertained (and hopefully in one place!) this month.

Play a game of "catch." Sit a few feet from your baby and roll a soft ball to him. Watch as he stops it, and cheer loudly for his amazing save. Encourage him to roll it back to you (you may need to step in with an assist). This fun activity not only helps to develop his gross motor skills but also teaches your little one how to take turns.

Introduce a shape sorter toy. Help sharpen your baby's problem-solving, critical thinking, and fine motor skills by handing him a shape sorter toy. Watch how he tries to figure out if the square shape can fit into the circle hole, or puzzle over why certain blocks won't fit into certain openings. In time, your baby will become a shape-matching pro.

Create a homemade shaking toy. Shake, rattle, and roll with homemade noise makers. Take empty water bottles or plastic containers with tight-fitting lids for safety and fill them with rice, dry pasta, or small toys to let your baby explore how different items make different sounds. Making a variety of these gives your baby a full band of instruments to play. Shaking helps your baby practice his grasping skills and hand-eye coordination while stimulating his hearing and sense of rhythm. Be forewarned, however—your hearing may also be stimulated, causing you to be ready for this toy to disappear at the end of the day!

Let your baby paint with water. Your cutie may not be ready for finger painting quite yet (and you may not be ready for the mess), but you can still help your baby channel his inner artist. Grab a small bowl of water, a chunky brush, and colored construction paper and let your baby create a masterpiece. Your peewee painter will have tons of fun watching the paper turn darker as he paints. Just be sure to take a picture of the artwork ASAP, because it won't look like much once it dries! This activity helps hone your little one's fine motor skills and unleashes his creative juices.

Introduce an activity table. Encourage your baby to pull up to stand with an activity table. Whether they have piano keys, shapes and sounds, numbers and letters, or animals, these endlessly entertaining toys teach lessons about colors, patterns, movement, music, shapes, and more, while promoting dexterity and brain connections. Plus, they'll buy you a few minutes to yourself to prep some dinner or catch up on messages.

Let your baby play with a push toy. If your baby has been crawling for a while, he may be ready to take a stand and even make some strides. Let him take some practice steps with a push toy (though stay close with a steadying hand to prevent tumbles; see page 273 for more on push toys). Even if your baby isn't ready to take the push toy for a stroll around the living room, there are enough fun buttons, activities, and sounds on the toy itself to keep a seated baby entertained and stimulated, too. Before you know it, your little cruiser will be pulling himself up to give it a go!

MAINTAINING ADULT FRIENDSHIPS

Accept that friendships will change

Plan regular friends' nights out

Set aside time for grown-up conversations

Be present when you're with friends

Include child-free friends in your parent life

Make important friendships a priority

A CLOSER LOOK

Perhaps you anticipated just how difficult it would be to keep up with your friends once your baby arrived. Or maybe you had no clue, but with baby care, work, and chores taking up all your time and mental energy, you fast realized that maintaining old friendships (or pursuing new ones) is a difficult task. Research shows that friendships are crucial when it comes to psychological well-being, and that goes double for moms and dads navigating the demands of parenthood. (It does take a village, after all.) Here are some tips to help keep your friendships strong.

Accept that friendships will change. Long gone are the days of a spontaneous coffee meetup on a Sunday morning or a happy hour after work that leads into a night on the town with your best friend. These days, making plans with friends looks more like this: You plan weeks in advance, send a calendar invite so neither of you forget, and then reschedule three times because your baby's nap times never seems to align with your plans. The reality is, friendships adapt as priorities and responsibilities do—and that's okay. Recognizing that changes to friendships aren't bad but to be expected can help you transition seamlessly into this new stage of life and your new social-life normal.

Plan regular friends' nights out. There's no way you can leave your baby for a night out with friends, right? Think again. If you push yourself to go, you'll realize how needed that quality friend time really is. When planning these quick recharges, aim for an attainable and realistic goal—say, a quarterly night out with your friends. You'll hopefully be able to forget about all the eating, sleeping, and pooping talk for at least a few hours, and get the refresh you're craving.

Set aside time for grown-up conversations. There are many ways you can make time for the important people in your life that don't require nights out or advance planning. Respond to texts or calls when your baby is sleeping or occupied with independent play, drive over to a friend's house with your napping baby for a quick car-side visit, or drop off a cup of coffee at their door when you and your baby are out on a walk. Send your pals messages of encouragement when you know they need it the most. Even a simple 5-minute gesture can mean a lot to both the giver and receiver, can help revive or maintain a friendship, and honestly, takes less time than changing a diaper blowout. Plus, it's a whole lot more rewarding.

Be present when you're with friends. Your baby is consuming every minute of your every day. But do yourself a favor when you're out with your friends: Be present with them, listen to them, and laugh with them. Be the friend they need as they talk about their breakups, troubles at work, or issues at home. And while your child's constipation issues may seem monumental to you, it may not be the best conversation starter. Put down your phone, push away your worries (your baby is fine with your partner or the babysitter), and simply enjoy being with your pals.

Include child-free friends in your parent life. You may not think your child-free friend would enjoy attending an event with babies everywhere or visiting you at home to catch up, but that's not always the case. Sometimes child-free friends cherish invitations to playdates and special kid events because it helps them feel like part of your life. Just because they don't have their own little ones to bring doesn't mean they won't be happy to be included in your family moments, big and small.

Make important friendships a priority. While your priority list these days may seem never-ending (taking care of your baby, cooking wholesome meals, being a good employee, keeping a clean house, showering every so often . . .), adding "maintaining important friendships" to that list will do wonders for your soul. You need friends in your life. They make you laugh, wipe away your tears, celebrate your significant moments, and offer support during hard times. It's worth carving out a few minutes when you can for these important relationships—even, or maybe especially, when you're feeling overwhelmed.

LEARN MORE

Here are some other topics in the chapters to come that may be relevant this month:
- Nap resistance (page 237)
- Dropping naps (page 265)
- Sleep hygiene (page 291)
- Food resistance (page 240)
- Food amounts (page 243)
- Dealing with a clingy baby (page 245)
- Separation anxiety (page 275)
- Baby fears (page 248)
- Biting, hitting, and hair pulling (page 297)
- Traveling with your baby (page 251)
- Baby toys (page 278)
- Language development (page 301)
- Screen time (page 293)
- Weaning from the breast (page 294)

MONTH TEN

As your baby heads into the last few months of the first year, you'll be witnessing some significant developmental strides. You'll catch a glimpse of your little one's increasing receptive language skills (the ability to understand words) by the way he or she reacts to what you say and responds through babbles, jargon, and gestures. You'll also notice emerging baby social skills: clapping hands, waving bye-bye, and "dancing" to music. Look for toys that help enhance what your baby is naturally learning about—object permanence and cause and effect. And rejoice at how your baby's personality shines through in every expressive interaction he or she has with you and with others—a great reminder that every baby is different, with a different temperament and different desires. Take the time to learn about your unique baby!

MONTH TEN OVERVIEW

NINE TO TEN MONTHS OLD

SLEEPING

12–15 HOURS
Total time your baby may sleep in a 24-hour day

2
Number of naps your baby may take each day

3–4 HOURS
Time your baby may be awake between naps

EATING

3–4
Number of liquid meals your baby may have each day

24–28 OUNCES
Total amount of breast milk or formula your baby may drink each day

2–3
Number of solid meals

GROWING

**14 LBS 9 OZ–22 LBS 15 OZ
25¾–29½ IN**
Average range of weight and height for a baby girl this age

**15 LBS 14 OZ–24 LBS 1 OZ
26¾–30 IN**
Average range of weight and height for a baby boy this age

A CLOSER LOOK

Your baby is a unique individual, on his or her own developmental timeline, growing at his or her own pace, with his or her own distinctive temperament, personality, desires, and needs. That means that how much (or how often) he sleeps, how many feedings she has, how tall he is, or how much she weighs will be unique to your little one.

This overview (and the other monthly overviews in this book) represents what a baby *might* be doing, eating, or gaining this month. But because every child is different, your baby won't necessarily fit perfectly into these averages. That's okay. Use these overviews as rough guides to help you gauge what might be happening with your baby each month, recognizing that the range of normal is wide. And then enjoy your baby wherever he or she happens to land.

WHEN YOUR BABY RESISTS NAPS

Work on nighttime sleep first

Stick to a flexible daytime schedule

Build up your baby's sleep pressure during wake windows

Have a pre-nap routine

Create the right environment

Know when it's time to drop a nap and when it's not

A CLOSER LOOK

Frustrated because your baby won't nap? *You* know your baby needs shut-eye during the day to recharge—why doesn't he? Here are some strategies you can try when your baby resists daytime snoozes.

Work on nighttime sleep first. The better your little one sleeps at night, the better he will sleep during the day. It's not surprising that babies over six months old who struggle to fall asleep at bedtime and have a difficult time staying asleep throughout the night will also have a much harder time settling in for naps during the day. The reason? Overtiredness makes it harder to sleep well in general. Help improve your baby's nighttime sleep with the tips on page 103.

Stick to a flexible daytime schedule. A daily schedule helps bring order and structure to your baby's day (and yours). Having a predictable rhythm to the day helps your little one know what to expect from you, what is expected of him, and what the day will bring—including regularly scheduled downtime in the form of naps. Irregularities in the schedule, on the other hand, will be confusing for your baby—it'll be hard for him to accept an unexpected nap when he stayed up and played with you the day before. But if he knows to expect two daily naps, he's less likely to protest when you lay him down.

Keep in mind that any schedule you implement should be flexible, not rigid. That means being open to adapting the day as needed, while still following a predictable framework. For instance, if the schedule says your baby typically has his morning nap at 10 AM, but your little snoozer slept unusually late in the morning, it may be necessary to push off the morning nap by 30 minutes. By the same token, if your baby woke up earlier than usual, an earlier nap (and hopefully a longer one) may be in the cards. An especially relaxed day may lead to shorter naps, while an overly exciting day may result in longer naps.

Build up your baby's sleep pressure during wake windows. Night sleep is governed largely by our circadian rhythm, but daytime sleep is controlled by something called sleep pressure, which builds the longer we stay awake. Babies don't need that much time between sleep episodes for the pressure to build, but if the time between naps (a.k.a. the wake window) is too short, your baby will not be tired enough to fall asleep, causing nap resistance.

Wake windows increase in length as your baby gets older, and the monthly overviews in this book give approximations for wake windows by age. But wake windows are just a guideline— it's always a good idea to be attuned to your baby's sleep cues (see page 55) to know when it's the right time for the next nap. Generally, the shortest awake time will be before the first nap of the day and the longest awake time will be between the last nap of the day and bedtime. Timing naps just right will help decrease your baby's resistance to them.

Have a pre-nap routine. Your little one needs a signal that nap time is approaching. So, adapt your baby's bedtime routine by creating a shorter, similarly soothing version that you can use before each nap. A pre-nap routine will help your baby wind down and transition from the activity of the day to sleep time. The pre-nap routine can include a diaper change, a cuddle and lullaby, and then putting your baby into the crib for sleep. Choose your own steps for your baby's nap routine and be consistent with these steps at each nap.

Create the right environment. The right nap environment will contribute to less resistance and better napping. Find what your child needs to fall asleep more easily. Is the light bothering him? Use room darkening shades. Is there too much noise outside his room? Try to keep the bustle of the house down or use a white noise machine in his room.

Does your baby typically nap in the car seat or stroller? Sure, the movement will almost definitely lull your tired little one into a snooze, but napping on the go past the newborn stage is less restorative and creates a problem when you're trying to stick to a schedule, since dozing off when out and about makes it much less likely that your baby will happily settle in for a nap once he's back home in the crib. Of course, life happens, and you can't always be home during nap time, but as much as you can, try to schedule your outings *after* nap time, when your baby is wide awake, rested, and able to take in and learn from his surroundings. And do your best to keep naps in the crib, where the environment is quieter and calmer than in the car or stroller.

Know when it's time to drop a nap and when it's not. While some babies resist naps when they're ready to drop one, don't mistake nap resistance for a sign that it's time to reduce the number of daily snoozes. See page 265 for information on dropping naps.

If you suspect your baby is resisting naps because he's going through a sleep regression, you can find helpful tips on page 215.

WHEN YOUR BABY DOESN'T WANT TO EAT FOOD

Offer more food variety and help build a tolerance for textures

Let your baby self-feed

Try a new location

Make mealtimes more positive

Make sure your baby is coming to the table hungry

Feed foods that fight constipation and/or address teething discomfort

Eat alongside your baby to model good eating habits

A CLOSER LOOK

Is your baby refusing her food? If you've only recently switched from purees to finger foods, your new eater may be unsure how to self-feed or hesitant to try the new non-purees in front of her. Or perhaps your baby has been a great eater since you started feeding solids a few months ago but suddenly is clamping her mouth shut and refusing to eat. What's up? And what can you do about it? Here are some tips.

Offer more food variety and help build a tolerance for textures. What's on your baby's menu? The same ten foods that you've been serving since she started solids? Your little one may be bored with the selection (and if you've been feeding mostly purees, with the consistency). It's time to shake things up by widening your baby's food repertoire. Resist the urge to feed only "baby food" and offer as much variety as possible—the sky's the limit, since you can offer your baby anything you yourself eat (except for a few select foods; see page 172).

If you've been feeding mostly purees and haven't yet transitioned to finger foods (a step usually recommended no later than eight to ten months old), your baby may find the texture of finger foods unfamiliar and have difficulty processing the sensory input from them, leading to eating resistance. The best way to help your baby build a tolerance for different textures is to offer a wide variety of them—bumpy broccoli florets, mushy avocado, slippery honeydew, flaky salmon, smooth yogurt, uneven egg omelet, crunchy whole grain toast—and to offer these foods again and again, even if your baby seems to balk at their textures the first few times she encounters them. Research shows it can take ten or more tries before a baby accepts a new food. Keep in mind, also, that making funny faces doesn't mean your baby doesn't like a food—it's just her way of saying, "Hmmm . . . this is interesting!"

Let your baby self-feed. Let your baby get her hands on finger foods—literally. Self-feeding is critical for so many reasons, not least because the more your baby is able to self-feed, the less likely she is to resist eating. If you're still spoon-feeding your baby at this age, you're not only preventing her from learning an important skill, but also preventing her from having autonomy at the table—something very important for healthy eating habits going forward.

Try a new location. Perhaps your baby gagged at the last meal and didn't enjoy that sensation, or maybe the high chair straps pinched her and now she balks as soon as you make a beeline for the seat. A baby who is unhappy in her high chair may be unwilling to eat. If you suspect a negative association with the high chair, take a break from it. Try holding your baby on your lap for the meal instead or lay out a picnic directly on the splat mat. These short-term tactics can help break the cycle of resistance because it brings the act of eating to a new environment. Once your baby is more readily accepting food again (hopefully within a few days), you should return to high chair eating—it's the safest place for your baby to eat.

Another option is to remove the high chair tray and bring her chair to the family table to eat alongside you—a good idea in general (see page 218 for reasons why). Or bring the high chair to a new location—the kitchen instead of the dining room, or the living room instead of the kitchen.

Make mealtimes more positive. Are you wiping your baby's chin between each bite? Shaking your head every time she drops a piece of food on the floor? Preventing your baby from spreading the yogurt all over the tray and squishing the ripe pear between her fingers? Forcing bites of food even when she shows signs of not wanting to eat? It's time to let meals get messy, remove all pressure to eat, and stop bringing emotion to the meal. Not only is messy eating okay, even desirable (see page 220 for reasons why), but preventing your baby from making a mess at mealtime can backfire, creating a negative association with eating and causing her to reject food.

Begging, encouraging, or forcing your baby to eat one more bite (or even praising her when she does) can also lead to negative associations with mealtime and set your baby up for food fights and picky eating to come. The best thing you can do at the table is feign indifference (yes . . . even if she doesn't eat anything!). Show no emotion whether she eats or not so that she's able to listen to her own appetite cues instead of feeling pressured to eat or compelled to fight you every step of the way. Make feeding times positive, connected, and responsive so your baby replaces any negative associations with positive ones.

Make sure your baby is coming to the table hungry. A baby's whose tummy is filled with formula or breast milk won't be hungry enough for a meal. Make sure you aren't serving liquid meals too close to table meals. Schedule milk feeds at least an hour before serving solids so your baby has built up an appetite by mealtime.

Feed foods that fight constipation and/or address teething discomfort. Teething, illness, and constipation can

HOW MUCH FOOD SHOULD YOUR BABY BE EATING?

Your baby should be eating as much solid food as she is interested in eating. Unlike for adults, there is no exact recommended portion size or amount of food per day for babies to eat. You'll see suggested ranges of a few tablespoons per food group (one to eight tablespoons each, for instance), and that's a fine estimate, but it's not an absolute, since some babies will eat less than that and other babies will each much more.

In other words, don't worry about amounts. That may sound crazy, but because there's such a wide range of appetites among babies (just as there are wide ranges of shapes and sizes), it's hard to determine the "right" portion size. What's more, different babies have different activity levels and metabolisms, making it difficult to standardize guidelines. Finally, your baby's intake will vary from time to time—growth spurts may increase her nutritional needs, while teething or illness might decrease her appetite—which means there will be a wide range of variation in the amount of food she requires from day to day and week to week.

Instead of focusing on how much your baby is eating at each meal, place your energy into the variety of foods your baby is consuming over the course of the week. And watch her cues instead of the tablespoons—babies are very capable of listening to their appetites, self-regulating, and letting you know when they're hungry or full. If your little one is gaining weight steadily, learning new skills, and happy, alert, and playful during the day, you'll know she's getting enough to eat, no measuring needed.

all put a dent in your baby's appetite. After all, the last thing a teething or sick baby wants to do is work hard at chewing new foods. The tips on page 121 can help with teething, and if your baby is constipated (you'll know because your baby's poop will be small round pellets that are hard to pass; see page 39), you can help fight it by serving the right kinds of foods—beans, lentils, chickpeas, berries, kiwi, chia, flax, whole grains, oatmeal, avocado, and ripe fruit (particularly the ones that start with the letter P: prunes, pears, plums, and peaches). Food refusal due to illness or teething is developmentally normal and nothing to worry about (this too shall pass).

Eat alongside your baby to model healthy eating habits.
Babies are born mimics, and most prefer to eat with company.
When eating together, offer your baby food from your plate, or
even eat food from her plate. Letting your baby feed you her food
may entice her to take a bite herself.

Most importantly, remind yourself that the majority of your baby's
nutrients in the first year come from breast milk or formula and
that eating solid food at this age, while important, is more for
gaining important eating skills than actual nutrients. That means
you don't have to stress about how much or how little your baby
is eating. Instead, focus on *how* your child is eating (self-feeding,
learning to manipulate food in her mouth, chewing larger pieces)
and on giving her lots of opportunity to learn.

DEALING WITH A CLINGY BABY

Take steps to
ease separation
anxiety

Offer opportunities
for self-guided
mobility

Provide stimulating
activities to
ease boredom

Encourage
autonomy

Offer comfort

Use a carrier

A CLOSER LOOK

Has your baby been clingier than ever lately? That's completely common at this age—a sign of burgeoning independence and the fear that comes with that newfound autonomy. Don't be alarmed if your previously happy-to-be-plopped-on-the-floor baby only wants to be in your arms. Here are some strategies you can implement to help your little one feel more comfortable with his growing freedom.

Take steps to ease separation anxiety. Your baby is now old enough to realize you're a separate person who can leave him behind, and that can scare him, which is why he clings to you with all his might. Separation anxiety is common toward the end of the first year, and the strategies on page 275 can help ease it.

Offer opportunities for self-guided mobility. Your baby's clinginess may stem from frustration with his limited mobility. He knows he wants to get somewhere but lacks the ability to get there on his own, so he calls for a rideshare. It's common for babies this age to use mom and dad for transportation and their own hands and knees (or feet) for exploration—but you still want to empower your baby to get where he wants to go on his own. Offer plenty of opportunities for crawling (see page 202) and cruising/walking (see page 272). If your baby has started pulling up but isn't yet taking steps while holding on, set up furniture in a way that allows your baby to cruise more easily from one low surface to another. A toy just out of reach on a sofa cushion can also encourage your baby to get moving, providing just enough impetus to propel him forward. If your baby is cruising already, a push toy he can use to move around the house can be a great next step . . . plus, get him where he wants to go without needing you as a transport service.

Provide stimulating activities to ease boredom. Is your little one asking to be held regularly due to boredom during floor play? Make floor time more exciting by introducing new toys, rotating out old ones, and occasionally playing alongside your baby. Check out play ideas for babies this age on pages 228, 255, and 278.

Encourage autonomy. Your baby wants you more than ever these days, and while you can (and should) give him as much of you as possible, you also want to make sure you don't smother him. Instead, encourage autonomy. That means letting your baby try to put the wrong piece in the wrong slot on the shape sorter (no need to rush in to "make it right"). Or allowing your baby to struggle a bit while trying to cruise instead of swooping in to pick him up and get him where he wants to go. Or letting him try to self-feed even if more food ends up on his lap than in his mouth. Trust that your baby, while dependent on you, is not helpless. The more opportunities your little one has for autonomy and independence in a safe environment, the more chances he'll get to learn that independence isn't so scary after all. The more uninterrupted space you can give your baby to discover and explore (and yes, make mistakes) without parental hovering, the less frequent and intense those bouts of clinginess will be. The reason: Once a child has experienced autonomy, he understands that he's capable of being on his own. If you jump in immediately to offer help or to do it all for your baby, he may believe he's incapable of even the smallest of things and cling to you even more.

Offer comfort. Though it's important to empower your little one toward autonomy, you'll also want to help your baby feel securely attached and safe by acknowledging and responding to his needs. Comfort him, giving him extra cuddles before bed when he's been especially clingy during the day and using words of love and understanding when he's sniffly. This is how your baby learns that he can trust you to be there for him in good times and in times of distress—the building blocks of healthy emotional regulation.

Use a carrier. Your baby may want to be held more than ever, but you still need your hands free to get things done. When your little one is feeling especially clingy, strike a balance between your own needs and his by placing him in a carrier while you go about your business. The days of him staying happily confined in a carrier or in your arms are numbered, so enjoy it while you can!

HELPING YOUR BABY HANDLE FEARS

Try to avoid
situations that cause
excess distress

Avoid ridiculing
the fear

Don't push your
baby to face
her fears

Consider offering
a comfort object

Be calm and reassuring
when settling your baby

Give your
baby time

A CLOSER LOOK

Babies aren't born with fears or phobias. It's not until they get older, usually somewhere between eight and twelve months old, that they begin to internalize their limitations and learn that the world can sometimes be a scary place. Because their immature brains are still developing, however, they haven't quite yet worked out what's truly dangerous and what isn't. Enter fear.

Fear in your baby isn't something to be fearful of—fear is a healthy emotion that protects her and helps her understand her environment. Fear of dogs, fear of strangers (even if that "stranger" is the regular babysitter or grandpa), or fear of loud noises (like the ones that come from the vacuum or a fire truck) are typical at this age. Here's how you can help your little one when she's feeling fearful.

Try to avoid situations that cause excess distress. When possible, work around your baby's fears to minimize distress. If you know the sound of the flushing toilet freaks out your baby, try to flush only when she's not nearby, and if the blender scares the heck out of her, wait until she's sleeping or blend out of earshot. If dogs are not her thing, don't visit the neighbor with the growling rottweiler. If stranger anxiety is high, ask relatives or friends to approach slowly and stay at a comfortable distance at first, while you allow your baby to acclimate from the safety of your lap.

Avoid ridiculing the fear. A video of your baby shaking in fear whenever you turn on the vacuum might get a lot of play on social media, but laughing at what frightens your little one or making fun of the fact that she's scared can erode her confidence in you and teach her that her emotions and worries aren't valid. Making fun of her fears will do nothing to help her overcome them faster.

Don't push your baby to face her fears. Your baby is too young to understand logic, so trying to reason with her or telling her, "There's nothing to be scared of . . . just pet the nice doggie" won't work at this age. Thrusting her into the arms of someone she doesn't want to be held by to get over her stranger anxiety won't make her any less hysterical. Let your little one take the lead when faced with something that frightens her. Give her the space and freedom to confront it when she's ready without any pushing from you.

Consider offering a comfort object. Known as transitional objects (because they help babies with transitions, such as the one from complete dependency to emerging independence) or security objects (because they bring a sense of security), a blankie, stuffed animal, or other "lovey" can help soothe your little one when she's feeling anxious. It's a portable representation of familiarity, comfort, and security—all things that can help her feel less frightened.

Be calm and reassuring when settling your baby. Your baby is looking to you to be the calm in the midst of her storm. Avoid overreacting to your baby's fearfulness, since that may reinforce the fear and make her think there is indeed something to be apprehensive about. She needs reassurance that you're there for her and will keep her safe, so support her by offering soothing words and gestures of comfort, without going overboard.

Give your baby time. Most babies outgrow their fears without much intervention. In time your baby will outgrow hers, too—though they may be replaced by toddler fears that seem equally irrational to you (monsters at night, being sucked down the tub drain, and so on).

TRAVELING WITH YOUR BABY

Plan travel around your baby's sleep schedule when possible

Check the weather and be sure to pack appropriate outfits and accessories

Stick to the same nap, bedtime, and feeding schedule that you have at home

If flying, gate check the stroller and use a car seat on the plane if possible

Feed during takeoff and landing to prevent your baby's ears from popping

Bring out snacks and activities to keep your baby entertained

A CLOSER LOOK

Traveling in general can be quite daunting—packing and unpacking, driving for hours on end if it's a road trip, and dealing with airport security lines and flight delays if you're flying. With a baby in tow, those challenges can multiply, making a getaway feel less like a vacation and more like a nightmare. But it doesn't have to be that way. The following strategies can help make traveling with your baby more manageable.

Plan travel around your baby's sleep schedule when possible.
The goal is to have your baby asleep during as much of the boring
traveling segments of your trip as possible. Think overnight flights
and long car rides during baby's nap time.

**Check the weather and be sure to pack appropriate outfits
and accessories.** If your destination will be cold, be sure to pack
appropriate layers and winter wear for your baby, including a hat.
Warm-weather destinations will require sunscreen with an SPF of
at least 30—though how and where you apply that sunscreen will
depend on the age of your baby. If your baby is over six months
old, you can apply sunscreen liberally over exposed skin. Babies
younger than six months should be kept covered up and in the
shade, with sunscreen applied only if it's impossible to keep your
baby out of the sun and then only on small, uncovered areas of
the body such as the face. Be sure to also have a wide-brimmed
hat for your baby if you'll be spending time in the sun. Bug
spray with less than 30 percent DEET is safe for babies over two
months old.

**Stick to the same nap, bedtime, and feeding schedule that
you have at home.** When at your destination, try to replicate the
home environment as much as possible. That means sticking as
best as you can to the schedule you've implemented at home.
Use the same bedtime and naptime routines and bring along
whatever your baby might need: favorite PJs, a sound machine,
a beloved pacifier—even a crib sheet from home (its familiar
smell might make it easier for your baby to sleep well in a new
environment). Don't forget to continue to use safe sleep practices
even when away from home.

Speaking of safety, be sure to do a thorough babyproofing
inspection when you arrive at your destination—whether it's
a hotel room or your cousin's house. Check to make sure the
crib meets current safety requirements and that the room you'll
be staying in is safe for your little adventure seeker. This will be
especially important if your baby is already mobile. Many hotels
offer babyproofing supplies like outlet covers, and some even
have baby gear like baby baths and monitors available on request.

**If flying, gate check the stroller and use a car seat on the
plane if possible.** When flying, use the lightest-weight stroller

you have (an umbrella stroller, for instance). It'll be helpful in the airport and at your destination, and can be checked at the gate before you get on the plane and then picked up on your way out—or, if the stroller is small enough, it can be stowed in the overhead compartment. Alternatively, you can use a baby carrier so your hands are free when navigating airport lines—plus you'll appreciate the flexibility of a carrier at your destination.

And yes, bringing a car seat on the plane is a hassle, but it's also the safest way for your baby to travel—and what's recommend by all experts. Plus, having a car seat will let you place your baby in a secure spot during the flight instead of having to struggle with a wiggly worm in your arms. You'll also be able to use it at your destination in your rental car or taxis. Remember, at this age you'll be positioning the car seat rear-facing, even on the plane.

A few more tips for flying: Pack essentials for the first day and night in your carry-on in case your luggage gets lost. And if you're traveling with a companion, have your partner board early with all the baby paraphernalia while you stay in the gate area with your little one until the last minute. This can be especially helpful if you think your baby will have a hard time staying seated for a good chunk of time—boarding, taxiing, and takeoff can last over an hour in many cases.

Feed during takeoff and landing to prevent your baby's ears from popping. To prevent ear discomfort from air pressure changes during takeoff and landing, offer your baby a bottle or cup to drink from. You can also breastfeed, but it's safest for your baby to be strapped into the car seat during these times. Sucking on a pacifier can also reduce ear discomfort. If your baby sleeps through, there's no need to wake him to drink or suck—especially because not all babies will experience discomfort.

Bring out snacks and activities to keep your baby entertained. Pack snacks and drinks or a full meal (depending on how long your travels will be) to keep your little one's tank full on the journey. And have on hand some of your baby's favorite soft plush toys to keep him busy. A trick of the road-warrior parent trade: Bring one or two new toys (surprise!) to occupy your baby's time and pique his curiosity, just in case the old favorites don't cut it.

No space left in the carry-on for toys? Finger play and clapping games don't take up space and are usually fan favorites.

One final reminder: If you're traveling internationally, check with your pediatrician to see if your baby needs any extra (or earlier) immunizations.

BABY JET LAG

Crossing time zones on your travels? Jet lag is no joke even for adults and can be very disruptive to a baby's schedule. Plan ahead by slowly shifting your baby's sleep schedule to match the new time zone beginning a few days before your departure. When you arrive at your destination, schedule meals and naps according to the new time zone as fast as possible. Exposing your baby to sunlight will help reset his internal clock, and making sure your baby is active during waking hours will help reset his schedule, too. It generally takes about one day for each hour of time change to get over jet lag, but most parents find they only have to deal with two or three days of jet lag misery in their babies regardless of the time difference. Younger babies usually acclimate faster since they tend to sleep more.

STIMULATING YOUR BABY IN THE TENTH MONTH

Bring your baby to different parts of the home to cruise along low furniture

Offer a container of safe household items for your baby to explore

Have conversations with your baby

Hand your baby a gift box to unwrap

Allow your baby to "paint" a mess-free masterpiece

Give your baby a homemade object permanence box

A CLOSER LOOK

Your once-wobbly baby has become an intrepid explorer seemingly overnight, testing her budding independence and your babyproofing skills. Here are some ideas to help your little one explore safely.

Bring your baby to different parts of the home to cruise along low furniture. Open up the world (or at least your babyproofed home) to your little cruiser. Letting your baby explore different rooms and different types of baby-safe low furniture helps boost her coordination and balance. Don't forget to keep an eye on her—while minor tumbles and slips are inevitable and nothing to stress about, you may need to step in occasionally to prevent serious injury. Read more about cruising and walking on page 272.

Offer a container of safe household items for your baby to explore. Gather a few safe household items—a wooden mixing spoon, a silicone spatula, a rubber whisk, a remote without batteries, plastic mixing bowls, empty formula cans or wipes boxes—and place them in a container or large basket for your baby to pull out and discover. This activity spices up your baby's playtime by keeping toy boredom at bay, works her fine motor skills, and stimulates that baby brain. Your little adventurer will have a blast being creative with each item and you'll get a kick out of watching her little mind at work.

Have conversations with your baby. Your baby's vocabulary might be limited to only a word or two (if that many) but that doesn't mean she can't hold a conversation. When you're spending time with your baby, whether sitting on the floor, running to the store together, or taking a walk, strike up a conversation with your baby babbler. Tell her about your day, your plans for later, what you need to buy, and what she's seeing on the street. But don't turn it into a mom or dad monologue. Pause and allow her the space to get a babble or word in. These conversation openers are paving the way for greater language skills, and before you know it, the two of you will be having real back-and-forth dialogues. See page 301 for more on building language skills.

Hand your baby a gift box to unwrap. It's not her birthday (yet), but there's no time like the present to offer your baby a present she can enjoy. And these days your little one will be thrilled with a box and some wrapping paper to tear, crumple, and toss in the air. No need to put anything inside the box—just having something to rip and crinkle is enough to make your baby's face light up. This is sensory play at its finest. If your baby seems more interested in eating the paper than playing with it, shelve this activity until she's older.

Allow your baby to "paint" a mess-free masterpiece.
Perhaps your baby is ready to graduate from painting with water, but mommy and daddy aren't yet ready to embrace the mess of real paint. Here's a way to let your baby create a colorful canvas without the mayhem: Pour some finger paint into a gallon-sized ziplock plastic bag, close it tightly, tape the top to the table or other work surface for added protection, and encourage your baby to move the paint around safely and neatly inside the bag. She'll love watching the colors come together as she taps into her artistic side and beefs up her brain power.

Give your baby a homemade object permanence box.
Your baby is now old enough to understand the idea of object permanence—that even when something is out of sight, it still exists. You've been cultivating her understanding of this concept by playing peekaboo, but this stimulating activity takes it to another level. Show your baby an empty tissue or diaper wipe box and then stuff a long colorful scarf into it so it's no longer visible. Next, reach into the box and slowly pull out the fabric. Your baby will be mesmerized by the magic trick you've just performed—and will delight in trying the trick herself, boosting her grabbing skills and reinforcing the concept of object permanence (something that will come in handy when separation anxiety rears its ugly head; see page 275).

THE MENTAL LOAD OF PARENTHOOD

You're juggling multiple roles and trying to perfect each one

You're responsible for nutritious family meals

You're everyone's schedule keeper

You're the housekeeper, closet organizer, laundromat, etc.

You've become an event coordinator

You spend your nights worrying

A CLOSER LOOK

As a new parent, you expected to change diapers, prep bottles or nurse, comfort your crying baby, and play on the floor alongside your cutie. But there's another part of the parenting job that you may not have expected—the invisible work that parents take on. This mental load of parenting—all the organizing, planning, scheduling, remembering, and worrying—is as overwhelming as those endless diaper changes and sleepless nights (if not more so), and it often consumes you from the time your baby wakes up until long after you've put your baby to bed. Here are some examples that highlight the weight of the mental load you might be feeling, and some tips to ease the burden.

You're juggling multiple roles and trying to perfect each one. You're not just a parent. You're also a partner, employee, boss, friend, and/or relative. Your responsibilities have grown, you have a lot of people relying on you, and it may feel like you're juggling a bunch of balls in the air hoping you don't drop any. It'll take time to find the right balance, but for now, focus on catching one ball at a time. Sure, you may (make that probably will) drop one here or there, but just brush it off and pick it right back up. Eventually you'll get the hang of the juggling act.

You're responsible for nutritious family meals. You may not be a trained chef, but you certainly feel like you're running a restaurant these days. Menu planning, grocery shopping, ingredient prepping, meal serving, and cleanup is a lot of responsibility to fall on your shoulders—and it's often the kind that goes unnoticed. But remember, being the family chef doesn't mean you need to whip up four-course meals every night. Focusing on serving simple (yet varied) ingredients can ease the burden. Meal planning on weekends for the week ahead can also make your life a little easier. So, too, can enlisting the help of your partner, other family members, or, occasionally, takeout.

You're everyone's schedule keeper. Between your partner's or your work trips, important meetings, baby's doctor appointments, day care closure days, upcoming gatherings, baby playdates, and more, your calendar seems to fill up months in advance. It's exhausting to manage your own life, and now you have to stay on top of your baby's, too. A color-coded calendar (online or the old-fashioned kind) can help keep everyone's comings and goings organized.

You're the housekeeper, closet organizer, laundromat, etc. Since you've become a parent, chores that felt manageable before now seem to have taken over your life. Laundry pre-baby was just a few loads a week; these days the washing machine never seems to catch a break. Tidying up used to take a few minutes, but now seems to take half a day. Grocery shopping used to be a quick trip to the store for a few basic items; now it involves generating a list that takes into account your baby's age and ever-changing stage of eating. The good news is you don't need to take on all these jobs alone. Your partner in parenting (if you have one) can (should) split the workload with you—both the physical part of it and the managerial/thinking part of it. If you're a single mom or dad (and even if you're not), you might consider outsourcing a job or two to hired help if you can.

You've become an event coordinator. These twelve months are filled with lots of firsts—first tooth, first steps, first holidays, and before you know it, first birthday. Your already-crowded brain may be overflowing with ideas for marking each occasion (or at least the significant ones) with a cute social media announcement or a big bash—and that's great if party planning is your jam. But here's a quick reality check: Your little one won't remember these celebrations—they're really for you. Certainly, if spending time and money to create these types of memories brings you joy, go for it. But if event coordinating stresses you out and you'd rather skip the whole hullabaloo (especially when it comes to a first birthday party in a few months' time), do that instead.

You spend your nights worrying. Your baby may be sleeping through the night (hooray!), but chances are, you're not. You've got a month's worth of to-dos swirling around in your brain, you're concerned about your baby's milestones, your relationship may not be at its peak, and all these worries are impacting your sleep. While a full night's sleep is probably a thing of the past once you become a parent, you can still take steps to power down your brain before bed to help you get the sleep your body craves. Download a meditation app and spend 10 or 20 minutes before bed finding your zen through mindful meditation. Or spend a few minutes journaling before hitting the sack—putting your thoughts on paper often helps stop the endless loop of nighttime worries. A soothing playlist, a good book, a warm bath, or some pre-bedtime yoga can also relax your mind (and body) enough so that you fall asleep more easily—and hopefully stay soundly asleep throughout the night.

LEARN MORE

Here are some other topics in the chapters to come that may be relevant this month:

- Dropping naps (page 265)
- Sleep hygiene (page 291)
- Separation anxiety (page 275)
- Biting, hitting, and hair pulling (page 297)
- Baby toys (page 278)
- Language development (page 301)
- Screen time (page 293)
- Walking (page 272)
- Weaning from the breast (page 294)

MONTH ELEVEN

Your little daredevil is finding that the world is one big adventure—and his or her need to explore and discover propels him or her on all fours and then toward pulling up, cruising, and possibly even a few solo steps. You'll notice how your little one is engaging all his or her senses in a more mature way to learn about the surrounding environment—manipulating toys and objects with more finesse, watching activity with more focus, listening to books with more concentration (except when he or she is squirming off your lap), and tasting food with more discernment. Also getting a boost this month are your baby's social skills (and social anxiety), language skills (particularly receptive language skills), and cognitive skills. Of course, if your gut is telling you that your baby may be lagging in some of these developmental milestones, bring it up to your baby's pediatrician. While every baby develops at his or her own pace, catching developmental delays early can make a big difference in outcomes, so don't be shy about your worries—even if you just end up getting reassured that everything is on track!

MONTH ELEVEN OVERVIEW
TEN TO ELEVEN MONTHS OLD

SLEEPING

12–15 HOURS
Total time your baby may sleep in a 24-hour day

2
Number of naps your baby may take each day

3–4 HOURS
Time your baby may be awake between naps

EATING

2–4
Number of liquid meals your baby may have each day

24 OUNCES
Total amount of breast milk or formula your baby may drink each day

3
Number of solid meals

GROWING

**15 LBS–23 LBS 9 OZ
26¼–30 IN**
Average range of weight and height for a baby girl this age

**16 LBS 9 OZ–24 LBS 11 OZ
27¼–30½ IN**
Average range of weight and height for a baby boy this age

A CLOSER LOOK

Your baby is a unique individual, on his or her own developmental timeline, growing at his or her own pace, with his or her own distinctive temperament, personality, desires, and needs. That means that how much (or how often) he sleeps, how many feedings she has, how tall he is, or how much she weighs will be unique to your little one.

This overview (and the other monthly overviews in this book) represents what a baby *might* be doing, eating, or gaining this month. But because every child is different, your baby won't necessarily fit perfectly into these averages. That's okay. Use these overviews as rough guides to help you gauge what might be happening with your baby each month, recognizing that the range of normal is wide. And then enjoy your baby wherever he or she happens to land.

DROPPING NAPS

Know the typical time frame for when babies drop naps

Make sure it's not a sleep regression or typical nap resistance

Look for signs of readiness to drop a nap

Take steps to make sure there's a smooth transition to fewer naps

Give your baby time to settle into the new schedule

Make sure you haven't dropped a nap prematurely

A CLOSER LOOK

Wondering when your baby will be ready to drop a nap? Sleep is crucial for babies in their first year and it's wise to avoid dropping any nap prematurely, since that can lead to overtiredness and behavioral issues, especially as your baby enters the toddler years. Be sure to continue offering nap time (or even a rest time) until you know for sure your baby is ready to drop a snooze. Here are some tips on how to do it.

Know the typical time frame for when babies drop naps.
Babies will usually transition from four to three naps around six months old, and then drop from three to two naps anytime

between six and twelve months. Most babies transition from two naps to one between twelve and twenty-four months, though the vast majority drop down to only one by eighteen months. The last nap usually doesn't get dropped until around age three. Of course, your little one could be ready to drop a nap well before the average age. Follow your baby's lead, but make a few adjustments to the nap schedule (like pushing sleep times up or back, for instance) before giving up on a nap completely.

Make sure it's not a sleep regression or typical nap resistance. Don't mistake a sleep regression (see page 215) or nap resistance (see page 237) for your baby being ready to drop a nap. Try the tips for dealing with those common sleep challenges before dropping a nap.

Look for signs of readiness to drop a nap. If your baby is within the expected time frame for dropping a nap and there hasn't been any improvement in his naps after trying the tips on pages 134, 216, and 237, look for *more than one* of these readiness signs that last for at least five to ten days to know it's time to give up a nap:

- Your baby takes a very long time to settle down for the nap. This could include prolonged fussing or talking/babbling in the crib.

- Your baby falls asleep easily at naps but wakes from them early (before 45 minutes).

- Your baby happily takes his morning nap but refuses (or has a hard time sleeping during) the afternoon nap.

- Your baby sleeps well for naps but takes a long time to go to sleep for the night, indicating that the last nap of the day may be interfering with nighttime sleep. (Bedtime ideally should be around 7 PM to 7:30 PM, and a nap that forces a later bedtime could mean it's time to drop that nap.)

- Your baby sleeps well during the day, settles in easily at bedtime, but then wakes in the middle of the night and stays awake for long periods—and these wakings can't be attributed to some other cause, such as teething, illness, travel, or a big transition.

- Your baby wakes exceptionally early in the morning when this wasn't an issue before (see page 191 for tips to help with early wake-ups before using this as a sign of readiness to drop a nap).

- Your baby can tolerate being awake for longer stretches (4 to 5 hours) between naps without any fussiness or cranky behavior. (As wake windows elongate, the later nap is often naturally dropped.)

Take steps to make sure there's a smooth transition to fewer naps. Dropping a nap won't always be smooth, but you can help ease the transition by moving bedtime earlier to compensate for the lost nap and then slowly, over the course of a few weeks, returning bedtime to its regular time. You can also institute a rest period or quiet time in place of the dropped nap, so your little bundle of energy still gets some downtime. Exposing your baby to natural sunlight during the time of the dropped nap can help signal his brain that it's awake time, easing the transition from his previous schedule. And as always, be sure you have a consistent bedtime and naptime routine so your baby knows when it's time for sleep.

Give your baby time to settle into the new schedule. The transition to one fewer nap needs time—sometimes a week or more. Your baby may go back to his previous nap schedule for a few days, then resume the new one. That's because your little baby's body has to get used to the new schedule. He also may not be ready for a complete transition—in other words, he may need just a little more than one nap, but two naps is too much. Watch closely for sleep cues (see page 55). If you observe eye rubbing, crankiness, yawning, and so on, a nap may need to be on the agenda on that particular day, even if you thought he was completely ready to give up that afternoon snooze. A rest period may also help bridge this gap.

Make sure you haven't dropped a nap prematurely. You'll know you've dropped a nap too soon if your baby's behavior changes (he gets grumpier, has more tantrums, is less happy) or if his sleep patterns change (he's more restless during naps and nighttime or falls asleep during meals or playtime). No worries if you dropped a nap too early—just reintroduce it back into the schedule until you see more readiness signs.

WEANING FROM THE BOTTLE

Get your baby used to a cup beginning at 6 months old

Aim to have your baby weaned from the bottle by 12 to 15 months old

Set bottle limits

Begin by replacing one bottle session a day with the cup

Make the change gradually . . .

. . . or go cold turkey

A CLOSER LOOK

How much does your little one love her bottle? If your baby is like most, she'll be firmly attached to her "ba-ba," and you may be dreading the moment you'll have to pry it out of her hands. But alas, that moment is nearing. Pediatricians recommend that you wean your baby off the bottle as soon as possible after her first birthday. That means you can (and should) start the weaning process before the first year ends. Here's how.

Get your baby used to a cup beginning at six months old. If you haven't introduced your baby to a cup (preferably an open cup or straw cup and not a sippy cup, which just replaces the bottle with another habit; see page 175), there's no time like the present to do so—and it's a crucial first step in the bottle weaning process.

Aim to have your baby weaned from the bottle by twelve to fifteen months old. Weaning from the bottle should happen around twelve months old and no later than fifteen months for several reasons.

First, babies tend to drink too much milk from their bottles after twelve months, and your baby won't need more than 16 to 20 ounces a day once she marks her first birthday.

Second, there's a higher risk of cavities, ear infections, and too much weight gain if bottle drinking continues long after the first year. Finally, the older a child is, the harder it is to get her to kick the bottle habit, which is why starting the weaning process early and aiming to complete it around or soon after the first birthday is a smart move.

Set bottle limits. Setting limits on bottle use will help with the weaning process. Don't let your soon-to-be toddler walk around with a bottle, and don't give her a bottle when she's in the stroller for your afternoon excursion to the park. Instead, try letting her drink from the bottle only when she's in her high chair or on your lap. She may start to resent the confinement the bottle requires and begin to prefer the cup, especially if you allow her slightly more freedom when drinking from the cup. Also, limiting how often your baby sees the bottle (by keeping it in a cabinet that she can't get to, for instance) will make it less likely that she'll ask for it, easing the weaning process.

Begin by replacing one bottle session a day with the cup. As your baby approaches her first birthday, choose one bottle session and swap in a cup. For instance, replace the middle-of-the-day bottle with a cup of breast milk or formula (or, after twelve months old, milk) at lunchtime or the first bottle of the day with a cup at breakfast. It's usually the final bottle of the day—the pre-bedtime one—that's given up last.

Make the change gradually . . . Wait a few days between replacing each additional bottle with a cup to allow for a gradual transition. Alternatively, pour less and less breast milk or formula (if your baby is under twelve months) or milk (if your baby has passed her first birthday) in the bottle each day. At the same time, increase the amount you offer in the cup at mealtimes.

. . . or go cold turkey. Though a gradual transition from bottle to cup works best for most babies, some tots (especially older ones who are already proficient in cup drinking) do well with a cold turkey approach. Have a goodbye party for the bottles, stash them away (or get rid of them), and make the switch in one fell swoop.

By the way, while nursing can continue for as long as you and your baby desire, if you pump and offer breast milk in a bottle, these same bottle weaning tips apply. You can continue to serve pumped breast milk in a cup beyond the first birthday.

SWITCHING FROM FORMULA TO MILK

If you're feeding your baby formula, it's time to start thinking ahead to the big shift from formula to milk. The AAP recommends that babies switch from formula to whole cow's milk or an equivalent alternative at a year old. (If you're breastfeeding, you can continue for as long as you'd like—though keep in mind that after age one your child should be getting the bulk of her nutrition from solid foods.) There's nothing magical about cow's milk—it's just an easy source of calcium and protein. Cow's milk is not a must-do if your toddler is getting adequate calcium, vitamin D, fats, and proteins from other food sources, though most parents find it's the easiest way for their child to net those nutrients.

Tempted to make the switch from formula to milk earlier? Don't. Formula has more nutrients than milk, and it's better suited for babies under age one. Tempted to stick with formula past twelve months old? Again, don't. Continuing to feed formula after the first birthday could provide your toddler with too many calories, making her less likely to eat a variety of healthier solid food. It could also increase your toddler's chances of gaining too much weight.

A week or two before your baby's first birthday, start by replacing one serving of formula per day with milk. If she resists, make the transition slower. Combine a small amount of milk with formula in a cup, then add a little more milk and a little less formula each day until it's all milk. And once you make the switch, give your toddler no more than 16 to 20 ounces of milk a day to make sure that milk is not ruining her appetite for solid food.

Prefer a nondairy alternative for your soon-to-be toddler? There are plenty to choose from, including pea milk, soy milk, oat milk, almond milk, and combo milk alternatives (like pea-almond-cashew milk). Not all measure up nutritionally to cow's milk, though, and some have a lot of added sugar. So, if you're choosing a nondairy alternative, check nutritional labels to make sure your baby is getting the calcium, vitamin D, and other nutrients she needs (without the additives she doesn't)—and if necessary, use other foods to fill in the gaps.

HELPING YOUR BABY LEARN TO WALK

Provide opportunities for cruising

Let your baby try a push toy

Encourage solo standing

Set your baby down into a standing position

Hold your baby while he takes a few practice steps

Expect a lot of falls at first

A CLOSER LOOK

Is your baby ready to take a big step forward? Somewhere around the first birthday (give or take a few months on either side), your baby will be ready to take those first steps. But don't stress about when those first steps happen. Your little one will learn to walk when he's ready—not when you want him to be. Some babies take their first solo steps well before they reach their first birthday, and others don't start walking until eighteen months—though the vast majority take their first steps between nine and fifteen months of age. Give your little one plenty of opportunity and practice, and eventually your tot will step out on his own. In the meantime, you can help encourage your little walker with these tips.

Provide opportunities for cruising. Cruising ("walking" while holding on to furniture) is the first step toward independent walking. Help your baby master this milestone by giving him lots of safe places to pull up on and cruise from—line up pieces of safe, low furniture (like an ottoman and a baby-friendly coffee table) close together so your baby can reach from one to the other. If your little one has mastered pulling up but not cruising, entice him with a toy just out of reach on the sofa so he needs to take a step or two to get it.

Let your baby try a push toy. A push toy can be a great aid for emerging walkers. This type of toy allows your baby to practice standing up and balancing, and enables him to see his legs and feet as he takes supported steps forward. You might need to hold the push toy at first for stability and so that the wheels don't spin out of control. You can also weigh it down so it doesn't slide forward as easily when your baby is still a newbie at using it. Starting off on carpet before moving to a hardwood or tile floor may help your baby get his footing a little easier. You can also give him readily available household objects to push around while on two feet—an empty laundry basket, a large cardboard box, or his own stroller (but make sure he's supervised so he doesn't get hurt).

Push toys described above are different from walkers—the wheeled toys your baby sits in the center of and moves across the floor using his feet. Not only has the AAP called for a ban on baby walkers out of safety concerns (they're already banned in Canada), but baby walkers don't help babies learn to walk. They put babies in an unnatural position and hinder progression toward independent walking because babies can't see their feet as they step. (Stationary activity centers are safer than walkers with wheels, but be sure to place limits on them, since too much time spent in containers will impede your baby's motor development.)

Encourage solo standing. Help your baby balance by getting him into a standing position, then letting go to see how long he can stand alone without him holding on to anything. It takes a lot of practice for a baby to learn how to balance in an upright posture. Once your little one can balance standing alone, he'll progress to shifting his weight while standing and then learning to walk independently.

Set your baby down into a standing position. When your baby is in your arms and you're ready to put him down, try not to always place him on the floor in a seated position. Instead, occasionally place him in a standing position so he gets used to bearing weight on his feet.

Hold your baby while he takes a few practice steps. You can encourage supported steps by holding your little pre-walker by the torso in a standing position and letting him take a few practice steps. While you can also hold his arms above his head as he takes those first steps, it could force your baby off balance, since his body naturally tilts forward when his arms are overhead. He'll do better with his arms out to the side to balance—think how you'd walk across a balance beam. Holding him with arms up is fine and won't cause any harm but it also won't teach walking. Favor trunk support when you can so that his center of gravity keeps him stable.

Expect a lot of falls at first. Tumbles and bumps and boo-boos will happen, but that's to be expected when your little one starts toddling on two feet. It's all part of the learning process, and your baby won't get hurt—he's got a diaper and baby fat to cushion him, after all. Offer lots of encouragement as your baby takes those first solo steps . . . and to prevent serious injury, make sure to babyproof areas in which your baby will be walking.

Wondering if now's a good time to get your new walker some adorable shoes? See page 299.

EASING SEPARATION ANXIETY

Let your baby separate on her own terms

Separate gradually

Leave something familiar with her

Don't sneak out

Keep goodbyes short and stay calm, even if your baby cries and clings

Lose the guilt and give it time

A CLOSER LOOK

Does this sound familiar? Your baby, who previously rarely give you a backward glance when you left the room, now screams at the top of her lungs and clutches you for dear life whenever you take a few steps away from her (the horror!). Sure, you've been playing object permanence games like peekaboo to help teach her that you're there even if she can't see you, but she's still a basket case whenever you leave. Welcome to separation anxiety, a very normal part of your child's development that typically makes its appearance between ten and eighteen months and, in some children, can last through the preschool years. Your baby is maturing, which means she more clearly understands that she's an autonomous person. This is a good thing because it helps her gain independence. But the flip side of this newfound freedom is the realization that there's a separation between her and the most important people in her life, the people she's dependent on—like you—and that creates tension and insecurity for her. So, she clings to you (see page 245) and cries when she's left with someone else. Or she develops sleeping problems. Or she refuses to play on her own. Or she never lets you leave her sight. It's a little flattering for you (wow, she loves you so much!) but also suffocating at times. Here are some ways to help ease your baby's separation anxiety.

Let your baby separate on her own terms. Your little explorer might hate it when you leave her, but there are times she'll be willing to leave you—and that's something to be encouraged. If she crawls or toddles into another (safe) room in the house, out of your sight, allow her that independence. Resist the urge to follow her, enabling her instead to strike out on her own so she gets comfortable being without you.

Separate gradually. Practice short stints of separation at home. At first, leave her side while she's playing but stay in sight. Next, leave the room but come back within a minute or so. Increase the length of the separations so your baby gets practice being without you. If you're leaving your baby with a babysitter or at day care for the first time (or first few times), don't separate immediately. Stay with your baby and the caregiver for a few minutes, then leave for a short while, building up to longer stays away. This gradual transition helps your baby feel safe and comfortable.

Leave something familiar with her. Does your baby have a security blanket, a special stuffed animal, or another comfort object? Bring it along to day care or let your baby tote it around when you leave. No comfort object? Any favorite toy, or even an article of clothing with your scent on it, can give your little one something familiar to turn to for support and comfort when you're away.

Don't sneak out. Sneaking out may seem like the path of least resistance, but if you don't give your baby warning of the impending separation, trust will be lost, and she'll become even clingier and more difficult during future separations. Instead, create some sort of goodbye routine that your baby can rely on to help with the transition, much like a bedtime routine. Blow a kiss, sing a special goodbye song, give a final cuddle, and remind her that you'll see her later (after lunch, when she wakes from her nap, etc.). Say goodbye with a big smile on your face, then leave. With time, following this routine at every separation will help reinforce for your baby that even though you're leaving, you'll always come back.

Keep goodbyes short and stay calm, even if your baby cries and clings. Your baby is looking for you to be a calming influence, so hide whatever mixed emotions you're feeling about the separation (it's not easy leaving your little one!) and be matter of fact. Avoid long drawn-out goodbyes—they just ramp up the emotions, and the big fuss will make your baby wonder if there is something to be worried about.

Lose the guilt and give it time. Though your baby might demand your presence 24/7, separations are inevitable (and healthy for both of you). So don't feel guilty when you run out for a quick errand, need to go to work, or are craving some me time. Your baby won't resent you or develop attachment issues; learning how to separate is a healthy developmental step that all babies go through as a part of growing up. And remind yourself that your baby won't have separation anxiety forever. One day you'll drop her off for a playdate, and she'll skip right into her friend's house without even giving you a wave.

BUYING TOYS FOR YOUR BABY

Offer a combination of quality open-ended and closed-ended toys

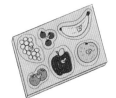

Look for toys that enhance fine motor skills, hand-eye coordination, and other developmental skills

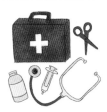

Choose toys that encourage imagination

Remember that the more a toy does, the less your child will be able to do with it

Decrease the quantity of toys and increase their quality

Rotate toys to limit distraction and increase focus

A CLOSER LOOK

Who's playing around? Your baby is—and that's a good thing because play is how your little one learns. No need to buy out the toy store to keep your baby occupied, though—simple household items like cardboard boxes, wooden spoons, pots, empty formula cans, and ice cube trays can dominate your baby's play space. But because you're sure to buy (or receive) plenty of toys during the first year, here are some things to look for when choosing the best toys for your little learner.

Offer a combination of quality open-ended and closed-ended toys. Toys that are open-ended give your baby endless opportunities to problem-solve, create, and imagine. A stuffed animal or doll is an open-ended toy because your little one can turn it into a friend, play pretend with it, and assign it feelings. Blocks allow for open-ended play because your baby can use them to build, learn about gravity, explore cause and effect, and more. Favor open-ended toys when choosing playthings for your little one.

There's also space in your little one's toy closet for some closed-ended, or structured, toys, however. These toys, unlike open-ended ones, come with limitations—they have specific intended outcomes that allow for only one way to play. Puzzles and shape sorters, for instance, are closed-ended toys because they have only one goal. But that isn't a bad thing. Quality closed-ended toys can give children a sense of mastery, the satisfaction of accomplishment, a sense of order, and opportunities for self-correction (such as when your little one realizes he put a piece in the wrong spot).

Look for toys that enhance fine motor skills, hand-eye coordination, and other developmental skills. Because play is how your little one learns, look for toys that boost brain development and motor skills. Help your baby work on his fine motor skills with toys like puzzles with knobs that are easily grasped and lifted, activity cubes with switches and beads on a track, lift-the-flap books, stacking toys, and textured balls. Enhance your baby's large motor skills with climbing toys, ride-on toys, push toys, and crawling tunnels. And give his hand-eye coordination a workout with shape sorters, toy pianos, and balls to roll back and forth.

Choose toys that encourage imagination. Imagination and creativity (the process of transforming imagination into reality) play a crucial role in your child's cognitive development. It's how he learns about himself and the world around him. Choose toys that let your little one flex his imagination muscle—role-play toys (doctor kit, tool bench, play kitchen, shopping cart), as well as dolls, stuffed animals, blocks, and more. It'll likely be a few months before your cutie is able to fully immerse in role-play games, but there's no harm in introducing these types of toys now.

Remember, the more a toy does, the less your child will be able to do with it. It can be tempting to purchase the toy that promises to do multiple things: It sings the alphabet! Plays twenty songs! Teaches seven colors! Lights up whenever baby comes near! But better to keep it out of your cart. Not only will these types of toys be overstimulating for your baby (and annoying for you), but they'll also stymie the creativity, learning, and curiosity that non-battery, lower-key toys encourage. Not to mention that when children become used to toys that do it all for them in such a flashy manner, they come to expect all toys to act that way, leading to boredom with the playthings that actually enable quality open-ended play.

Decrease the quantity of toys and increase their quality.
A room full of playthings may seem like a child's dream, but when it comes to toys, less is more. Having fewer toys promotes deeper, more creative play, more mindfulness when playing, an appreciation for toys and playtime, and less mental fatigue during play. Plus, young children tend to spend more time playing with each toy when they have fewer toys to choose from. So, decrease the number of toys you have for your child and work on increasing their quality.

Rotate toys to limit distraction and increase focus. Buckets, bins, and shelves stuffed full of toys can overwhelm babies, who may respond by dumping the toys out instead of engaging with them. Plus, too many toys can be too distracting for your baby, resulting in a lack of focus during play. Implement a rotation system, limiting the number of toys that are available at any one time and changing up the selection on a regular basis. A toy rotation system helps refresh your baby's curiosity and keeps him engaged.

When it comes to your baby's toys, always keep safety in mind. Avoid jumpers and seated walkers on wheels, and limit time in stationary entertainment centers or other containers. And remember to keep toys with small parts out of reach—anything that can fit through a toilet paper roll is a choking hazard.

STIMULATING YOUR BABY IN THE ELEVENTH MONTH

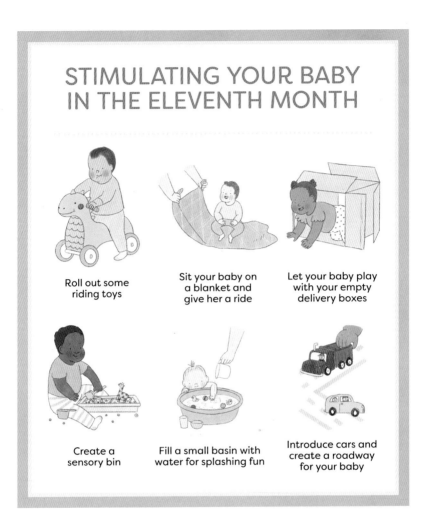

Roll out some riding toys

Sit your baby on a blanket and give her a ride

Let your baby play with your empty delivery boxes

Create a sensory bin

Fill a small basin with water for splashing fun

Introduce cars and create a roadway for your baby

A CLOSER LOOK

It's amazing how quickly time has flown by and how much your little one has grown. As your baby enters the last months of being, well, a baby, be sure to take note of her incredible physical and cognitive developments. She's on the move (possibly even on two feet), feeding herself, speaking a few words, grabbing everything she can get her hands on, and showing off her personality. Here's how you can stimulate your baby's growing mind and body this month.

Roll out some riding toys. Your baby is mastering push toys, but don't stop there. Beginning around this age, she'll also love going for a ride using her own power. Look for sturdy ride-on toys that are low to the ground. A handle for mom or dad to push is a bonus and allows you to lend a helping hand as your baby learns coordination, balance, and spatial awareness.

Sit your baby on a blanket and give her a ride. Treat your baby to a "magic carpet ride." With your little Aladdin seated in the middle of a large, soft blanket, grab the two top corners and gently pull your baby on a journey. This activity works best on a hardwood or tile floor, and helps your baby work on her core strength and balance.

Let your baby play with your empty delivery boxes. Doing a lot of shopping online now that you've got a baby keeping you close to home? Your bank account may not be thrilled, but your baby will love having all those delivery boxes to sit in, crawl through, dump toys into, and bang on. This simple and free (well, technically not free!) activity offers your baby opportunities for open-ended exploration and creativity.

Create a sensory bin. These super-simple, easy-to-make bins can keep little kids entertained for what feels like hours. Fill a shallow plastic bin with differently textured, shaped, and colored items like scarves, extra-large pom poms, balls, and/or giant pasta shells, plus a few different toys or safe kitchen utensils, and then let your baby explore. She'll have tons of fun scooping, sifting, and stirring. A sensory bin offers babies the opportunity to fill-and-dump, play hide-and-seek, and grasp and manipulate items—plus, it helps boost their attention span. Sensory bins also encourage little ones to use their senses while playing, which makes it a winning activity.

Remember, because babies tend to put everything in their mouths, these sensory bins should contain only age-appropriate toys too large to present a choking hazard. Alternately, try an edible sensory bin using Cheerios or well-cooked spaghetti.

Fill a small basin with water for splashing fun. Your baby is likely used to playing during her nightly bath, but she can have water fun during the day, too. Fill a small bin with water and add some floating toys like rubber ducks, a baby doll for your baby to "wash," some plastic ball-pit balls, or a small bucket to make a "waterfall" (great for learning cause and effect).

Remember to always supervise any type of water play closely to ensure your baby's safety (even a few inches of water presents a drowning hazard).

Introduce cars and create a roadway for your baby. *Vroom vroom!* Put your baby in the driver's seat with large, easy-to-grasp cars and trucks perfect for little hands—your baby will love seeing where the road of her imagination takes her. Amp up this activity by adding a roadway rug or blanket or creating streets with tape on the floor. Your little one will be up and down testing out new traffic patterns and ruling the road!

THINGS THAT CHANGE FOR THE BETTER WHEN YOU BECOME A PARENT

You become more financially responsible

You're able to function on much less sleep

You eat healthier

You develop more patience

You gain confidence

You're full of love

A CLOSER LOOK

You've been a parent for nearly a year, so you've probably noticed lots of changes in your life—from not being able to use the bathroom alone to the mounds and mounds of laundry that pile up each week. While you may be mourning some of the things you lost (say, a full night's sleep or the ability to show up anywhere on time), you might also notice some of the many upsides to being a parent. Here are just a few of those upsides, though you're sure to experience plenty others as well.

You become more financially responsible. Babies in their first year cost a lot. Between diapers, strollers, toys, nursery paraphernalia, day care, clothes, and more, you've been shelling out a lot of cash to support your little one. While you may have been able to spend freely in your pre-baby days—going to dinner and a show whenever the mood struck, springing for the latest trendy outfit just because—these days you might find you're more financially careful: choosing to set aside money for your baby's education instead of buying a pair of must-have boots on a whim; prioritizing household expenses over splurging on the latest tech gadget; socking away money for retirement instead of indulging in a second daily latte at the coffee shop.

You're able to function on much less sleep. Perhaps you were always the type who needed a full 8 hours of sleep to be productive. These days, a full night's sleep is a luxury you rarely get, and yet you've learned how to keep moving, carry on coherent conversations, and do what needs to be done on just a few hours of shut-eye. Who knew you'd be able to accomplish so much on so little sleep? The goal, of course, is to get quality sleep again (eventually), but for now you're doing great!

You eat healthier. Because you're motivated to feed your hungry little one the healthiest diet possible, the choices on your menu may have improved, too. You might be cooking at home a bit more instead of going out for fast food, stocking the kitchen with more fruits and veggies than sweets, and thinking about balanced eating rather than diet cola and chips.

You develop more patience. You may not be a patient person by nature, but now that you're a parent, a greater sense of patience may be emerging. Cases in point: returning to your baby's room thirty times in one night to replace his pacifier, reacting calmly rather than with frustration when your baby whines, not losing it when your baby flings his entire lovingly prepared lunch from the high chair, and resisting the urge to complete puzzles for your baby when he's struggling to figure them out. You may have moments (or days . . . or weeks) of frustration (and of course you're still a work in progress), but if you take a step back, you'll likely see that you've become a little more relaxed and patient—with your baby and with yourself.

You gain confidence. You've learned on the job how to be a parent and you're doing great. It takes time to gain confidence as a parent (see page 74), but every day you're feeling more capable, learning to trust yourself and your instincts more, and finding an inner strength that assures you that you can tackle (almost) anything.

You're full of love. Shocked at how much you're willing to do for your baby? At how, despite the challenges and uncertainty and frustrations and exhaustion, you still give parenting and your baby your all? That's what being a parent is all about—and you do it because you're overflowing with love for your baby. Who knew your heart could be so full?

LEARN MORE

Here are some other topics in the chapter to come that may be relevant this month:

- Sleep hygiene (page 291)
- Biting, hitting, and hair pulling (page 297)
- Language development (page 301)
- Weaning from the breast (page 294)
- Baby shoes (page 299)

MONTH TWELVE

Welcome to month twelve—the last month your baby will still technically be considered a baby (after the first birthday, he or she becomes a toddler!). It's time to celebrate how far your little one has come: from helpless infant to independently mobile (crawling, cruising, and maybe even walking); from only being able to cry for communication to interacting with signs, gestures, babbles, and perhaps even a word or two; from eating a liquid-only diet to eating nearly everything, nearly independently. Embrace these developments and honor your baby's achievements. You and your baby have come a long way, and you deserve a pat on the back for getting through this very challenging (and very exhausting) first year. And remember, while your little one's baby era may be about to end, he or she will always be your baby!

MONTH TWELVE OVERVIEW

ELEVEN TO TWELVE MONTHS OLD

SLEEPING

12–15 HOURS
Total time your baby may sleep in a 24-hour day

2
Number of naps your baby may take each day

3–4 HOURS
Time your baby may be awake between naps

EATING

2–3
Number of liquid meals your baby may have each day

16–24 OUNCES
Total amount of breast milk or formula your baby may drink each day

3 (+ 1–2)
Number of solid meals + possible number of snacks per day

GROWING

15 LBS 7 OZ–24 LBS 4 OZ
26¾–30½ IN
Average range of weight and height for a baby girl this age

17 LBS–25 LBS 6 OZ
27½–31 IN
Average range of weight and height for a baby boy this age

A CLOSER LOOK

Your baby is a unique individual, on his or her own developmental timeline, growing at his or her own pace, with his or her own distinctive temperament, personality, desires, and needs. That means that how much (or how often) he sleeps, how many feedings she has, how tall he is, or how much she weighs will be unique to your little one.

This overview (and the other monthly overviews in this book) represents what a baby *might* be doing, eating, or gaining this month. But because every child is different, your baby won't necessarily fit perfectly into these averages. That's okay. Use this overview as a rough guide to help you gauge what might be happening with your baby this month, recognizing that the range of normal is wide. And then enjoy your baby wherever he or she happens to land.

MILESTONES CHECK-IN

As your baby rounds out the first year, he or she will be hitting lots of milestones. It's likely that your little one will be doing everything on the list below and much more, but if your baby seems to be lagging behind, speak up! Remember, flagging developmental delays is important for identifying children who may benefit from additional evaluation and, if necessary, intervention. Early identification can lead to earlier intervention, which can make a world of difference when it comes to your little one's learning and development.

Seventy-five percent of babies will be able to do at least the following by the end of the first year:

- Wave bye-bye
- Play games like patty-cake
- Call you by name ("mama" or "dada")
- Understand "no" (demonstrated by stopping when you say it, or at least pausing briefly)
- Look for an object you've hidden
- Put something into a container
- Pull up to stand
- Cruise (walk holding on to furniture)
- Drink from an open cup (with some help from you)
- Use the pincer grasp (pick something up between thumb and pointer finger)

Don't forget to use your baby's adjusted age if he or she was born early!

PROMOTING GOOD SLEEP HYGIENE

Keep your baby active but not overstimulated during the day

Store stimulating toys away from the crib

Create the right sleep environment

Go screen-free for at least 30 minutes before bedtime

Keep bedtime consistent

Always have a bedtime routine

A CLOSER LOOK

You've made it through the newborn stage of no sleep, through the early months of broken sleep, and through sleep regressions and nap refusals, and at this stage, hopefully, your baby's sleep is at least somewhat predictable and mostly consolidated. The goal now is for your baby to sleep a full (or nearly full) 11 to 12 hours each night, with two quality naps each day (though whether reality matches this goal is a different story). The sleep hygiene tips below will help lay the groundwork for years of healthy sleep to come.

Keep your baby active but not overstimulated during the day. Daily activity, including some outdoor time (weather permitting), will help build up sleep pressure between naps and before bedtime (see page 238 to learn more about sleep pressure). But be sure all that activity isn't too overstimulating, especially close to sleep times, since that could make it harder for your little one to settle down.

Store stimulating toys away from the crib. Exciting, bright, loud, or light-up toys or objects that are within view of your baby's crib can be a distraction, making it harder for your little one to fall asleep. Try to keep only quiet toys in view of the sleep area—books, blocks, puzzles, and stuffed animals. If you're able to separate your baby's room from the play area, even better.

And remember, all toys, including stuffed animals, should be left out of the crib until after the first birthday. Pillows and blankets aren't needed until your baby switches to a bed (though you can add a blanket to the crib after twelve months if you want).

Create the right sleep environment. A cool, dark, and noise-free bedroom can help optimize sleep. A sound machine set to low can be helpful to block out external noise, but don't feel compelled to add one to the nursery if your baby doesn't need it. It's not a must-have.

Speaking of your baby's sleeping environment, now is not the time to transition your baby out of the crib and into a bed. It's best to wait until your baby is around two and a half to three years old, or taller than thirty-five inches, before making the switch. For now, just make sure the crib mattress is at the lowest level to prevent escape.

Go screen-free for at least 30 minutes before bedtime. At this age, your baby should be exposed to either minimal or no screen time (see the box on the next page). If your baby does engage in TV-watching or iPad scrolling, be sure it's not happening close to bedtime. Screen time can overstimulate your baby, making it harder for him to fall asleep and stay asleep.

Keep bedtime consistent. Thanks to their natural circadian rhythms, babies tend to downshift around 6:45 PM to 7:45 PM. Instead of fighting this internal clock, aim for your baby to hit the sack at approximately 7 PM to 7:30 PM (it's the bedtime sweet spot!). Babies who miss this time frame can end up getting a second wind thanks to an increase in the stress hormone cortisol, making going to sleep and staying asleep difficult.

Always have a bedtime routine. It's hard for your always-on-the-go baby to transition from the busy day to the quiet night without getting time to wind down, which is why a bedtime routine continues to be important.

SCREEN TIME FOR BABIES

Eager to plop your baby in front of the television or your device to keep him occupied while you make dinner or take care of laundry folding? The AAP recommends that babies under eighteen months have no screen time at all. Even after eighteen months, screen use should be limited to 15 to 30 minutes a day, and the AAP says it's best for you to sit alongside your baby and interact with him while he watches, to help him understand what he's seeing.

Seem unrealistic? No need to feel guilty if you have no choice but to keep your baby busy for a few minutes with an interactive color game app or high-quality educational programming while you get something else done. Short stints in front of a screen won't harm him. It's only when a baby spends lots and lots of time in front of the television that the downsides start to multiply. Children in general learn from personal interactions, facial expressions, body language, vocal intonations, and the give-and-take of conversations. TV-watching is passive and one-sided, and babies (who don't comprehend what's happening on the screen anyway) and toddlers learn less from screens than from interacting with adults. Video chatting is fine—it provides social interaction, which is why it's not considered screen time—but watching TV or playing games on a screen, even educational ones, takes babies away from the more important brain-developing activities they should be doing. Even leaving a television on in the background can be enough to delay language development, since research shows parents speak fewer words when there's a TV on, and fewer words means less learning.

Bottom line: Try to limit or avoid screen time for your little one as best you can. But drop the screen time guilt. Short bursts in front of the TV are not worrisome, and as long as your interactions with your baby are more frequent than your baby's time with an iPad or screen, occasional screen time is nothing to feel guilty about.

WEANING FROM THE BREAST

Wean gradually

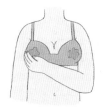

Going cold turkey can be painful and lead to engorgement, plugged ducts, or mastitis

Drop one nursing session at a time

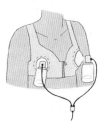

If you're pumping, lengthen the time between sessions and decrease pumping time at each session

Give extra snuggles and kisses to make up for the deceased physical contact

Use distraction

A CLOSER LOOK

The AAP and WHO recommend exclusive breastfeeding for the first six months and then continued breastfeeding (along with serving solid food) for as long as mutually desired—even if that's into the second year or beyond. So, if you're not ready to call it quits yet, there's no need to wean. When you *are* ready to wean, if you have no choice but to wean, or if your baby decides *she* wants to wean, these strategies can help you do it comfortably.

Wean gradually. Weaning off the breast should be a gradual process, both for your comfort (see below) and to help your baby acclimate. By this age, your baby is starting to get more of her nutrients from solid foods than from breast milk, but the comfort that comes from nipping at the breast will be hard to give up. That's why a slow, gradual process will be easier on your baby.

Going cold turkey can be painful and lead to engorgement, plugged ducts, or mastitis. An abrupt stop to breastfeeding can cause pain from engorgement and clogged milk ducts. Mastitis (a breast infection) can also sometimes occur when weaning happens cold turkey. Slow and steady is best for both your baby and you.

Drop one nursing session at a time. To wean gradually, reduce the number of times you're bringing your baby to the breast each day over the course of a week or more. Say your little one is nursing five times a day. Start by going down to four times a day for a few days, then three times a day, and so on, continuing to drop one nursing session every few days (or weeks). You can replace each nursing session with a bottle or cup of formula (before twelve months), a cup of milk (after twelve months), previously expressed and frozen breast milk (at any age), or a snack (for toddlers). If your baby is nearly a year old, it doesn't make sense to offer a bottle, since you'll be weaning off the bottle at twelve months anyway (see page 268).

If you're pumping, lengthen the time between sessions and decrease pumping time at each session. If you've been pumping, take a two-pronged weaning approach: Stretch out the time between pumping sessions by an additional hour (or more) every few days until you're able to drop them one by one, and pump for a shorter amount of time at each session. Your breasts will get the message that milk isn't needed anymore and shut down production.

Give extra snuggles and kisses to make up for the decreased physical contact. When weaning happens, your baby misses out on the snuggles, close skin-to-skin contact, and special attention that comes with nursing. Make up for that lost closeness by offering more touch time during the day—extra hugs, more kisses, additional cuddles. It'll help the weaning process proceed more smoothly. But don't worry if your baby doesn't seem to need it. Some babies move on from weaning without needing any adjustment time or extra touchpoints—and that's perfectly normal, too.

Use distraction. Some babies who are especially attached to the breast and the comfort it provides may give you a hard time when weaning begins. Use distraction during times that were previously set aside for nursing: Bring out a special toy, read a book, or engage your baby in a game or activity. It'll hopefully be enough to distract your baby from what's under your shirt and make her forget what she was clamoring for.

WHEN YOUR BABY BITES...
OR HITS... OR PULLS HAIR

Babies bite, hit, or pull hair as part of communication and exploration

Your big reaction to his behavior makes your baby think it's a game

Stay calm and say, "That hurts"

Remove your baby from the activity or situation where the behavior is happening

Distract your baby with another activity or toy

Prevent aggressive behavior by avoiding common triggers like hunger or overtiredness

A CLOSER LOOK

Ouch! You've got a baby vampire with a sharp bite . . . or a baby slugger with a strong arm . . . or a baby hair aficionado with a penchant for pulling your tresses. While any "aggressive" behavior from your little one isn't much fun for you, it does present you with an opportunity to start teaching him about right and wrong and what's okay to do and what's not. Your baby is too young to follow any rules consistently—and maybe even too young to understand them completely—but you can certainly start laying down the seeds of discipline and limits now.

Babies bite, hit, or pull hair as part of communication and exploration. Biting, hitting, and hair pulling are often methods of communication—your baby doesn't yet have the words to voice his thoughts or needs but he does have the ability to express himself through physical actions. Babies are also exploring their capabilities—*When I pull Mommy's hair her head moves! I wonder what happens when I use my teeth to chomp on the babysitter's arm! My dad yells when I hit him and that's cool!*—and they don't realize that these behaviors can hurt or are inappropriate.

Your big reaction to his behavior makes your baby think it's a game. Your baby isn't quite sure what he's doing the first time he takes a nip on your cheek, finger, or arm, or the first time he hits you or pulls your hair. But when he does and subsequently gets an outsized reaction from you—a loud yelp and maybe even a laugh—he thinks of it as a fun game to be repeated. That's why your reaction (or more accurately, non-reaction) will be crucial.

Stay calm and say, "That hurts." End nipping with a firm "No biting. Biting hurts." Stop the hitting with a reminder that hitting is not appropriate. Same for hair pulling. And stay calm when issuing the limit. Any type of big reaction—positive or negative—will reinforce the behavior instead of putting an end to it.

Remove your baby from the activity or situation where the behavior is happening. If your baby is biting while in your arms, lower him to the floor. If he's biting during a feeding, stop the feeding. If he's hitting another child or you while playing, remove him from the scene. If he's pulling your hair, tie back your hair.

Distract your baby with another activity or toy. Engage your baby in another activity or with another toy as a distraction to prevent a repeat offense. Most babies this age are easily sidetracked when a shiny new activity is presented to them, and that can quickly put a stop to unwanted behavior.

Prevent aggressive behavior by avoiding common triggers like hunger or overtiredness. Babies (and, as you'll soon see, toddlers) tend to act with less control when hungry or tired. Because negative behaviors are exacerbated when it's been a long time since a meal or a nap, be sure to stick to a regular nap and feeding schedule to keep hunger and tiredness away.

WHY YOUR BABY SHOULD SKIP SHOES INDOORS

Walking barefoot helps strengthen the feet and toes

New walkers have better balance when barefoot

Going barefoot on varied surfaces helps babies learn to maneuver their bodies in different settings

Tight, stiff shoes can interfere with proper foot development

When choosing shoes for outdoors, look for ones that are lightweight, breathable, and flexible

Socks under the shoes should fit well without bunching or wrinkling

A CLOSER LOOK

Tiny sneakers, itty-bitty boots, and miniature sandals are irresistibly cute and fun to buy. But avoid the temptation to dress your new (or emerging) walker in shoes all the time. Your baby is better off going shoeless when indoors, and here's why.

Walking barefoot helps strengthen the foot and toes. Your baby's feet undergo tremendous changes in the first few years of life as they prepare to bear weight and take those first toddles, runs, and climbs. Bare feet get more sensory input, and that sensory input is what tells the muscles and ligaments in the foot to develop and strengthen.

New walkers have better balance when barefoot. When babies and toddlers walk barefoot, they tend to keep their heads up more. That's thanks to the feedback they get from their feet, which orients them to the ground and helps them balance. Wearing shoes, however, blocks that sensory information, so babies have to look down more often. This puts them off balance and leads to more frequent topples.

Going barefoot on varied surfaces helps babies learn to maneuver their bodies in different settings. Being barefoot boosts coordination because it lets your baby learn about her position in relation to the space around her, enabling her to better organize her movements. Walking barefoot on all types of indoor and outdoor surfaces—carpet, tile, hardwood, grass, sand, and even mud—gives little ones the confidence to maneuver their bodies in lots of different settings, plus makes them less prone to injury.

Tight, stiff shoes can interfere with proper foot development. Need yet another reason babies are better off shoeless? Shoes that are tight, stiff, or inflexible can pinch toes, restrict the spread of toes (which is what helps tots stay balanced), and interfere with the proper development of the foot, preventing the foot from growing and strengthening as it should.

When choosing shoes for outdoors, look for ones that are lightweight, breathable, and flexible. While no shoes are needed indoors, shoes are often necessary to protect your baby's delicate feet from dirt and injury when outdoors. Choose shoes that are lightweight, breathable, and flexible in the front. Avoid high-tops since they restrict ankle movement. And look for nonslip soles with good traction so your baby doesn't lose her footing.

Socks under the shoes should fit well without bunching or wrinkling. Any wrinkles can dig into your baby's feet, causing discomfort.

While barefoot is still best when indoors so that your baby can feel the floor, wearing socks indoors when it's cold is fine. However, make sure they have nonskid bottoms for safety.

YOUR BABY'S LANGUAGE DEVELOPMENT

Pointing and gesturing to make needs known are forms of communication

Babies start using jargon and word approximations after 10 months old

Your baby's first words may appear close to the first birthday

Most 12-month-olds will be able to say one word

You can count something as a word if your baby uses it consistently, intentionally, and independently

By 12 months, your baby will be able to respond to simple, one-step directions

A CLOSER LOOK

In the span of under a year, your baby has gone from cooing (breathy, throaty sounds beginning at two to three months) to vocal explorations (squeals, growls, and raspberries at around four to six months) to babbling (repeated consonant and vowel sounds, like "ba-ba-ba-ba," that are produced in the front of the mouth at around seven to nine months old). What can you expect in the language department as your baby nears his first birthday?

Pointing and gesturing to make needs known are forms of communication. By now, your baby may be well on his way to communicating with you—not with words but with gestures (see page 180 for information about baby signs). Clapping, waving, putting his arms up, and blowing kisses may already be part of his communication repertoire. (You'll notice these gestures more frequently after nine months old.) Pointing and shaking his head "no" often appear around the first birthday. You may also notice, by month twelve, your baby paying attention to where you're looking as well as where you're pointing—another important foundational communication skill.

Babies start using jargon and word approximations after ten months old. Does your baby sometimes sound like he's speaking gibberish? That gibberish, called jargon by speech-language experts, sounds like adult conversation but without words—it has a mix of consonant and vowel sounds, like "bo-ga-da-ma," and the same sing-song quality that regular language has. Listen, too, for word approximations at this age—simplified versions of words with meaning like "muh" for more, "da" for down, "cu" for cup, "uh" for up, and "ba" for ball.

Your baby's first words may appear close to the first birthday. The first birthday comes not just with cake, but also, often, a word or two. Time to celebrate!

Most twelve-month-olds will be able to say one word. When it comes to language milestones, pediatricians and speech therapists will want your twelve-month-old to have a least one word. The average one-year-old will be able to say five or more words. Some very advanced talkers will be saying lots more than that!

You can count something as a word if your baby uses it consistently, intentionally, and independently. When listening for words, what counts? Does "duh" for dog count? Yes! That's a word approximation, and since it's used intentionally, it's considered a word. Exclamatory words, like "uh-oh," also count, as do animal sounds, like "moo." Even baby signs count as words. If your baby is using a sound, sign, or word consistently, intentionally, and independently, you can consider it a word.

By twelve months, your baby will be able to respond to simple, one-step directions. Receptive language (the ability to understand) comes before expressive language (the ability to speak)—so even if your baby is only saying a word or two at his first birthday, he's likely able to understand fifty or more. In fact, most babies this age can respond to simple verbal requests, such as "Come here," "Roll the ball," "Let's get into the stroller," or "It's time for your bath" . . . though whether they'll actually do what you're asking is another story!

BILINGUAL BABY

Eager to raise a bilingual baby? There's no better time to introduce a second language to your little one than when you're introducing the first. While it's common for bilingual children first learning to speak to have smaller vocabularies in one or both languages compared to monolingual children, if you count up all the words your little one has, the total for both languages will likely be similar to that of a child who only speaks one. Indeed, research shows that exposing your child to two languages does not cause a language delay. So, don't hesitate to introduce a second language if you'd like your little one to grow up bilingual.

STIMULATING YOUR BABY IN THE TWELFTH MONTH

Give your baby window clings to stick and unstick

Hand your baby a busy board with latches, snaps, zippers, and knobs

Sort toys by colors to teach your baby different shades

Make edible play dough for your baby to squeeze and shape

Push your baby on a tricycle

Offer role-play toys

A CLOSER LOOK

Time certainly has flown—your baby is about to turn one! As you're gearing up for the big birthday celebration, you can try out these stimulating activities for your almost-toddler.

Give your baby window clings to stick and unstick. Give your baby's pincer grasp and hand-eye coordination a workout with this fun activity. Buy some thick gel or foam window clings and let your little one grab them, stick them onto a window or mirror, unstick them, and repeat. Window clings are a fun and easy activity to set up, and one that'll keep her occupied in the same place for a good amount of time, buying you a reprieve from running after your now-very-mobile baby. They can also provide great opportunities for lessons about shapes and colors!

Hand your baby a busy board with latches, snaps, zippers, and knobs. Busy boards are perfect for your busy babe! Most of the latches, snaps, buttons, and zippers will be too advanced for even your smarty pants at this age, but the neurons in her brain will be firing fast as her mind works overtime trying to figure out how to manipulate all those different closures. And a few months from now, you'll be amazed at how her dexterity has improved!

Sort toys by colors to teach your baby different shades. Repurpose your little one's favorite toys to play a game of color sorting—separating toys into piles made up of similar colors. Name the red pile, the blue pile, the green pile, and let your baby explore the rainbow. Challenge your baby by moving some toys around and encourage her to reunite each toy with its color family. It'll take time before your baby catches on, but you'll both have fun with this multicolored activity in the meantime.

Make edible play dough for your baby to squeeze and shape. Play dough is an awesome sensory toy for your baby, and making an edible version is the perfect solution for a little one who still likes to put everything in her mouth. Your baby will have lots of fun squeezing, squishing, rolling, and shaping the dough with her little hands in this awesome sensory activity. If she's spending more time eating the dough than playing with it, though, wait until she's older before trying this activity again.

Push your baby on a tricycle. Your one-year-old may not be able to pedal a bike just yet, but there are tons of options to get her started riding. Try a balance bike, letting her use her feet to propel the bike along (look for one that's sturdy, with enough wheels to provide ample support). Or try a grow-with-baby tricycle that has an option for you to push her until she can move it with her own two feet. Bike riding is a great way to help your baby develop her coordination, balance, and muscles. Once she's using one independently outdoors, be sure she wears a helmet for safety!

Offer role-play toys. Your imaginative baby will love to stretch her creative juices with pretend-play toys in the coming months. And because there's nothing more exciting for a baby than copying mom or dad, role-play toys tend to become fast favorites, especially when you get involved in the game. Offer up a play kitchen, pretend dishes and food, dolls, a playhouse, a workbench, a doctor kit, a pretend store, a toy phone . . . and let your baby's imagination run wild.

FINDING MOMENTS OF JOY WITH YOUR BABY

Feeling the warmth of your baby's sweet cuddles

Listening to your baby's laughter

Hearing the adorable way your baby speaks

Witnessing how your baby's eyes light up when he sees something new or interesting

Watching your baby's face when he sleeps

Observing your baby's personality shine through

A CLOSER LOOK

Congratulations! You've made it through a whole year of parenting your sweet baby. It hasn't always been easy—there have been plenty of difficulties and frustrations, and yes, plenty of tears from the both of you. But there's likely also been more moments of laughter, exhilaration, and joy than you can count. Tapping into these moments of delight, especially during the hard times, will remind you why being a parent is so special.

Feeling the warmth of your baby's sweet cuddles. There's nothing more magical than when your adorable baby climbs into your lap, rests his head on your chest, and just sits together with you in silence. Those cuddles may not come as often as they did in the newborn stage, but when they do, they are as yummy as can be.

Listening to your baby's laughter. The most precious sound in the world is your baby's sweet belly laughs—something you'll be hearing often these days. Your little one thinks so many things are funny, but you're the one who makes him laugh the hardest. Enjoy every giggle you get.

Hearing the adorable way your baby speaks. There's nothing more adorable than baby jargon and mispronounced words that only you can decipher. Before you know it, your baby will be pronouncing words correctly, so enjoy the gobbledygook now while you can.

Witnessing how your baby's eyes light up when he sees something new or interesting. The curious mind of a baby knows no bounds. Watching his eyes light up at the wonders he discovers can warm the heart of even the most jaded adult. As you observe your baby exult in, learn from, and analyze the world around him, take a second to rediscover all these amazing things yourself.

Watching your baby's face when he sleeps. There are frustrating days as a parent, to be sure. But as you watch your (finally) sleeping little cherub, the peaceful look on his face is enough to make you forget the craziness of the day—and leave you eager to start it all over again tomorrow.

Observing your baby's personality shine through. Don't look now, but you have a walking, talking, attitude-filled little one with a personality bigger than life. Your baby's individuality shines through in everything he does, and you'll delight in those antics and traits that are all his own. You'll also get a kick when his mannerisms mimic yours. Cherish these moments—your baby's blossoming personality will bring you more joy than you ever could have imagined.

INDEX

ACKNOWLEDGMENTS

As solitary as book writing is, it's never done alone. It's probably too cliché in the context of a parenting book to say that it takes a village to nurture a book from idea to manuscript to published copy, but I'll say it anyway. I am blessed that so many people have been a part of my life and my life as an author. Thank you to:

My brilliant editor Leah Wilson, who believed in this book from the beginning and whose targeted and insightful editing made everything inside these pages better.

Glenn Yeffeth, for your support and leadership, and the entire publishing team at BenBella Books, including Adrienne Lang, Alicia Kania, Susan Welte, Madeline Grigg, Sarah Avinger, Morgan Carr, Jennifer Canzoneri, Kim Broderick, Kit Sweeney, and Leah Baxter.

Kara Western, for the incredible illustrations of beyond adorable babies and extremely relatable moms, dads, and caregivers that bring each parenting topic to life.

My agent, Stacey Glick, who saw the potential and the need for this book, championed it, and found it a wonderful home.

My fabulous followers on social media and my coaching clients who keep me on my toes (and on top of the latest research). Thank you also to my fellow social media parenting experts who have supported me and who have become virtual and real friends.

David Leichtman and Alex Kaplan, for being there when I needed it most.

My friends and family, including my parents, siblings, and siblings-in-law, for their listening ears and sage advice . . . and for encouraging me to follow my passion.

My wonderful children (and children-in-law), Daniella and Ben, Arianne and Jeremy, Kira and Zev, and Sophia, and my adorable granddaughter, Zara (who arrived just in time to test the tips in this book while I was writing it)—you help remind me every day what is most important in life. I am forever thankful for your boundless enthusiasm, encouragement, feedback, and love.

Jay, my incredible husband. I knew (literally) from our first date that I couldn't go through life without you by my side. Words cannot adequately express what you mean to me and how much I love you. I am beyond grateful to you and for you.

SOURCES

For references and sources, see:
sharonmazel.com/bite-sized-parenting-sources

ABOUT
THE AUTHOR

Sharon Mazel is an internationally recognized parenting and pregnancy expert, author, journalist, speaker, parenting coach, and mom of four with over twenty-five years of experience in the field. She reaches hundreds of thousands of new and expectant parents with her popular parenting and pregnancy guidance on social media, parenting coaching, e-guides and online resources, blogs, and parenting courses. Sharon's social media has been called one of the "Most Educational IG Accounts" for new parents and one of the "Best Instagram Accounts for New Moms."

Sharon began her career as a television journalist and producer. After leaving the world of television news, Sharon focused her writing efforts on parenting and pregnancy topics, including spending two decades working on a *New York Times* bestselling pregnancy and parenting book series. Sharon's writing and guidance have been widely published online and in numerous publications including *Parenting* magazine, *BabyTalk* magazine, *The Washington Post*, and others. She was also the executive producer of an educational video series for the Yale University Child Study Center. Sharon graduated from Barnard College, Columbia University, and received a master's degree in journalism from Columbia University's Graduate School of Journalism.

Find out more about Sharon on her website, sharonmazel.com, and follow along on social media for more bite-sized parenting tips and information on Instagram (instagram.com/sharonmazel), Facebook (facebook.com/SharonMazel), and Twitter (twitter.com/sharonmazel).